C0-ANA-943

This book* is a

Loyola
request
reprint

LOYOLA UNIVERSITY PRESS
Chicago, Illinois
is pleased to make
this out-of-print book
available once again
to its old friends

* Reprinted by arrangement
with the author
and/or the original publisher.
This book is now sold only by
Loyola University Press.

IÑIGO DE LOYOLA

TO HIS EXCELLENCY
Most Reverend Walter A. Foery, D.D.

RELEASE

IÑIGO DE LOYOLA

by

PEDRO LETURIA, S.J.

*Dean of the Faculty of Ecclesiastical
History, Gregorian University*

BXXQ 7466 .L65   ST. JOSEPH'S UNIVERSITY   STX

Inigo de Loyola;

3 9353 00016 3392

TRANSLATED BY
ALOYSIUS J. OWEN, S.J.

*Reissued by
Loyola
University Press,
Chicago, in the
Loyola request
reprint series,
October 1965*

Bx

BXXQ 4700

L .L7

L453

05916

Copyright, 1949, by

LE MOYNE COLLEGE PRESS

All rights reserved, including the right to repro-
duce this book or portions thereof in any form.

Permissu Superiorum:

John J. McMahon, S.J.

Provincial: New York Province

Nihil Obstat:

Edward A. Ryan, S.J.

Censor deputatus

Imprimatur:

✠ Walter A. Foery, D.D.

Bishop of Syracuse

PRINTED IN U. S. A.

CONTENTS

thwarted by the *Comuneros* of Castile. Iñigo's activities in Najera and Guipuzcoa. 60-64; 4. The military expedition from Guipuzcoa to Pamplona, and the wounding of Iñigo. 64-74; 5. Convalescent dreams of knightly deeds. 74-82.

CHAPTER IV. THE KNIGHT OF CHRIST AND OF THE VIRGIN 83-106

1. Ignatius' reading at Loyola: the *Flos Sanctorum* and the *Vita Christi*. 83-87; 2. Early influence of the *Flos Sanctorum*: Saint Francis, Saint Dominic, and Saint Onuphrius. 87-93; 3. The "King of the Saints," by Fray Gauberto M. Vagad, and his "Royal Standard". 93-97; 4. The key to Ignatius' conversion: reflection and experience in discerning spirits. 97-101; 5. The crown: decision to go on pilgrimage to Jerusalem, and the apparition of Our Lady. 102-106.

CHAPTER V. THE FIRST RETREATANT AT LOYOLA....... 107-125

1. Iñigo's domestic apostolate. 107-111; 2. The germ of the Exercises in the retreat at Loyola. 111-115; 3. The Ignatian election at the Castle. 115-120; 4. The departure. 120-125.

CHAPTER VI. OUR LADY'S PILGRIM.................. 126-147

1. The chronology of the journey. 126-127; 2. The route through Navarre and Aragon. 127-132; 3. Fear of recognition, and the vigil at Aranzazu. 132-136; 4. Chivalrous idealism: the adventure with the Moor near Pedrola. 136-140; How the idea of making the vigil come to Iñigo. 140-144; 6. The confessor at Montserrat. 144-147.

Photograph taken from death-mask.

Introduction by Author

I. MARCH 1936

1. Juan de Aquemendi and Pedro Garcia, notaries of Azpeitia, mention Saint Ignatius by his full name at least twice. They cite him as a witness in legal documents of May 18th and of July 23rd, 1535, by the name of: *Iñigo Lopez de Loyola*. Martin, his brother, shortly afterwards registers in the inventory of the family estate "the act by which *Iñigo Lopez de Loyola* states that he has received his share of the patrimony, and renounces the right to demand anything further." It is not surprising, then, that the Municipal Council of Azpeitia in 1595, Father Ribadeneira in his "Manuscript History of the Spanish Assistency", and the attorney, Lorenzo de Paulis, in 1605 frequently use that name: *Yñigo Lopez, Ignatius seu Inicus Lopez*.[1]

It was customary during this period for brothers to apportion among themselves the various names occurring in the family genealogy. Ignatius' eldest brother was called *Juan Perez de Loyola* after an ancestor of that name who lived around 1280. His elder brother was named *Martin Garcia de Oñaz*[2] after Lope Garcia who lived around 1260. Finally, Ignatius along with his priest brother Pero[3] used the name *Lopez* which had been in the family since 1221. They combined it with the title of the family estate which has been immortalized by history: both are *Lopez de Loyola*.[4]

The founder of the Society of Jesus kept pruning his ancient and noble name so that not even the *Iñigo* was left. Apart from the legal documents mentioned, there remains, as far as is known, no other record of the *Lopez* except a dubious reading in the

---

[1]Lizarralde (I), p. 138; Perez Arregui (I), p. 167; Cros, *opusc.* I, pp. 39, 46; *Scripta*, II, pp. 249, 529; Ribadeneira, *Hist. mms.*: "Saint Ignatius used to write *Yñigo;* later *Iñigo*, which we retain in this book, prevailed".
[2]Martin succeeded to the title when Juan was slain during the Neapolitan wars.
[3]The Pero or Pedro particularly associated with Ignatius' worldly life.
[4]Dudon, pp. 608-609, 612-613.

indictment drawn up at the trial at Alcala in 1527.[5] Ignatius himself rarely used *Loyola* even though others did so.[6] He kept *Iñigo* along with *Ignatius* from 1537 on. A little later he dropped it entirely in favor of *Ignatius*, probably out of devotion to Saint Ignatius of Antioch who had been so devoted to the Name of Jesus.[7]

2. We retain the full name in the title of our book because it summarizes the purpose and extent of the work. We do not intend to give the entire life story of the author of the Exercises or of the founder of the Society of Jesus. We shall only describe the complete Courtier in his worldly life and also in his Christian childhood, in his life as a convert, penitent, and exercitant. We shall depict Ignatius as he transforms himself from a knight of the king into a Knight of Christ. We shall follow him as he consecrates himself to the Virgin's service by a vow of chastity and sketches in his own experiences the future Exercises. For the scion of Loyola had no need to divest himself of his courtly garments, or to unbuckle his knightly sword in order to receive the summons to serve his heavenly King.

We shall follow him throughout the years of his formation and transformation until he is no longer Iñigo Lopez de Loyola but simply Iñigo, or better, the anonymous Pilgrim of the "Autobiography".

This work has a further purpose, one which gives it some claim to originality. It proposes to place the Courtier Iñigo in the setting of his country and century. It neither omits the lights or the shadows as it traces how he transformed himself in them, or, how under the effect of grace, they formed and transformed him. We have followed the example set in the seventeenth century by Father Gabriel Henao, and in our own by Father Jose Adrian de Lizarralde, O.F.M., Father Juan Perez Arregui, S.J., Father Paul Dudon, S.J., and Dom Anselmo Albareda, O.S.B. We have tried to steep ourselves in the atmosphere of Guipuzcoa, Castile, Navarre, and Montserrat. For there the founder of the Society of Jesus was born, reared, formed, and transformed.[8]

---

[5] *Scripta* I, pp. 622-624.
[6] Constituciones I, pp. 8, 13-14. Cf. for the signatures of the founders of the Society in official documents.
[7] Tacchi-Venturi II, pp. 7-8; Rahner (II), pp. 14-15.
[8] We are gratetul to Fausto Arocena (San Sebastian), Joaquin de Yrizar (Azcoitia), and Father Jose Zunzunegui (Vitoria) for their friendly collaboration in this book.

In order to do this we frequently had to follow paths that led through many nations and centuries, and to venture at times into the domain of the romances and books of chivalry. The explanation of certain incidents, or the ballad that made them immortal, is often to be found there.

Whenever we have been unable to reach certitude we have designated the probability of our views by qualifying our statements. This has enabled us to satisfy the demands of criticism without shearing the wings of hypothesis which motivates further research and inspires psychological synthesis.

3. Our primary source is the "Autobiography". Ignatius dictated it toward the close of his life to Father Gonzalez de Camara when he and Father Nadal insisted that he write an account of his experiences.[9]

Its authenticity and trustworthiness as the basis for all Ignatian biography are corroborated by comparison with other early documents. Each word of the concise and terse "Autobiography" contains a fact, or opens up a wide perspective. It has been rightly remarked[10] that in the field of modern biography it constitutes one of the best examples, not of richness and color of style, but of force and objectivity in its psychological acumen.

We had to refer to other contemporaneous sources and to recent works although we had intended to prescind from them. But lest certain statements might appear unfounded and even absurd, we were forced to multiply citations beyond our first intention. We have given in parenthesis in the text the number and page of the "Autobiography". For other references we have merely given in footnotes the name of the author of the work cited, with a numeral in parenthesis if we refer to more than one work by the same author, and a numeral designating the page. Any obscurity caused by this brevity will be overcome by consulting the complete bibliography at the end.

4. We have no need to insist that the sole aim of our book is to depict what kind of a man the "Courtier" Loyola was, and why. We have omitted certain impassioned polemics of the present day. If these pages help to a better understanding of a great personage

---

[9]Cf. Bibliography under "Acta".
[10]Feder (II), pp. 11, 120. Contains a reference to Fueter, p. 275.

and great Saint, their purpose will have been attained. The author would welcome correction based on documentation.

The Finger of Divine Providence and the Light of Grace are so evident in Iñigo's transformation from knight of a king into Knight of Christ that it is enough to seek the truth about his life to find therein the symbol and slogan of all his actions: the Holy Name of Jesus, Son of God and Saviour of the world.

Rome, Gregorian University,

March 17, 1936.

II. May 1939

Three years have passed since the above was written. Three years will have been completed in July, since publication was begun at Barcelona.[11] In those three years centuries have been compressed due to the tremendous events that have left their mark on Catholic Spain.

This telescoping of centuries has for the most part been staged in its epic grandeur and searing tragedy among the mountains and valleys that witnessed the childhood of Iñigo de Loyola. The drama has been presented amidst the scenes of his peaceful pursuits and military achievements. It took place along these winding roads which symbolized one faith and one devotion for Spain, leading Mary's Pilgrim from Loyola to Aranzazu, thence to Navarrete, from Navarrete to Lerida, and from there to Montserrat.

There before the altar of the Blessed Mother and the divine Child Ignatius laid down the burden of his sinful life. There he offered the fruits of his heroic conversion and was dubbed Knight of Christ and sent on a spiritual world-wide quest. A century later Lope de Vega envisioned him ascending the mountain:

> No se ha de preciar España
> de Pelayo ni del Cid,
> sino de Loyola solo
> porque a ser su sol venís . . . (T. I.)

---

[11]This delay was an advantage technically. In the summer of 1937 the author was able to consult Father Cros' documents at Toulouse through the kindness of Fathers Fernando Cavallera and Paul Dudon. Thus he could incorporate several valuable texts in Chapter I. During the Spanish War a first edition was published in Montevideo (*Mosca Hnos*). The present edition (Barcelona) is the second revised and augmented.

May the intercession of that *"Sol de España"* convert his ascent and descent from Montserrat into a symbol for the regeneration and future greatness of his glorious country.

Rome,
May 8, 1939.

T.I. (Spain has no need to boast/of Pelayo/nor of the Cid/but only of Loyola/for you came to be her sun.)

CHAPTER I

THE LOYOLA HERITAGE

1. The name *Loyola* has become universal after four centuries. But it is forgotten that etymologically it is derived from the Basque.

Its Basque etymology was definitively established as far back as the seventeenth century by the Jesuit etymologist Father Gabriel Henao. He refuted the fantastic derivation proposed by Father Engelgrave.[1] If this refutation had been kept in mind today, the picturesque origin suggested by a famous German historian would not have been accepted; namely, his *"lupus in olla"* i.e. "Wolf at the pot", an allusion to the Loyola escutcheon.

The Basque word *Loyola* has no connection with the Castilian "lobo en olla" nor was the family name of military origin. It was a place name common to various regions of the Basque country.[2] Father Henao in the seventeenth century and Father Villalta in 1895, pointed out the three most important instances in Biscaya and in Guipuzcoa: a region of Arrazua near Guernica, the alluvial flats of Urumea, now a suburb of San Sebastian, and the lowlands of the Urola half-way between Azpeitia and Azcoitia where Saint Ignatius was born.[3]

The topography of these regions confirms the probable conclusions of etymology. As we pointed out elsewhere,[4] *loi* means mud, while *ola* may be interpreted either as a simple locative suffix, or as a compound of *ol* meaning abundance plus the article *a*. In either case the meaning suits the nature of the lowlands or alluvial flats mentioned above: *muddy site, abundance of mud or of mud flats*. Zeuss and most philogists ascribe a similar etymology to *Lutetia Parisiorum* (Paris) i.e. from *lutum* (mud).

---

[1] Engelgrave, p. 21.
[2] Huonder, p. 3.
[3] Henao-Villalta VII, p. 23; III, p. 131; Mujica, (I), pp. 106, 108; Echegaray, (II), p. 773. However *Loyolaechea* in Palencia, derived from Loyola in Azpeitia, owes its name to military prowess. Cf. Henao-Villalta, VI, p. 277.
[4] AHSI, 2 (1933) p. 314.

The topographical nature of this etymology directs the historian to a fact of importance. The name *Loyola*, as the generality of Basque names, derives not from comparatively recent military deeds, but from the primitive agricultural character of the land.[5]

Even of more importance than the *"Lobos y la olla,"* rudely depicted over the gateway to the Castle on an escutcheon that antedates the Castle itself, are the lowlands of Urola and the mountains of Oñaz. On these lowlands and in these mountains were born the rural and patriarchal institutions whence Loyola derived its title to nobility.

The learned Jesuit Larramendi said in the eighteenth century of all Guipuzcoan families: "On the hills and on the farms is where all the castles and houses of the nobility of Guipuzcoa were located, and thence they drew their title to nobility."[6] The same may be said of Saint Ignatius' forebears.

It is enough to observe, as Father Polanco did as early as the sixteenth century, the location of the famous Castle and the rural nature of the Loyola heritage.

2. Saint Ignatius' secretary, Polanco, whose family came from Polanco in la Montaña,[7] remarks: "Both houses (those of Oñaz and of Loyola are in the district (though not within the town limits) of Azpeitia. For it is customary in that region for its noble houses to be situated outside the towns in the manner of villas."[8]

The Castle of Loyola, though it was linked in later days to the nearby Azpeitia, did not make use of the town for its own protection, nor did it serve as a protection for the town. It was not like many other frowning strongholds of the nobility throughout Europe which reared their walls on the ruins of some ancient Roman settlement, nor did it group at its feet the dwellings of serfs and tenants to form the more or less feudal town of the Middle Ages.

The Castle of Loyola stood isolated on the plain, as did that of Oñaz on the mountain. For both houses began in the primi-

---

[5]Oñate, p. 696; Ziesemer, pp. 41-42.
[6]Guerra, (I), Intro.; (II), p. 6.
[7]*Pol. Compl.*, II, p. 835.
[8]*Chron.* I, p. 9.

tive farm settlements on plain and mountain. Their modest growth made them prominent among their neighbors, but they never forgot their rustic origin. Rather they rooted themselves more deeply in the countryside, and created their primitive and rural estate by acquiring ancient farmlands and by improving their original holdings. Thus at Loyola as in other districts rose the *Aide Nagusiak*, the *Parientes Mayores* of the Basque country.[9]

The archaic manor-house of Loyola became the stronghold of the fourteenth century in later and less idyllic times. But even then it was not, as in the case of Xavier, a real castle with walled-in precincts, a court of arms, and turrets surmounted by a tower of homage. Loyola had but a simple tower and stood alone amidst orchards and gardens. It served but as a defense against rival factions or neighboring villages.[10]

Even the pride of its watchtower was humbled before Ignatius' time. In 1457 its defenses were destroyed by the "Brotherhood", (*Hermandad*), of the Guipuzcoan towns favored by royal decrees of Henry IV. A later decree, given at Segovia on July 26, 1460, permitted castles to be restored. The King insisted upon two conditions: that they be not built on their former sites, and "that they be flat without towers or fortifications of any kind."[11]

Loyola was exempted from the first condition, but the second was strictly enforced. Juan Perez de Loyola, Saint Ignatius' grandfather, added two stories of brick to what remained of the old castle. The turrets at the four corners were in no way intended for defense, but served merely to harmonize the former stronghold with the modern castle. Expert opinion on Guipuzcoan architecture has found indications of an architect from Andalusia or from Castile in the arabesques and brick arches which were previously unknown in the Province. Thus Loyola is the earliest instance of that Moorish style which was soon to be imitated throughout Guipuzcoa.[12] The will made in 1538 by the Saint's brother, Martin Garcia de Oñaz, reflects the home and the customs which they both knew in childhood. Martin bequeaths to his

[9]Gorosabel, I, pp. 279 ff.; Guerra, (I), p. 409; Boehmer, (1), p. 7.
[10]Yrizar, (I), p. 12.
[11]Dudon, p. 12, note 2.
[12]Yrizar, (II), p. 10; Echegaray, (II), p. 9.

heirs, besides certain objects of silver and gold which belonged
to the dining room and the chapel, "two pack-mules and a
mare . . . , three casks of my own cider that are in the press,
as well as the cider in the casks mentioned in the said patent of
patrimony . . . , likewise all my clothing, jewelry and household
effects, beds, furniture, and all kinds of stock on all the farm-
settlements, except that of Zuganeta and Ameznabar which belong
to my son Beltran . . . , and the revenue from the farm settlement
of Aguanza and the stock thereof, also the ash groves I have about
the above-mentioned house of Loyola, cultivated and to be
cultivated."[13]

The same rustic note is found in other contemporaneous
sources. The deed establishing the patrimony in 1536 mentions
"the house and estate of Loyola with its garden, dovecote, wine
press and mills near the said estate."[14]   In 1569 Juan Perez de
Yarza of Azpeitia speaks of "the farm settlements and mountain
land in the neighborhood of the house and in sight of it."[15]   In
1551 Father Pedro de Tablares remarks that the house "is in the
country . . . situated between (Azpeitia and Azcoitia), approximately a league from both. It is in so delightful a site that I
doubt that another can be found more pleasing to behold. Loyola
stands completely encircled by woods and all kinds of fruit trees
which are so thick that one can hardly see the house until one
comes to the very gateway.[16]   Father Henao adds that "among
these orchards is "an ancient evergreen oak that towers above the
roof at one corner of the house."[17]   Potenciana de Loyola gives
the final touch by recalling the hunting dogs which were there
when Ignatius was at Loyola.[18]

All this rusticity may come as a surprise to those who look
upon Loyola as a mountain fastness, its masters, marauders, as
notorious for their depredations as for the moral failings revealed
in their wills.

This error is partly due to the false idea of the *Parientes
Mayores*. The misconception results from Lope Garcia de
Salazar's "Chronicle" and those inspired by it. "Those fierce

---

[13]*Chron.*, I, pp. 508-509.
[14]Fita, (I), p. 555.
[15]Henao-Villalta, VII, p. 387.
[16]Perez, Arregui (I), p. 17.
[17]*Chron.*, I, p. 531.
[18]*Scripta*, II, 193.

marauders", justly observes Juan Carlos de Guerra, "were not so bad as they were painted. The Chronicle is biased. They were industrious, pious, charitable, just and honest in their accounts. There is documentary proof of this."[19] They preserved the age-old institution, the farm-settlement, by "respecting the choice the farmers made among their children for continuing the lease-hold," and by maintaining their patrimony intact down through the centuries.[20]

This was true of Loyola. It is shown, not only from the rustic character of its dove-cotes, mills, and presses, but even more from the very nature of the properties that constituted the heritage.

3. A decree of May 5, 1518 issued by Queen Juana and her son, Charles, summarizes the properties of the heritage: "It has been reported to US that you hold the houses at Oñez and at Loyola and (the monastery) at San Sebastian Soreasa (sic), and revenue of two thousand maravedis, as well as several iron works and farm settlements and mills and mountain land and meadows and forests of oak and chestnut, apple orchards and other properties and possessions. . . . [21]

In this enumeration we see the survival of the patriarchal organization set up by the *Aide Nagusiak* which ante-dated the founding of the towns. If we supplement this data with other documents, we find three types of properties in the Loyola heritage: agricultural, industrial and ecclesiastical.

The first type is the basis of the others. In the patent of the patrimony, 1536, we find first enumerated the properties of the house at *Oñaz* with its fields and woods, "besides all the farm-settlements thereof, together with its gardens, usances, and outlets, pastures and water and all else that pertains to the above mentioned."

Then come the properties at *Loyola* which appear in the patrimony with nine farm settlements and numerous farms, gardens and woods. Martin, Ignatius' brother, distinguishes what is in the country or at Beyzama and Urrestilla from what has been built or bought later in the town of Azpeitia. He also makes a distinction between what belonged to the original

---

[19]Oñate, pp. 713-714; RIEV, 26 (1935), pp. 481-482; documentary confirmation.
[20]Oñate, pp. 73-74.
[21]Fita, (I), pp. 546. 553-555.

heritage and later additions made by his father, Beltran, for instance, the property at Ibarrola[22], or what he himself bought, the house and land at Arguizabe and at Insola.[23] Finally, there are some other properties which he does not include in the patrimony, for they are shared with other families, such as at Eguibar and Recarte, or they have heavy charges laid on them, such as the house and shrine at Eguimendia which was under lien to Catalina de Olozaga.[24]

In 1569 Juan Perez de Yarza of Azpeitia describes this rural estate which was dotted with farm settlements, rich in lush meadows and verdant forests: "The twenty farm settlements extend some two leagues from the manor and castle of Loyola. You can go from one to another without entering the limits of other properties except so much as in some parts is public property. There are many which are so large that their arable land produces a sizeable return. The estate has rights also over many private dwellings within the jurisdiction of the manor."[25]

The good Azpeitian is somewhat over-enthusiastic. For he himself admits that the annual income from the rural properties did not exceed seven hundred *escudos*.[26] We know that the revenue which Juan de Borgia received from La Reina amounted to over three thousand five hundred "from the wheat crop alone"[27], and that Martin Garcia de Loyola was reported to have an income of some fourteen thousand . . . [28] However the honest Guipuzcoan saw in that rural patrimony the survival of primitive institutions dear to his countrymen, those institutions that lend such charms to the farm settlements that to this day nestle in the valleys and on the mountainsides of Azpeitia and Azcoitia.

Saint Ignatius regarded the Loyola heritage as considerable. In order to move his brother, Martin, to the practice of virtue he wrote him: "For God has granted you *an abundance of temporal things* that through them you might gain eternal blessings. . . . Therefore you should not show yourself niggardly

---

[22]Fita, (I), pp. 557-558.
[23]Fita, (I), pp. 556, 559-560.
[24]Fita, (I), pp. 560-561.
[25]Henao-Villalta, VII, p. 386.
[26]Henao-Villalta, VII, p. 385.
[27]Henao-Villalta, VII, p. 390.
[28]Henao-Villalta, VII, p. 384.

toward *God Our Lord Who has been so generous toward you*"[29].

The second class of properties, the beginnings of indigenous industry, likewise reveal the traditional character of the patrimony.

Gonzalo de Berceo had sung: *"Fierro traen de Araba e caños de acero,"* in reference not only to Biscaya but also to Guipuzcoa and Alava.[30] For the iron wrought in its forests and in the mills on its streams marks the earliest essays at such industry in the Basque country. So it is not surprising that there were iron-works on so ancient a patrimony as Loyola. In 1405 Beltran Yañez mentions in his will "the wheels or mills which belong to the said holdings (of the Castle)", and the "favors of the King in regard to the iron-works at Barrenola and Aranaz."[31] In 1467 mention is made of the iron-works at Ibayderaga.[32] By 1536 the mills and the iron-works have multiplied but they still retain their rural character. This is shown in the patent of patrimony where it is stated that there are "the iron-works at Hubisusaga with their buildings, wheel-tires, mill pond, and all the rights and privileges relating to the cutting of wood on the mountain, the clearing of land, pasturage, and water rights within the limits of Beyzama."[33]

We also learn from this document that the annuity in perpetuity, which is referred to in the royal decree of 1518, concerned the two iron works at Zumaya: those mentioned in 1405 and 1464 which were at Barrenola and at Aranaz. The king, apparently Henry III, had granted to Beltran Yañez and his heirs an annuity of two thousand maravedis on the "tithe" payable to the Crown "on the iron that should be forged" in these works.[34] Perez de Yarza, in 1569, does not mention this annuity but seems to speak instead of the revenue of two hundred ducats from a minor actuary post in the administration of Guipuzcoa which was substituted for it.[35] However it was still part of the heritage in 1518 and 1536 and was so incorporated by Charles V and Martin.

The third type of properties in the Loyola heritage is made up of ecclesiastical properties. This class throws light on the primi-

[29]*Epist. et Instruct.,* I, p. 81.
[30]Isasti, pp. 232-235; Gonzalez, pp. 105, 151, 158; Luciano Serrano, pp. 103-105: "De ferro de Alava", taken from the records of San Millan de la Cogolla, 1025. It is clear that by Alava was meant the three Basque regions.
[31]Henao-Villalta, VI, pp. 289, 290-302.
[32]Dudon, p. 21.
[33]Fita, (I), p. 558.
[34]Fita, (I), p. 558.
[35]Henao-Villalta, VII, p. 386.

tive organization both religious and social of the shrines, monasteries and villages of Guipuzcoa.

4. Even to this day the shrines scattered among the valleys and mountains near Loyola are characteristic of the countryside. We know of no less than ten which have belonged to the heritage of Loyola since the fourteenth century.

More striking than their number is their distribution among the farm settlements and the way in which their structures harmonize with the architecture of those settlements.

Yrizar, an authority on this subject, has written: "It is very easy to compare the shrines, sanctuaries and village churches from a structural and decorative standpoint with the farm settlements and their adjuncts. They are of all types. The simplest have neither porch nor choir, and their roofs have but two sides. They are really sheds (*txabolas*) with a rude statue in a niche. Sometimes they have roofs with four sides, and then they are more palatial in appearance. Some have porches only at the entrance, while others have a porch that extends around the entire shrine. When religious cult acquires a certain development there is a very simple type of choir over the entrance in most cases; in the more sumptuous, it is extended on both sides. The farm-settlement is an integral part of the Basque countryside. I cannot conceive of one without its corresponding shrine."[36]

That was true too of Loyola and its surroundings. It is difficult to assert that some of those that bordered Azpeitia existed before the town was founded in 1310. This holds for the shrine of Magdalen and of San Pedro de Elormendi near the manor of Emparan.[37] Others, however, such as Nuestra Señora de Olaz and Nuestra Señora de Elosiaga on the mountain, and San Martin de Urrestilla on the plain, probably antedate the founding of Azpeitia.

As Father Lizarralde says: "We can only guess at the history of other similar shrines in the country. They were undoubtedly reared by the famous confraternities which, as is well known, were established before the founding of the towns. They were the shrines of their respective patrons during their resistance to

---

[36]Yrizar, (II), p. 14.
[37]Lizarralde, (I), p. 63.

the arrogant pretensions of the hated *Parientes Mayores.*[38] The *Parientes*, too, had their shrines for the religious service of their families and adherents, shrines which were, perhaps, even more ancient than those of the brotherhoods. There was the shrine of San Juan de Oñaz near the old farm settlement of the family, and that of San Pedro de Eguimendia or Loyola, which is very close to the Castle.[39]

Father Lizarralde has deduced that such shrines of the confraternities as well as of the nobility, before the towns were founded, were used from time immemorial for religious services dependent on the diocese of Pamplona.[40]

The royal Monastery of San Sebastian de Soreasu was preeminent as far back as the thirteenth century. It was within the parish limits of Azpeitia and had formerly belonged to the Templars.[41] Around the beginning of the fourteenth century the church and its possessions had been confiscated by the King of Castile, Ferdinand IV, who had begun to appropriate their properties as early as 1308, before the total suppression of the Templars by Clement V.[42] In 1311 the monarch already spoke of "my monastery of Soreasu with its mountains and springs and lands with pastures and all rights belonging to said monastery."[43]

The date 1311 brings us to the founding of the town of Salvatierra de Iraurgui or Azpeitia.

Before this time three classes of towns existed in Guipuzcoa. The most ancient were maritime: San Sebastian, Fuenterrabia, Guetaria, Motrico, and Zarauz, 1150-1237. Next came the towns on the Navarrese frontier: Tolosa, Villafranca, and Segura, 1259. Finally there were the agricultural and urban towns of the interior: Mondragon, Vergara, and ancient Deva on Mount Iciar.[44]

Azpeitia belongs to this third category. It was founded Feb-

---

[38]Lizarralde, (I), p. 60.
[39]Perez Arregui, (I), pp. 8-9, 90.
[40]Lizarralde, (I), p. 3; Zunzunegui, pp. 185-193. Describes the ecclesiastical organization of Guipuzcoa under the diocese of Pamplona.
[41]Lizarralde, (I), p. 57; Cros, *Sect. Docum. Azpeitia*, mms. of 1649 in parish church of Azpeitia: "There is an old tradition that the said church with all its tithes . . . was owned by the Templars until their suppression in Spain and France. After the suppression the said church and tithes accrued to the Crown of Castile by grant of Clement V."
[42]Finke, pp. 372-373. It does not seem possible to admit a concession by Clement V as supposed in the "Memorial of Azpeitia". The King acted from 1308 on his own authority as did other monarchs.
[43]Henao-Villalta, VI, p. 288.
[44]Echegaray, (I), pp. 341-353, 373, 376 ff.

ruary 20, 1310 by Ferdinand IV.[45]   In this type of town there
was even greater opposition to the *Parientes mayores* than in the
others.   This is seen in the case of the church and lands of the
monastery of San Sebastian which was one of the bases of the
foundation of Azpeitia.   The King in 1311 granted to the Council
of the new town patronage over the revenues and tithes of the
monastery.   He prohibited them, however, under pain of for-
feiture from alienating these rights.[46]

Beltran Yañez de Loyola, the restorer of the Castle, used this
clause from 1387 to 1394 to supplant by royal favor the Town
Council's right to that patronage.   The occasion of this manoeuvre
was as follows.   Around 1387 "the offensive of the Basque
bishops against lay patronage" reached Azpeitia[47]   The curate
of San Sebastian, Pelerin Gomez, appeared in Azpeitia with a
decree of the bishop of Pamplona which appointed him Rector
of the church.   This decree had been issued without previous
agreement or mention of the rights of presentation which the
town possessed.[48]

The town vigorously opposed the measure.   The names of
Pedro Ochoa de Loyola and Lope Ochoa de Oñaz figure among
the opponents.   None the less, the Council was obliged to yield
in the face of two grants by Clement VII which Pelerin obtained
on May twenty-first and August twenty-first of 1388 at the
Pontifical Court in Avignon.   Beltran de Loyola saw that the
time had now come to win the King's favor.   He opposed the
Avignon Pope's Bulls and supported the supposed rights of the
Crown.   He displayed great energy, not stopping at violence, in
their defense.   Henry III commended him saying: "You have
defended and protected, and you defend and protect the said
monastery and you have done and do great deeds and strive to
protect and defend the royal right and prerogative that belongs
to me in the said monastery."[49]

The outcome was easy to foresee.   Beltran and his heirs were

---

[45]Echegaray, (I), pp. 409-410.
[46]Henao-Villalta, VI, pp. 228, 118. Note in the following that the Loyolas' patronage over the church of Azpeitia does not derive feudally, but by grants and
conflicts of an absolutist character.
[47]RIEV, 26 (1935), p. 484.
[48]Henao-Villalta, VI, pp. 122-125, 299. In the following we have extracted data
from the original documents in the Pontifical Register of the Vatican, especially
the Bull of Benedict XIII of September 20, 1415 which grants the patronage to
the Loyolas.
[49]Henao-Villalta, VI, p. 118.

invested by the monarch with the patronage and right to receive the church tithes under the same terms previously enjoyed by the Council. A solemn royal letters patent confirmed them in this right on April 28, 1394. A long and stormy period of conflict followed between the Loyolas, supported by part of the townsfolk and by the royal authority, and Pelerin Gomez and his successors, supported by the Bishop of Pamplona and the Papal Court at Avignon. The conflict lasted more than twenty-five years, years of excommunications and interdict of the church and town of Azpeitia.

Finally on February 6, 1414 an agreement was reached at Pamplona due to the petition of Sancha, lady of Loyola, and of Martin de Erquicia, rector of the parish. The Apostolic Administrator of the diocese, Lanciloto de Navarra, granted the lords of Loyola the patronage over the parochial church of Azpeitia on condition that they submit to previous pontifical Bulls and recognize Erquicia as legitimate rector. In the official document Lanciloto says that this was done: "with the hope that other laymen who in like manner unjustly hold churches, would imitate the example of the aforesaid lord of Loyola," Lope Garcia de Lazcano.[50]

Peace came to the valley when the lord of Loyola acknowledged Erquicia as rector of the parish on March eighteenth, and the latter, as well as the Council and the townsfolk, accepted the Lord of the Castle as the legitimate patron of the church and its possessions. The solemn Bull of confirmation issued by Benedict XIII on September twentieth, 1415 gave definitive form to the privilege.[51]

The patronage, thus confirmed, lasted up to the time of Saint Ignatius despite occasional litigation and disputes.[52] The lord of Loyola had such power of intervention in the functioning of the parish that Father Tablares, S.J., says with intended exaggeration that "he has the power of a bishop in the church. . . ."[53] He received three quarters of its tithes amounting to a revenue of some thousand ducats a year, more than the seven hundred

[50]Zunzunegui, p. 187: from this expression and from other data rightly infers that not only the town of Azpeitia but also the Loyolas had hitherto acted rather as *masters* than *patrons* of the church.
[51]Henao-Villalta, VI, pp. 121-126: taken directly from the register of the Bull at the Vatican.
[52]RIEV, loc. cit., pp. 489-490.
[53]Henao-Villalta, VI, p. 112.

accruing from the rural patrimony.[54] He had the right of presenting nominees for the bishopric, the rectorship, and all the
benefices of the parish.[55] He laid down rules and regulations in
conformity with the canons for the reform of the clergy and the
people.[56] He regaled the newly ordained priests with a banquet
at the Castle. . . .[57] Besides having the right to be buried in
the principal tomb in the church, he also had "the right to
another tomb next to Saint Michael's altar, for the burial of
priests of his line . . .", as Martin Garcia says in 1536.[58] These
privileges were extended to the ten country shrines which, from
the founding of the town, had been dependent on the parish
church of San Sebastian de Soreasu.

The most solemn religious services were held in that church.
For instance in 1535 the ordinances concerning the poor were
promulgated at the High Mass. We are told that "almost all the
inhabitants of the town and its environs were present. The
ordinances had to be read aloud word for word in Basque so that
all might know of them, and that there might be no excuse for
pretended ignorance."[59]

Despite this centralization the shrines retain much of their
former cult and autonomy and even appear in documents designated as "suffragan."[60] They have their own chaplains who say
Mass on fixed days, and celebrate High Mass during the
Rogation Days, and from time to time preach outdoors even from
the branches of a tree.[61] The Blessed Sacrament was reserved
for *Viaticum* in the larger ones and in them the funerals of the
nearby farm settlements took place.

These shrines were given local color by the *seroras* or *freiras*
(sisterhoods) which had survived especially in the Basque
country down to this period. The sisterhoods were groups of
devout women who wore a religious garb but lived outside
cloister and were not bound by religious rule. They lived at
the shrine after their appointment had been presented to the
patron and the municipality.[62] They were quite numerous and

[54]Henao-Villalta, VII, p. 381.
[55]Henao-Villalta, VI, pp. 111-113.
[56]Dudon, pp. 24-25.
[57]Coster, p. 58.
[58]Fita, (I), p. 559.
[59]*Scripta*, I, p. 543
[60]Henao-Villalta, VI, p. 127.
[61]Perez Arregui, p. 147; *Scripta*, II, p. 206.
[62]Lizarralde, (I), pp. 8, 9; 15, 16; Henao-Villalta, VI, pp. 114, 127-140.

highly esteemed in Guipuzcoa. This is easy to understand when we recall that no convent except that of the Augustinians of San Bartolome at San Sebastian, which dated from before the thirteenth century, existed in the Province up to the sixteenth century. Nor is there any record of any male religious foundation before the sixteenth century, apart from the suppressed Templars, and foundations attempted by the Mercedarians, Dominicans, and Conventual Franciscans at Aranzazu.[63]

The sisterhoods at times worked in the fields, taught or engaged in works of charity.[64] But their main duty was to take care of the shrines. They saw to the lamps in the shrine, cleaned and dusted it and its ornaments, prepared wine and hosts for the Holy Sacrifice, rang the bell at the proper times and supervised the behavior of the women at burials and processions.[65]

This service was regarded as an honor and many ladies of the house of Loyola performed it.[66] Saint Ignatius' niece, Potenciana, served at the shrine and hospital of Magdalen, and his aunt, Maria Lopez de Emparan y Loyola, served at San Pedro de Elormendi. The latter was one of the foundresses of the Franciscan convent in Azpeitia.[67]

An interesting clause in Martin's will shows the importance of the shrines in the religious life of the town and reveals how directly they were affected by the Loyola patronage rights.

The clause was doubtless inspired by Saint Ignatius who wished to introduce in 1535 the custom of praying for those in mortal sin and of begging grace that they might not fall into it. He asked to have bells rung nine times in strokes of three, a practice unknown in the valley. Since he was acquainted with the organization of the shrines and the parish, he requested his brother as patron to dispose of his share of the Loyola inheritance for this purpose.[68] Martin agreed and *ordered* and *prescribed* in his will that the parish bell be rung "at mid-day every day in the world" in the manner suggested by his brother, and put aside two gold *escudos* annually for the sacristan or his substitute.

As was to be expected, both brothers were mindful of the

[63]Gorosabel, IV, pp. 251-256 ff; V, pp. 216 ff; Gonzalez pp. 28 ff.
[64]Lizarralde, (I), pp. 72, 15.
[65]Lizarralde, (I), pp. 9 ff.
[66]Dudon, p. 25.
[67]Dudon, p. 70.
[68]*Scripta*, II, p. 193; *Chron.*, I, p. 132.

inhabitants of the farm settlements. The will continues: "And that God our Lord may be better served, I bid, and it is my will that the sisterhoods, each in their shrine, shall ring the bell at the said time at mid-day every day, that those on the land may join in prayer . . . , and for this each sisterhood shall receive annually one *real*. The yearly charge upon my estate and upon my heirs is *two gold ducats* and ten Castilian *reales* which are valued at thirty-four *maravedis* each."[69]

He concludes with these words which complete the picture of the environment: "I assign for carrying out said obligation the farm at Aguirre, (which is opposite that of Izarraitz), along with its appurtenances which I wish, and it is my will, be set aside and hypothecated for the fulfillment of same. And I desire, and order that it be not commuted into another pious work even though the Holy Father now reigning or his successors should allow it."[70]

This symphony of shrine bells accompanying the parish bell as a call to penance and prayer, which was to be perpetuated by farm revenues, was very appropriate to the religious and social conditions of the country and of the Loyola patrimony. This was especially true during the period of transition from the fifteenth to the sixteenth century.

5. Laxness of morals, which was so wide-spread in Europe, had penetrated even to these remote valleys. The Catholic reform which was started by Queen Isabella did not entirely immunize them. We have but to look at the list of illegitimate children recorded in the Loyola wills, and recall the concubinage, dissension and inertia of the clergy in Azpeitia.[71] Truly, then, the ringing of bells at the shrines and at the church was a summons to prayer and penance.

Their notes are the prelude to the Catholic Reformation. They fortified the living, robust, almost instinctive faith, hope, and charity that survived in the countryside. These virtues had been handed down through age-old institutions which had been uncontaminated by Jews, Mohammedans, "New Christians," and heretics.

---

[69] *Chron.*, I, p. 311.
[70] *Chr. ι.*, I, p. 312.
[71] *Scripta*, I, p. 90; Tacchi-Venturi, p. 9; Lizarralde, I, p. 80.

That was the Guipuzcoan's greatest boast in the fifteenth and sixteenth centuries. To preserve that faith their Councils passed an Ordinance around 1483, which was incorporated into their laws in 1527. The Ordinance read: "New Christians converted from Jewry or Mohammedanism as well as their descendants" are forbidden to come into the Province. . . . [72] We can appreciate, then, Father Araoz' indignation when Father Ribadeneira wrote in 1572: "that he had corrected many errors in that region (Azpeitia)." Father Araoz takes him to task asserting: "There are none there. Rather he should have said that he had settled many conflicts and rivalries, and corrected vices. But to say 'errors' may offend the inhabitants of that region."[73]

This purity and naturalness of faith appears in the Loyolas' public actions. They humbly confessed their sins in their wills; out of charity and contrition they left legacies to Santiago in Galicia and to Guadalupe, and they sincerely and tenderly invoked Our Lord and Our Blessed Lady.[74] Iñigo's eldest brother, Juan Perez de Loyola, addressed Her as "Most glorious Virgin Mary, whom I have ever held to be my Lady, and Helper, and Advocate in all my actions, and to whom I now most devoutly offer with sincere heart myself, as slave and servant, body and soul, and of whose mercy I ask, as devoutly as I can, that She protect me from all danger and from all sin, and guide and console me, and grant me the grace and benediction, through Our Lord Jesus Christ, that I may live in safety and die in repentance."[75]

An equally sincere and candid faith breathes in the hymns and ballads of Juan de Anchieta, a native of Urestilla. He was Master of the Royal Chapel and Rector of San Sebastian de Soreasu from 1498 to 1518, that is to say, during Iñigo's childhood and youth.[76]

Up to 1515 Anchieta did not reside as a rule in Azpeitia. He

---

[72]*Nueva recopilación* . . . , p. 478; Cf. Pulgar, pp. 149-150; Henao-Villalta, V, pp. 263-264; Gorosabel, I, pp. 317 ff.
[73]*Scripta*, I, p. 727.
[74]Dudon, p. 24.
[75]Cros, *Docum. Arch. Notar. de Azpeitia.*
[76]Lizarralde, (I), pp. 84, 85; Barbieri, num. 298: *Doncella madre de Dios, / Estrella, guiadnos vos . . . / Guiadnos a do subió / El, y la cruz do murió / De la cual El descendió / A los infiernos por nos.* (Maiden Mother of God / Star, guide us / guide us where mounted / He, and the cross on which he died / from which He descended to Hell for us.) num. 328: *Visitaréis el sepulcro / muy santo con alegría, / feriendo los vuestros pechos / con humildad todavía, / llorando de vuestros ojos / con gemidos de porfía.* (You will visit the Sepulcher / very holy, with joy / striking your breast / ever with humility / your eyes weeping / constantly groaning.) These two ballads represent early influences on Iñigo's devotion to Mary, and the idea of a pilgrimage to Jerusalem.

stayed at Court, and governed his parish through his vicars, Domingo de Mendizabel and Pedro de Izaguirre.[77] Iñigo may have met him in Azpeitia, for he visited his church from time to time, and was a friend of the Loyolas, at least up to 1510. Doubtless, then, Iñigo would have heard of his pastor's poetry.

An outburst of devotion along the banks of the Urola was noticeable toward the end of the fifteenth century. Since the middle of the century anagrams of Jesus and Mary had crowned the fretted steeples of the Burgos Cathedral, and the Name of Jesus echoed in a thousand forms throughout Castile, Biscaya and Guipuzcoa.[78] Father Lizarralde has given abundant data for Biscaya to which we add details concerning the country and town of Saint Ignatius.[79]

The anagram of the Name of Jesus dating around the end of the fifteenth century is sculptured on a gateway at Elgueta.[80] Another is found in the accounts of the *Pariente Mayor*, Martin Yañez de Artazubiaga.[81] It was used by the notaries of Azpeitia, Juan Martinez de Alzaga and Juan de Aquemendi, friends of Iñigo, instead of the customary flourishes in their writings[82] There is an instance in a contract for the making of hosts. The contract was drawn up between the parish of Azpeitia and Maestro Peronal, clock-maker, on July 3, 1530. It stipulated that "the Name of Jesus is to be stamped thereon," and this as a condition for the payment of 17 reales they offered him.[83] It is not to be wondered at then that Iñigo's brother, Martin begged of the Saviour in his will that He deign "to guide him and keep him so that it (his will) be well begun, continued and ended to the glory and praise of *His Holy Name*, Jesus Christ."[84]

Three ladies of pure Basque origin imparted a new religious tone to the environs of the valley in the fifteenth century. They were Saint Ignatius' mother, Marina Sanchez de Licona, Martin's wife, Magdalena de Araoz, who came to Loyola while Iñigo was still a child, and his cousin, Maria Lopez de Emparan, a member of the sisterhood at San Pedro de Elormendi.

[77]Lizarralde, (I), pp. 86, 94.
[78]Olmedo, p. 152. His article complements the data given for Spain by Mariotti, pp. 153 ff.
[79]Lizarralde, *Andra Mari en Vizcaya* (Bilbao, 1934), pp. 95 ff.
[80]Acknowledgment to Lizarralde.
[81]Oñate, p. 714.
[82]Olmedo, 148-149.
[83]Cros, *Docum. Arch. Not. Azp.*
[84]Fita, (I), p. 552.

Iñigo's mother brought with her not only the pious tradition of her ancestors at Ondarroa and Lequeitio in Biscaya, but also that of the town of Azcoitia. Her father, Doctor Martin de Licona, was the patron of the church there and in 1466 drew up the regulations which governed it.[85] In 1503 Juan Perez de Licona, probably Marina's brother, founded the first Reformed Franciscan monastery in Guipuzcoa. It was "San Francisco de Sasiola and was located two leagues from Ondarroa and half a league from the town of Deva."[86]

Magdalena de Araoz, lady of honor at the Court of Queen Isabella, enriched the Castle with a gift that lent it a Marian tone. She brought with her the panel of the Annunciation that the Queen had given her. It had been presented to the Queen by the Basque family of the Ladrones de Guevara, also related to the Loyolas.[87] The panel still embellishes the "primitive oratory" of the Santa Casa. It is highly probable that Magdalena also brought the books which were, one day, to influence Iñigo de Loyola so decisively, the *Flos Sanctorum* and the *Vita Christi*.

Maria Lopez de Emparan, his cousin, was one of the sisterhood at San Pedro Elormendi. She was a devout lady who, under the direction of the Franciscans of Bermeo and later of Sasiola, founded the first convent of religious in those valleys and mountains. She founded it at the end of the fifteenth century while Iñigo was still a child. It was known as the convent of the Isabellites, or of la Concepcion, an institution of prayer and penance in Azpeitia even to this day.[88] Her initiative indicates a notable advance from the backward ecclesiastical organization of the parish and of the Loyola patrimony, as well as a renewal of devotion to the Holy Name and to the Seraphic Saint. However a conflict arose over jurisdiction and revenues between the exempt Mendicants and the parish and its patrons. We shall see in the following chapter the importance of this for the young Iñigo.

Summarizing the characteristics of the social and religious environment of Loyola and Azpeitia at the dawn of the fourteenth century, we find there a certain archaic, patriarchal, and rustic note. The superior culture and religious organization which

---

[85]Dudon, p. 25.
[86]Lizarralde, (I), p. 69.
[87]Dudon, pp. 608, 25; this seems the best reply to his observations.
[88]Lizarralde, (I), pp. 64 ff.

radiated from Burgos, Pamplona, and Bermeo were beginning to infiltrate. But there is ever present the sound, simple, though slow, growth of the ancient farm settlement of Guipuzcoa. This was the backwater in which divine Providence placed the childhood of Iñigo de Loyola.

6. It is remarkable that, apart from his baptism at the church in Azpeitia as befitted the patron's son,[89] the first two and only events of his birth and childhood that have come down to us are concerned with a farm-settlement, Eguibar, and with a villager, his nurse.

This villager was Maria de Garin, the wife of a smith named Errazti after one of the Loyola farm-settlements.[90] One of her sons later became an excellent priest and confessor due to the Saint's personal intervention,[91] despite "his somewhat ugly and crooked face."

Saint Ignatius' nurse was known as such in Azpeitia in 1535.[92] Her historical importance, however, is not confined to her having nursed the founder of the Society of Jesus. She was to affect Ignatian biography in another way.

Saint Ignatius apparently contradicts himself in speaking of his age. He stated he was converted when he was twenty-six. That would put his birth in 1495. Again, in 1555 he said he was sixty-two which would date his birth in 1493.[93] Some clarification had to be made, and investigations were conducted in Azpeitia, probably before the Saint's death.[94] His parents were dead, and there was no record of his baptism. They asked his nurse if Ignatius was sixty-two in 1555 as he had said. Her answer was prompt: Iñigo was two years older, i.e., he was born in 1491: *"Nutrix tamen ejus duos (annos) addebat,"* as his secretary expressly states.[95] Despite the skepticism of Polanco himself and of some recent historians the nurse's testimony prevailed in the first "Life" of the Saint written by Ribadeneira in 1572 and in the lessons of

---

[89]Tacchi-Venturi, II, p. 7: the pastor at that time was Juan de Zabala, (1486-1498). He it was who probably baptized the child.
[90]*Scripta,* II, p. 192; Fita, (I), p. 558; Cros for the nurse's name.
[91]*Scripta,* (II), p. 192, 233.
[92]Leturia, (I), pp. 47-48.
[93]*Scripta,* (II), p. 23. The investigation was repeated at Azpeitia in 1571 for on his tombstone was written: *"Aetatis suae 65"*, i.e. born in 1491. Cf. Astrain, I, pp. 7-8.
[94]Chron.,VI, p. 44.
[95]Ibid., I, p. 9; Cf. Ribadeneira, II, pp. 185-187.

the Breviary. The famous secretary concludes: *"ejus nutricis sententiam secuti videntur."*

The nurse was probably right. There is a certificate dated October 23, 1505 among the protocols by the notary of Azpeitia, Domingo de Egurza, in which Iñigo appears as a witness. It reads: "present as witnesses for this purpose were summoned Iñigo de Goyaz, and Domingo de Garagarza, and *Inego de Loyola*, inhabitants of the said town."[96] Since a witness must be fourteen to testify validly in Castile and Guipuzcoa we arrive at 1491, which confirms the nurse's two additional years.

There is more about this nurse of Azpeitia. She lived at the farm settlement of Eguibar, a quarter of a kilometer from the Castle. It was at Eguibar, and not at the Santa Casa, that she nursed Iñigo. There is documentary evidence, though not entirely convincing, of this tradition which is found in the sixteenth century. This evidence is contained in two inscriptions, one in Basque and one in Castilian, which appear on the walls of Eguibar.[97] Other data shows that the child's stay at the farm settlement, or at least his relations and those of the Loyolas with Eguibar were lengthy and intimate.

This is shown by the fact that the inhabitants of Eguibar easily recognized him when he returned to Azpeitia after several years' absence. His intention was to enter incognito that he might stay at the hospital and not at the Castle. He was successful up to a point for no one recognized him at the hospital or at many of the houses where he begged alms.[98] But Juan and Catalina de Eguibar recognized him at once. The former knew him at sight when he saw him through a crack in the door at the inn in Iturrioz;[99] the latter at the very moment he appeared at her door as a beggar seeking alms.[100] They ran right away to inform his brother, Martin; Juan even interrupted his trip to Behovia and retraced his steps from Iturrioz to Azpeitia.[101]

We do not know how long he stayed at Eguibar, or what happened while he was there. Nor do we know the length of his stay at Loyola before he left for Arevalo. We may be sure, how-

---

[96]Cros, *Doc. Arch. Not. Azp.*; This is now published in *Fontes narrativi*, pp. 21-22, where may be found the discussion on the date of Iñigo's birth.
[97]Perez Arregui, (I), pp. 34-35.
[98]Perez Arregui, (I), p. 121.
[99]*Scripta*, II, p. 190.
[100]*Scripta*, II, p. 232.
[101]*Scripta*, II, p. 190; Fita, (I), pp. 556, 260.

ever, that he did not leave around 1496 "when he was only five
or six,"[102] but several years later. It may have been between 1504
and 1507 when his father, Beltran, died. The boy could already
read and write when he left to go to Arevalo.[103] Saint Ignatius'
Castilian was always halting and incorrect. This would be hard
to explain if he had been educated from the age of five in the
heart of Castile.[104] Further, whenever the Saint or Polanco, Maffei
or Ribadeneira refer to his stay at Court they use the expression
"at the Court of His Catholic Majesty." They would not have
done so, but would have said "at the Court of their Catholic
Majesties." For the Queen did not die until 1504.[105] So Iñigo
must have been at the Court some time after 1504.

An unpublished text by Nadal confirms this. It states that
Iñigo spent his childhood at home tutored by his parents and a
teacher: *"pueritiam domi exegit, sub parentum ac 'paedagogi'
cura."*[106] Tacchi-Venturi and Dudon suggest that the child may
have been destined by his father for a church career. He would,
then, have begun such rudimentary studies as would permit him
to receive the tonsure immediately, and soon enjoy some parish
benefice. We know that as early as 1515 the youth claimed the
privileges of tonsure, and his accusers were unable to deny
them.[107] At any rate, we think it is certain he did not leave
Azpeitia before his twelfth or thirteenth year.

The boy Iñigo must have spent his life for twelve or thirteen
years, partly at the Castle, partly at Eguibar. He heard his father
and elder brothers speak fairly correct Castilian, while his mother
and nurse spoke Basque. He delighted in the doves and white
flour at the Castle, and gorged himself on the roast chestnuts so
typical of the farms. He assisted at High Mass and Solemn
vespers in the parish church, dressed as befitted the son of the
patron, and then, in rustic clothes, visited the shrines of Olaz and
Elosiaga. He sang the modern courtly tunes composed by
Anchieta, but preferred the familiar songs and dances of the
country folk. He sat under the harsh ferule of one of the curates
of Azpeitia who came to the Castle to teach him the rudiments of

---

[102]Tacchi-Venturi, pp.8-9; Dudon, p. 23: vs. Fita and Perez Arregui, pp. 36-37.
[103]*Chron.*, I, p. 10.
[104]Coster, p. 7.
[105]*Scripta*, I, p. 68, 744, 750; II, p. 972; *Chron.*, I, p. 10.
[106]*Nat. Apol. ad Doct. Paris.*, fol. 106 r.
[107]Astrain, I, p. 86, note 5; Tacchi-Venturi, p. 9; Dudon, pp. 23-24.

Latin grammar, and when the lessons were over eagerly joined in raids on the Loyola orchards or those of others. . . .

Most of the details we have given are characteristic of the environment, and are further confirmed by later reminiscences scattered throughout the sources. We might have recounted them one by one,[108] but we prefer to group them under certain headings which will help us understand their effect upon his character.

7. First of all there is that sturdy, simple faith so typical of his native land and family. Saint Ignatius and his closest collaborators later on appeal to it as a guarantee of his orthodoxy. Iñigo answered the vicar Figueroa in Alcala who asked him if he kept the Sabbath: "There are no Jews in my country."[109] The Majorcan, Father Nadal, wrote in defense of the "Exercises" in 1554 that "Ignatius is a Spaniard from the first families in the province of Guipuzcoa in Cantabria where the faith is kept so incorrupt. Its inhabitants' zeal and constancy have been so great from time immemorial that they do not allow any "New Christian" to live there. There is no record from the very beginnings of Christianity of anyone who was noted or suspected of heresy. This should have been enough to ward off any suspicion from him."[110]

While the child lived with his parents at Loyola he was imbued with this staunch faith and profound piety. The two principal witnesses who tell of his visits to the church and shrines, of his attendance at Mass and at the Divine Office, and of his obedience and good behaviour expressly limit their testimony "to the time he lived with his parents,"[111] and "to his childhood and adolescence at the said Castle of Loyola."[112] We do not think that sound criticism can object to this picture of him if it is limited to his life at Loyola up to 1507. This is, too, a further confirmation that Iñigo did not leave so soon for Arevalo.

We have already seen how this piety practiced by his family and in his country was accompanied by a certain moral laxness. This was true of Iñigo. However, even in the stormiest phase of

---

[108]Ribadeneira, *Vida., Lib. II, cap. V*: somewhat legendary account; Astrain, I, p. 84.
[109]*Chron.*, I, p. 37: *"Nec in patria mea Judaei esse solent."*
[110]Nat., IV, pp. 825-826.
[111]*Scripta*, II, p. 868, art. 2º.
[112]*Scripta*, II, p. 529, art. 2º.

his life, the traditional devotion to the shrines and ancient oratory of the family lived on. It was also united with a reverence for the Holy Name that banned from his lips the slightest blasphemy[113] and led him to perform his religious duties as a Christian.

Years later the pious Bishop of Calahorra, Bernal Diaz de Luco, who was a native of Alava, and later won fame at the Council of Trent, reminded the founder of the Society of Jesus how much he owed his native land and his family in this matter. He urged him to remedy the lack of instruction among the Basque clergy by sending preachers who could speak their language. He wrote: "Your Reverence owes in charity more to that land than to any other . . . , and there is no other region in the whole world to which you are under greater obligation."[114] The Saint replied: "Your Lordship acts always as the angel of the Basques, whom we are undeniably bound by peculiar obliga- tion to help. I have done my best to send there (to Guipuzcoa) some who speak Basque (Araoz and Ochoa), and others who though they do not speak the language may help for the edification of souls."[115] One of the latter group was Saint Francis Borgia who went to Oñate for his ordination, and said his First Mass at Loyola Castle. . . .

Years later in his reminiscences the Saint recalled incidents that touched upon his life in the country. They are the second group of details that affected his character.

Father Gonzalez de Camara relates that the aged founder had almost completely lost his sense of taste. He tells us "For a treat we sometimes gave him a few roasted chestnuts. He evidently enjoyed them, for they are fruit of his native land where he was brought up."[116]

It may seem even more surprising that the scion of Loyola should remember the Basque songs and dances of his childhood. Yet Ribadeneira expressly mentions this. He relates that a certain person, who was afflicted by melancholy, came to Saint Ignatius for direction. He conceived the strange notion of asking him to sing and dance for him as he used to do in Biscaya (i. e. in the

---

[113]*Fontes narrativi*, p. 156.
[114]*Ep. mixt.*, I, p. 210; V, p. 720.
[115]*Ep. et Instruct.*, III, pp. 319-320.
[116]*Fontes narrativi*, pp. 641-642.

Basque country). He said that if Ignatius would do this he would
be greatly consoled and relieved. The Saint must have been
amused by the request, but granted it on condition that it would
not be repeated. Then he sang and danced so well that the
patient was rid of his melancholy. Afterwards he improved, and
within a few days was completely cured.[117] A note by Father
Lancicius leads us to believe that this incident occurred in 1538
at Monte-Cassino. There the Saint gave Doctor Ortiz the
"Exercises" during Lent of that year.[118]

This glimpse of Iñigo's childhood enables us the better to
appreciate his fondness for music. The author of the "Exercises"
and of the "Constitutions" appreciated fine music, not only as a
page at Arevalo, but even as General at Rome. He enjoyed hearing
church music which benefited his health, and helped him overcome melancholy. Father Camara says that to regain his spirits
he would summon Father Frusio to his room, and have him play
a while on the clavichord, or again, he would call on a simple but
devout lay brother to sing to him. This brother had a sweet
voice, and formerly had been guide to a blind man. So he would
come to the Saint's room, and sing to him "many pious hymns in
the style they are sung by the blind."[119]

This will doubtless astound those who regard the founder of the
Society of Jesus merely as a converted soldier, or presume that
he rejected choir in the Society due to his failure to appreciate
liturgical music.[120] Documentary evidence and the very environment of his childhood prove just the contrary. Ignatius told
Ribadeneira in 1544, when he had returned from Saint Joseph's
in Rome where he had listened to the organ: "If I were to follow
my own tastes and inclination, I would impose choir and the chant
on the Society."[121]

Ignatius also appreciated the country and nature. Though we
do not hear he stood in awe before the massive ruins or the
grandiose architecture of Rome, we do learn that his spirit ex-
panded before the beauty of flowers and the starry skies.[122]

Though his ministries kept him in cities almost all his life, he

---

[117]Portillo, pp. 295-296.
[118]Lancicio, *Opuscula.*
[119]*Fontes narrativi*, pp. 636-637.
[120]Constant, p. 6.
[121]*Scripta*, I, p. 418.
[122]*Scripta*, I, p. 43; Ribadeneira, *Vida., Lib. I, Cap. II.*

appreciated, as no other religious founder, the physical and
spiritual advantages of houses in the country.[123] Even while he
was in the city, he spent as much time in the gardens and orchards
of Rome as his occupations allowed. Father Coudret, who
attended him for seven months before 1548, informs us: "When
he was writing the Constitutions . . . in order to be more at ease
he would retire on pleasant days to a friend's garden, and there
would write on a table in the garden. . . ."[124]

A third effect which the blood and education of Loyola left on
Ignatius' soul was his language and style.

It is certain that Iñigo learned Basque as a child. To hold
otherwise would be to disregard everything that historical sources
have told us of the environment of Azpeitia and of the farm settlements. This is confirmed by Father Araoz' practice of writing
him letters in which he employed Basque whenever the matter
was confidential. For instance, in a letter of 1546 he speaks of
receiving into the Society "gente berria," i. e. "New Christians."[125]
Again when in 1545 he refers to a delicate question in Portugal
he writes: "Las causas principales eztitut scrivicen," i. e., I do not
write them. Evidently he uses Basque as a kind of code, for it
was their common tongue.[126]

When the Saint preached in 1535 from the cherry tree at
Nuestra Señora de Elosiaga he undoubtedly spoke in Basque, for
the farmers and their womenfolk understood him perfectly.[127] He
probably heard confessions, and gave spiritual direction in Basque.
This must be so in the case of his spiritual child, Mateo, the
Biscayan, of whom Ribadeneira says he knew his own language
and a little Castilian.[128]

However, for the understanding of Ignatius, and for the
exegesis of his writings, his direct use of Basque is not important.
No letter of his in that language has come down to us. The
importance lies in the influence that Basque syntax and
morphology exerted upon the Castilian of the "Exercises," of his
"Spiritual Diary," and of other works exclusively written by him.

An Italian critic has recently said of the "Exercises": "The

---

[123]Scripta, I, pp. 238-239, 500.
[124]Scripta, p. 572.
[125]Ep. Mixt., V, p. 643.
[126]Ep. Mixt., I, p. 197.
[127]Scripta, II, p. 206; Boehmer, I, p. 167, note 2.
[128]Scripta, I, p. 391; II, p. 14.

exuberance of the Spanish character is not found in Loyola's style. It is ever simple, chaste, concise almost to the point of anacoluthon and elipsis, as incisive and precise as that of a German speaking Castilian.[129] Father Feder's criticism is acute. He is the German translator of the Saint's "Spiritual Diary," and speaking of this work he tells us: "The translation has been quite difficult for us since Ignatius was a Basque, and had never mastered Castilian."[130]

Father Placido Mujica confirms Feder's observation. Many of the irregularities and peculiarities of Saint Ignatius' language are to be explained by his lack of literary formation. They are to be ascribed to certain popular expressions used among soldiers with which he was familiar as a youth, and to reminiscences of Latin, French, and Italian which he later added to his vocabulary without, however, ever succeeding in amalgamating them. But the principal key to his peculiar style lies in the Basque which explains his continual ellipses, his substantival infinitives, his incorrect use of reflexives, his strange use or omission of articles and pronouns, his hyperbaton, and almost word for word translation of some phrases.[131]

Yet the stamp of his language and formation is revealed not so much by grammatical technicalities, as by the very spirit of his style. That style, so foreign to coloration and embroidery, is concentrated, interior, psychological.

Here we touch upon the last and most profound effect produced on Ignatius by the Castle and the farm settlement. All who have studied, even superficially, the incontestable traits of what in Ignatius' day were known as Biscayan or Cantabrian[132] agree on his fundamental characteristics. They were his personal concentration, his reflective spirit, his slow but courageous expansiveness, sure of itself yet lacking in color of expression, and as a result of all this, his formidable firmness of will. The Portuguese, Simon Rodriguez alluded to this when he remarked to Father Camara in 1553: "You must realize that Father Ignatius . . . is a Biscayan, and once he decides upon something . . ."[133]

---

[129]Bondioli, p. 35.
[130]Feder, (I), p. vi.
[131]Mujica, pp. 53-62.
[132]Gorosabel, I, pp. 343-344; Guerra (I), p. v; Oñate, p. 494. Apraiz; Ziesemer, pp. 120-122, though we reject some of his ideas.
[133]Ep. mixt. III, p. 34; Fontes narrativi, p. 539, note 21.

We need not insist upon that concentrated psychology or on that iron will. They will be evident in the deeds which remain for us to narrate.

The personality and the achievements of Saint Ignatius are primarily and above all else the effect of grace. If natural disposing causes are sought, it is not enough to repeat and exaggerate his military training in its rigid and courtly context. We must bring out, too, the penetrating solitary observer who was at the same time introspective and realistic, at once assimilator and originator. This we shall see in the process of his conversion and in the genesis of the "Exercises" and of the "Constitutions."[134] The fact remains that antedating the heraldic *lobos* of his lineage were the fields and chestnut groves of his native mountains and meadows. Before the imperial drums of Charles V echoed in Loyola, the rustic bells of the shrines had left their mark on Ignatius' soul. . . .

---

[134]It may have been this typical diversity of temperament and language that induced the Provençal F. Coduri to group the founders of the Society thus in 1539: "*allique ex nobis essent galli, alii hispani, alii sabaudi, alii cantabri.*" That Coduri and not Ignatius is the author cf. Const. I, pp. xxxvii-xxxviii.

CHAPTER II

LOYOLA AND CASTILE

1. The *military* traditions of the Oñaz and of the Loyolas do not derive originally from brilliant feats against the Moors, who never reached their mountains, but from the sorry rivalry between Guipuzcoa and Navarre, regions bound by ties of blood and religion.

We know little of Saint Ignatius' ancestors until around 1200, the time of the definitive political separation of these regions. A few names of no historical significance are mentioned in connection with the beginnings of the family patrimony and with the internecine strife. Father Cros' researches have not advanced beyond Father Henao's findings in the seventeenth century.[1]

Campion has found in Navarrese sources of about the year 1200 the first concrete information concerning the military prowess of the Oñaz. They engaged in the mutual bloody raids along the Navarrese-Guipuzcoan border. The accounts that have come down to us, written by hostile pens, describe them in no flattering terms. Juan Lopiz de Urroz considers the Oñaz, who in one of their raids on the valley of Larraun had carried off some pigs, as *"ladrones pésimos."*[2]

This antagonism toward Navarre became involved with hostility toward France at the end of the thirteenth century. Prior to 1274, Gascons were well liked in Guipuzcoa. There was a large Gascon settlement at San Sebastian, where streets, fountains, and mountains were named after them, and their language was familiar.[3] But from 1274 to 1328 French sovereigns effectively ruler over Pamplona, a situation which led them to adopt a hostile tone toward Guipuzcoa, and opened up to them the possibility of a full-scale. attack upon Castile.

This situation developed into the battle of Beotibar in 1321, which definitively inclined Guipuzcoan policy toward the King of

---

[1]Henao-Villalta, VI, p. 215, 253; Dudon, pp. 19, 608-609.
[2]Campion (II), for the year 1309.
[3]Echegaray, (I), p. 347.

Castile. This accounts for the deep mark Beotíbar has left on songs and ballads. In the Basque songs, studied by Juan Carlos de Guerra,[4] is the record of the foreigner who approaches the mountains of Tolosa only to flee never to return. There actually were Gascons and French in the rearguard of the invading army under their commanding general Pons de Morentain.[5] The ballad composed by the Galician, Rodrigo Yañez, twenty-eight years later,[6] stresses the mountain strategy and indomitable valor of the *Lepuscanos* (Guipuzcoans).

It was necessary to mention these details for Beotíbar is the heraldic consecration of the Oñaz and Loyola line. The paladins in the fray were Gil Lopez de Oñaz and Juan Perez de Loyola along with his five brothers, apparently the origin of the seven bands on the Oñaz escutcheon.[7] Beotíbar was decisive for the future policy and fealty of the line.

However, there was not constant enmity between Guipuzcoa, and France and Navarre. After the danger of invasion had passed, and the dynasty of Navarre had become nationalized, France does not re-appear in the history of the Loyolas until the end of the fifteenth century. Navarre is hardly mentioned except when the Oñaz intervened in the bloody civil strife between the Beaumontais and the Agramontais,[8] and in law suits brought before the Bishop of Pamplona, to whose diocese Azpeitia belonged. When there is a resurgence of hostility toward the close of the fifteenth century, it is on a more universal scale, and is of quite a different character.

The policy followed by the Loyolas after Beotibar is loyalty to the King of Castile. The house of Loyola had served the King of Castile as its lord at a decisive moment. It was now receiving his protection and favor, and on him it based its expectations for the future. This explains the meridional trend of the Loyolas from 1321 on.

Beltran Yañez de Loyola, the immediate successor of the heroes

---

[4]Guerra, (II), in 1923.
[5]Henao-Villalta, VI, pp. 266-267.
[6]Yañez, Stanzas 53-71: *Las calderas que tenian / con sus sogas las ataron, / de piedras las henchían / e del monte las echaban . . . / levaron los arrancados / e callaban e ferían / de asconetas e de dardos / muy grandes golpes hasían.* (What cauldrons they had / they tied with ropes / and filled with stones / and hurled them down the mountain . . . / they wore their headress / and were quiet and struck / with arrows and javelins / mighty blows they made.)
[7]Henao-Villalta, VI, p. 274 ff.
[8]Henao-Villalta, p. 255.

of Beotibar, took part in the frontier struggles with the Moors
of Andalusia, and formed ties with the Castilian nobility. He
had been reared at the house of the powerful Castilian noble,
Diego García de Zuniga, and apparently was related to his wife,
Juana Garcia de Leiva.[9] Henry III said of Beltran in 1394,
that he wished to reward him "for the many good and loyal
services you performed for King Juan I, my father and my
sovereign, whom may God pardon, and which you now perform
in like manner for me each day."[10]

These achievements were not of epic grandeur, as neither were
those of the Crown from 1350 on. The King was involved in all
kinds of internal dissension, which was reflected in Guipuzcoa.
After the victory of Beotibar in 1321, and the services rendered
the King on the Moorish frontier and at the Court in later
decades, there arose, in the fifteenth century, the struggle of the
towns against the *Parientes Mayores* and strife among the
Parientes themselves. This internal conflict has been described
in the "Chronicles" of Garcia de Salazar and in the "Ordinances"
of Azcoitia of 1484.[11]

In 1457 Henry IV called it "violence and destruction, robbery
and murder, affronts and mutinies, arson and sieges of towns,
harboring and abetting of evil-doers . . . "[12] A somber picture
that is comparable only to what was going on during the same
period in Navarre between the Beaumontais and the Agramontais,
in France between the Burgundians and the Armagnacs, in England between the Red and the White Rose. It is but one more
act of the terrifying drama staged throughout Europe in what
Huizinga calls "the Autumn of the Middle Ages." During these
terrible times sacramental absolution was denied an enemy on the
scaffold, and those condemned to be quartered were "bought",
as if they were holy relics, in order to regale the populace with
the spectacle of their sufferings. . . .[13]

The situation in Guipuzcoa, though it had not reached such
extremes, was sufficiently chaotic to demand the intervention of
the Crown. The towns of Azcoitia, Azpeitia, Deva, Motrico,

---

[9]Henao-Villalta, pp. 285-286.
[10]Henao-Villalta, p. 117; Zunzunegui, p. 189, note 58. He records Beltran's par-
ticipation in the King's name, at the fixing of the Navarre-Guipuzcoa boundary
in 1389 and 1392.
[11]Echegaray, (I), pp. 112 ff, 198 ff.
[12]Henao-Villalta, VI, p. 338.
[13]Huizinga, pp. 23-24.

Guetaria, Tolosa, Villafranca, and Segura had formed a "Brotherhood" against the *Parientes Mayores*. In 1456 the latter replied with a barbarous defiance in which there is hardly a sign of concern for social order, save for a profession of respect for the authority of the Crown: "We are motivated," they say, "by loyalty and the fidelity we owe the said King," and attack the organizers of the "Brotherhood" "as his enemies and our own."[14]

On April 21, 1457, Henry IV, induced by his Basque counsellor, Miguel Lucas de Iranzo, decided in favor of the towns against the *Parientes*.[15] The condemned heard the sentence read at Santo Domingo in the presence of the Archbishop of Seville and of the most distinguished counts and marquises. It reviewed the crimes committed "with little fear of God and of myself;" imposed the penalty of death incurred along with "infamy of family and line;" and finally, proffered relative clemency "in view of the services your ancestors rendered the Kings of glorious memory, my progenitors." This relative clemency was coupled with the warning that, in case of renewed insubordination or rebellion, "your heads are to be severed by a sharp iron knife."[16]

Juan Perez de Loyola, Saint Ignatius' grandfather, was one of those sentenced to a very long term of exile. He was "banished for four years to the town of Ximena" in Andalusia, "where he was to remain for the service of God and my own, in defense of the Catholic Faith, warring with your persons and with your horses, and arms, and at your expense, against the enemies of the said Catholic Faith. . . ."[17] In addition the Tower at Loyola was razed.

Neither Juan Perez, nor his father, Lope Garcia de Lascano, had neglected the family patrimony. Besides participating in the activities which resulted in the firm establishment of the signorial regime, Lope Garcia had transferred herds of cattle from Peña de Allende to Oñaz, and Juan Perez had increased the farms, herds and woods of the estate, as we previously mentioned.[18] But both of them had taken part in many of the disorders of the province, especially at Segura and Mondragon.[19]

[14]Henao-Villalta, VI, p. 331.
[15]Mújica (II), pp. viii, 59 ff.
[16]Henao-Villalta, VI, pp. 339-340.
[17]Henao-Villalta, VI, p. 339.
[18]RIEV, p. 26 (1935), pp. 482 ff.; Henao-Villalta, pp. 298-304; Dudon, p. 21.
[19]Echegaray, (I), pp. 373-379, 386-387.

Heinrich Boehmer, a Protestant biographer of Saint Ignatius, is surprised that Juan did not withdraw in a pique to his woodlands on his return from banishment.[20] The truth is that neither honor nor self-interest counselled it. Due to new favors granted by the Crown on July twenty-sixth, 1460, Juan was able to pass on to his son, Beltran, the family keep which was now transformed into a castle, along with the former privileges and the family heritage. The son rivalled the towns and the Province Council in fidelity to the King, which precisely at that time, had been granted their charters of nobility.[21] For the Loyolas, it was the dawn of a period of expansion and unforeseen greatness.

2. The reign of the Catholic Kings was characterized not only by the absence of internal strife, but also by the rise of universalist ideals. Such ideals had hitherto been lacking in the Loyola military tradition. From 1480 on, the family had spread throughout the old and new world within a few decades. Beltran received favors from their Majesties during the Granada crusade;[22] Juan, his eldest, together with another brother, succumbed during the Naples campaign in 1498;[23] Hernando left for the Indies in 1510, and died in South America;[24] Martin, his heir on the death of the first-born, took part in the battle of Belate against the French;[25] another son, whose name we do not know, went off to Hungary, and perished fighting the Turk around 1542.[26]

It is hardly possible to reflect more concisely within a single family the profound and heroic change that had taken place in Castile and Guipuzcoa under the Catholic Kings and Cisneros. Therein breathed the spirit of a world-wide crusade, a spirit to which, two years before Saint Ignatius' birth, Juan de Anchieta, a native of Urrestilla and later pastor of Azpeitia, gave poetic form.

Ferdinand and Isabella were besieging Baza in 1489, when they received this menacing message from the Sultan of Constan-

---

[20]Boehmer, I, p. 10.
[21]Guerra, (II), pp. xix-xxi; Mujica, (II), pp. viii-ix, 60 ff.
[22]Chron., I, pp. 516-517.
[23]Chron., p. 517; Dudon, pp. 26, 613; Navarrete, II, pp. 91-92, 97, 107, 110, 120-121. Juan had fitted a caravel of two hundred and twenty tons. Before going to Naples he took part with it under General Iñigo de Arbieta in the Armada of the Indies in 1493 and in various operations in Africa.
[24]Henao-Villalta, VI, p. 350; Dudon, p. 23.
[25]Henao-Villalta, pp. VII, 7.
[26]Chron., II, p. 267.

tinople: "For the vexations suffered by the Mohammedans of Granada, reprisals would be taken on the Christians of Palestine." Then it was that Anchieta put to music the ballad, *"En memoria de Alixandre."*[27] The eyes of the poet beheld, behind Granada, the holy city of Jerusalem where, at the Holy Sepulchre, there awaited the Catholic Kings an Imperial Crown. . . .

There was more than poetic illusion in the bard's inflamed imagination. The taking of Granada was felt in the Mediterranean from Oran to Algiers. That other crusade of discovery, which unexpectedly came to continue the crusades and in a certain sense to hinder them, brought under the Crown the islands and lands overseas.

This environment explains the increasing popularity of novels of chivalry. According to Menendez Pelayo this literary genre was of foreign importation and did not take root in Castile, since it was considered extravagant, until the conquest of Granada and the discoveries overseas. Then appeared the revisions of the old "Amadis of Gaul" in the typically Castilian and modern version by Garcia Ordoñez de Montalvo, the first known edition published in 1508.[28] In the prologue, the author alludes to the points of contact his work has with the spirit which motivated the great enterprise of the taking of Granda.

The author says: "If in the days of those great orators, the Kingdom of Granada had been conquered by our most courageous and Catholic King Ferdinand, what flowers, what roses would not have been strewn by them to eulogize the bravery of the knights in the fray, in skirmishes and hand-to-hand combat, and in all the other trials and labors of such a war. They would have praised, too, the reasoned address made by His Majesty to the leaders assembled in the royal tent, and the obedient response they gave. Especially would they have lauded his great merit for

---

[27]Barbieri, no. 318: *Caminad, Emperadores, / nacidos en muy buen día / que lo que es imposible / con fe posible sería. / Moros son los enemigos, / Santiago es nuestro guía; / ya tremen en Tremecén / y lloran en la Turquía. / Las llaves con la obediencia / Vos darán en la Suría, / visitaréis el sepulcro / muy santo con alegría. / El Pontífice de Roma/las coronas vos pornia/cantando "Gloria en excelsis"/al que en tierra paz envía.* (Forward, Emperor and Empress / auspiciously born / by faith the impossible / becomes possible / The Moor is the foe / Santiago is our guide / Already they tremble in Tremecen / and weep in Turkey. / The keys with obedience / they give you in Syria / You will visit the Sepulcher / most holy with great joy / The Roman Pontiff / will crown you / singing: "Gloria in excelsis" / to the one who upon earth brings peace.)

[28]Menendez Pelayo, pp. 161, 273, 210. The Seville edition has but three books and is not the definitive work which later influenced the entire country, that is Ordoñoz' edition.

having undertaken and carried out so Catholic a campaign."[29]

The "Amadis" sums up and heightens the atmosphere which the men of that age breathed both inside and outside of Spain. For the heroic loyalty of Amadis toward his King, Lisuarte, and toward his Lady, Oriana, his chivalrous struggles on land and sea against giants, dragons, wizards, and legions of enemies, his amorous impulses and moral laxness, were joined to an ingenuous but ardent faith. In Spain alone, up to 1521, there were five editions of this work, which for the longest time and most profoundly has left its mark not only on the domains of fantasy, but also on that of social mores."[30] There appeared in the same period twenty-nine novels of like theme.[31] Boehmer records sixty in French, thirty-four in German, twenty-one Italian, and three English versions up to mid nineteenth century.[32] This confirms Menendez Pelayo's judgment: "that the influence and spread of books of chivalry was not a Spanish, but a European phenomenon. They were the dying rays of the setting sun of the Middle Ages.[33]

The popularity of chivalrous novels was preceded and accompanied by the flowering of a sounder and deeper-rooted type of Castilian poetry. This poetry which was of two classes, popular and humanistic, was largely motivated by religion and ascetics. In turn it, too, was accompanied by a flowering of music and song. There is no need to multiply details of a fact which we shall soon encounter in Ignatius' youth and later on in his conversion. It will be enough to mention in a general way the "Cancionero" of Fray Ambrosio Montesino. He was the favorite poet of Isabella and of her ladies and advisers, to whom the songs are dedicated and in whose palaces they were sung to ancient popular tunes.[34] Mention may be made also of the charming account which Fernando de Oviedo gives in his "Libro de la Camara del Príncipe don Juan" on the education of the Prince and of the Princesses.

Guipuzcoa was more open to these currents than in previous periods. This was due not only to the introduction of the printing press and the importance of the Basque shipping for communica-

[29]Ed. Gayangos, p. xci.
[30]Menéndez Pelayo, p. 189.
[31]Ed. Gayangos, LXIII; Cejador, p. 206; Boehmer, pp. 299-301.
[32]Boehmer, p. 301.
[33]Menéndez Pelayo, p. 255; Huizinga, pp. 32 ff.
[34]Ed. Sancha, pp. 401 ff. prologue and dedications to various ballads.

tion between Castile and England and Flanders, but also because a great many of her sons were reared in Castilian homes during the reign of Ferdinand and Isabella. The famous chronicler, Fernando del Pulgar, has left some curious data on this point in a letter to Cardinal Mendoza written probably between 1480 and 1483.

He writes that at that time he had at his house "four Guipuzcoans" and that "more than forty honorable married men are in the region whom (he) reared and established." This was not unusual. He adds a bit ironically, "the homes of the merchants and lawyers here are crowded with Guipuzcoans. Some are contented with posts as lackeys, but the majority try to become lawyers and secretaries, and still others are reared as nobles "learning to joust" at the palace of the Marquis Iñigo Lopez de Mendoza." He concludes: "You now find more Guipuzcoans at the homes of Fernan Alvarez or of Alfonso de Avila, secretaries, than in your own or in that of the Lord High Constable, even though you are both from their country."[35]

The effects of this intercourse between Guipuzcoa and Castile were not limited to warfare and literature. Advances in agriculture, architecture, and education in the Basque country date from the last years of the fifteenth century and the first decades of the sixteenth. This was due to the turning over of more land for cultivation, the construction and reconstruction in stone of farm buildings and homesteads, the introduction of corn, and to the establishment of convents and monasteries, or orphanages and churches, and of more or less stable centers of education and learning.[36]

There were few who imitated Lope Garcia de Salazar in mid fifteenth century. From his castle at Muñatones he endeavored to obtain books and histories of the world. He had them sought for throughout the provinces and houses of Christian kings and princes, at home and abroad, at (his) own expense, by merchants and mariners.[37] However it is to be noted that the rudimentary Guipuzcoan libraries contained books on subjects more serious than chivalry. Iñigo, for instance, could not get "*Amadis*" and

[35]Pulgar, pp. 14-150. The Mendozas came originally from Álava; Guerra, (II), p. 327.
[36]Echegaray (I), pp. 7-8; Malaxechevarria, pp. 191-198. The advance in studies was far behind that of economics and religion; Lafitte-Obineta in Oñate, pp. 260 ff.
[37]Echegaray (I), p. 36: text and commentary.

"Esplandian," but he did get the richly bound recent works of devotion, at Loyola Castle.

But there is no doubt that the war-like atmosphere, with its note of chivalrous exaltation, penetrated the Basque towns at the beginning of the sixteenth century. Even peaceful and remote Azpeitia was able to mobilize rapidly, in 1521, more than a hundred experienced militia men well provided with pikes and "musket-balls" which had been manufactured in the town itself by Domingo de Arregui.[38] Guipuzcoa made the best pikes and breast-plates on the Peninsula. This military ardor crept into the fashions of the day, and in 1500 the Catholic Kings were constrained to check the extravagant military style of men and women who wore "lachets tipped with ferrules, chapes of swords, daggers and silver knives, according to the local custom."[39] And finally, names taken from novels of chivalry, such as Tristan, Presebal, Montesin, and Floristan, began to be introduced into certain respectable families, for instance, the Leguizamon and the Butron of Biscaya.[40]

In such an environment the outburst of military ardor among the Saint's brothers, and his own desire to "become a soldier," are perfectly understandable.

3. We have already mentioned in the first chapter that, Beltran had at first intended Iñigo to follow an ecclesiastical career, and that he probably received the tonsure at Azpeitia. But the younger son soon revealed his true character. The unpublished dialogues of Nadal tell us that, "though educated with distinction as a noble at his home, he did not devote himself to studies, but moved by a generous ardor, dedicated himself, in conformity with the traditions of the nobility of Spain, to win the favor of the King and of the grandees, and to signalize himself in military glory."[41] It was true of him then, as later on, "that he was not attracted to study which cost him tremendous effort of the will."[42]

This militant ambition in his son was most opportune for Beltran. Between 1504 and 1507 he had received an invitation from his friend in Castile, Juan Velazquez de Cuellar, the Chief

---

[38]*Repartimientos,* fols. 115, 117 v., 118 v.
[39]Gorosabel I, p. 340.
[40]Guerra in Oñate, p. 707.
[41]*Nat. Dial.,* p. 47 v.
[42]*Scripta,* I, p. 394.

Treasurer of the Royal Court since 1495, to send him one of his sons. Velazquez offered to maintain him at his home as one of his own family, and be his patron at the Court.[43] This invitation was not only opportune, but also renewed the ancient bond between the Loyolas and the Castilian nobility. It may be recalled that Beltran Yañez de Loyola had been educated in like manner at the home of his relatives, the Zuñigas, in the fourteenth century. This time, too, the wife of the Castilian nobleman, Maria Velasco, was related to Saint Ignatius' mother.[44] Iñigo, then, was chosen by his father and so went off to Arevalo in Castile.

The first thing we know of the future founder's life at Velazquez' home is the gratitude he still felt after many years. The Saint in 1547 requested the Licentiate Mercado to give to one of Velazquez' grandsons his "humble regards, as from one formerly inferior to him, and still so, and to his father, (Gutierre Velazquez) ; and to his entire family, of which he now has such fond memories and will continue to have in Our Lord."[45]

The Treasurer "was an intelligent, virtuous, generous and Christian man; of fine appearance and of scrupulous conscience. He governed, as over his own domain, the fortresses of Arevalo and Madrigal, and dealt so kindly toward the inhabitants . . . that in "Old Castile" there were no villages that were better treated."[46] He was not only a soldier and an able administrator, but also a patron of letters, and a benefactor of the Church, as were most of the nobles about Isabella. He had founded the convent and hospital of the Poor Clares in Arevalo.[47] Both in the reign of the Catholic Kings and later of Queen Juana and Archduke Phillip, he was in high favor at Court where he was obliged to remain for long periods.[48]

This favor did not lessen when Ferdinand the Catholic married Queen Germaine de Foix, Louis XII's niece. Maria, Velazquez's wife, won the Queen's confidence so that "she could not spend a day without her, while María attended and fêted her at great expense." Carvajal, a contemporary, adds: "even more than was proper," alluding probably to the stout queen's reputa-

---

[43]*Scripta*, II, p. 471; Fita (II), p. 498.
[44]Henao-Villalta, VII, pp. 179-182.
[45]*Ep. et Instruct.*, I, p. 705.
[46]Sandoval, I, pp. 260-261.
[47]Sandoval, I, p. 500; Gómez Rodriguez (I), pp.. 10-11.
[48]Fita (II), pp. 503, 498.

tion for heavy drinking: *"pinguis et bene pota,"* as Peter Martyr wrote in his *Letters*.[49]

The page Iñigo must have seen or heard of another royal personage, the Princess Catalina. She was the posthumous daughter of King Philip I, and was born at Torquemada on January fourteenth, 1507. She later became the wife of John III of Portugal, the great benefactor of the Society of Jesus.[50] The most beautiful of Philip's children, and the one that most resembled her father, she aroused special sympathy and commiseration because of her unhappy childhood. Her mother, the mad Queen Juana, did not permit her to leave her side at Arcos and Tordesillas, but brought her up in the seclusion and poverty in which she herself lived. The child's clothing was a skirt of plain cloth, a kind of leathern mantle, and a white headress. She was allowed no other amusement except to view from a high window the children of Tordesillas at play. The poor recluse would try to attract their attention by tossing coins from her window.[51] The King came to see her occasionally when he visited Queen Juana, and once brought Queen Germaine along with him.[52]

Velazquez and his wife undoubtedly accompanied him, and some special affection must have sprung up between the Princess and Maria. For we know that in 1525 she accompanied the young Princess, as her chief lady of honor, on her journey to Portugal. She never left her, and when she died at her post in 1540, she left her august lady "one of the thirty pieces of silver for which Christ Our Lord was sold, which Queen Isabella had given her."[53] We say nothing of the taste shown by the lady, nor do we vouch for the authenticity of her gift.

This intimacy of Velazquez and his wife with queens and princesses, shows that Iñigo, on coming to the Treasurer's palace, found himself in a court atmosphere. This is what he means when he says in his "Autobiography" that he was serving at His Catholic Majesty's Court," although he was never King Ferdinand's page.[54] At Arevalo, the courtesy he had acquired at the

---

[49]Fita, (II), pp. 504, 516; Martyr, no. 638, p. 352.
[50]Fita, (II), p. 506; Cedillo, p. 165.
[51]Rodriguez-Villa, pp. 186, 220, 272.
[52]Rodriguez-Villa, pp. 233-234, 238.
[53]Fita, (II), p. 6.
[54]*Scripta*, I, pp. 68, 750.

family Castle became polished and elegant.[55] This courtesy and elegance, purified of all worldly defect, is revealed in his letters to the Duke of Gandia, to John III, to bishops and princes throughout Europe. It is also manifested in his appreciation of "proper address and conversation" for winning souls. Father Palmio, who was Minister at Rome for some time, testifies that, at his table there breathed a certain "courtly" air, coupled with simplicity and frugality, especially when the Saint was entertaining persons of quality.[56]

While at Arevalo, Iñigo became acquainted with the literature of the period. We have already mentioned Velazquez' interest in learning. We do not mean by this that he was a scholar devoted to studies or fond of theological and juridical discussions, but rather that he appreciated and encouraged the literature of the Spanish Renaissance then in its glory. His wife and his mother-in-law, Maria de Guevara, had similar tastes. The latter was a pious Basque woman who lived at this time in seclusion with her ladies in a little house next to the hospital of San Miguel at Arevalo. Before the convent of the Poor Clares was founded by the Treasurer, (1514-1515), Maria devoted herself as a Franciscan of the Third Order to works of piety and charity. The Castilian editor of *"Llibre de les dones"*[57] praised her twice in his *"Carro de las donas"* and Fray Ambrosio Montesino dedicated to her[58] his finest stanza to the Virgin in his *"Cancionero,"* a companion piece to one on the Passion and Our Lady of Sorrows, which he dedicated to Guiomar de Castro, the Duke of Najera's mother.[59] The stanza addressed to Maria was to be sung to the air of a well-known popular ballad: *"Aquel pastorcito, madre, . . . que no viene."*[60]

These ballads, which were probably composed during Isabella's reign, were published in 1508, while Iñigo was in Arevalo and at

---

[55]*Nat. Apol. ad Doct. Paris,* fol. 106 r. *"pie ac nobiliter edcuatus."*
[56]Tacchi-Venturi, I, p. 615. Text wherein Father Palmio described it thus: *"Parsimonia et frugalitate Ignatii mensa splendescebat, nescio quid aulicum tamen redolebat; duo enim tresve aderant qui ministrarent, praesertim cum externi homines adhiberentur convivae. Pocula autem adeo eleganter ministrabantur ut ne in aulis quidem id fieri posset elegantius atque concinnius."*
[57]Henao-Villalta, VII, pp. 179-180. Texts. The anonymous Castilian editor records that the author of this Catalan work is the Illustrious Franciscan, Fray Francisco Eximenis.
[58]Ed. Sancha, p. 461. (This stanza may have been dedicated to her, or to one of her nieces, Marina.)
[59]Ed. Sancha, p. 424.
[60]Ed. Sancha, p. 461.

the Court. The *"Cancionero"* was dedicated to King Ferdinand, and was published at his request.[61] It is likely that the stanza to Our Lady was sung in the presence of Maria de Guevara and her children.[62] (Appendix I)

It is probable, too, that the two ballads, which Montesino dedicated to his spiritual father, Saint Francis, were sung in Maria's retreat and on the feast days of the Poor Clares. They had been composed at the request of the Archbishops of Toledo, Pero Gonzalez de Mendoza and of his successor, the then Fray Francisco Jimenez de Cisneros, and reprinted in the *"Cancionero"* in 1508.[63] (Appendix I) The ballad, which was dedicated to the Duchess of Najera, must have been sung if not at Arevalo, then at Navarrete or at Najera, where the ladies of the Duke's deceased mother must surely have sung it. . . . Its theme is the "Way of the Cross," or a "Treatise on the Way and Suffering of Christ as He went up to Golgotha." In it the poet Montesino contrasts the vices of the court with the love and compassion for the *"Dolorosa"* and the *"Ecce Homo."* The keynote is struck in the prologue.[64] (Appendix I.)

At Arevalo, Iñigo not only learned to appreciate the literature of his day, but also perfected his penmanship, and even tried his hand at composition. Ignatius himself tells us that he became "quite a fair writer."[65] We know he had learned to write at Loyola, but now his hand-writing showed those firm and elegant traits which are typical of the Renascence, and invite comparison with that of the scriveners and lawyers of the period.

However, there was more to his efforts than mere caligraphy. Polanco says that, before his conversion, Iñigo had composed a poem in honor of Saint Peter.[66] Father Araoz, a relative of his and acquainted with many at the Court who still remembered Iñigo, adds that, "when he was depressed he composed a prayer to Our Lady, and refrained from playing music on Fridays and Saturdays."[67] This presumes an elementary knowledge of music, and even if there is no question of a prayer in verse, as the

---

[61]Ed. Sancha, p. 401 ff. This is stated expressly in the prologue.
[62]Ed. Sancha, p. 461 ff.
[63]Ed. Sancha, pp. 431-432.
[64]Ed. Sancha, p. 420, p. 425. Cisneros.
[65]*Sripta* I, p. 43. Quotation from Ignatius.
[66]*Chron.* I, p. 13. Not in the primitive Castilian life but in the *"Vita Latina."*
[67]*Scripta*, I, p. 726.

parallel with the poem to Saint Peter seems to indicate, it does imply a written literary composition.

Heinrich Boehmer remarks that the poem and the prayer could not have been literary gems, for there is no trace of them in the various collections of the period.[68] Father Araoz ironically remarks: "It would be interesting to see how a man, who found such difficulty writing prose, would express himself in verse."[69] Yet, the very fact of their composition leads us to conclude that Iñigo received some rudimentary instruction in literature and music, which was an obligatory complement in the formation of a future courtier.[70] Iñigo may have received this instruction at Velazquez' home, or at María's retreat, at the Royal Chapel under the direction of Juan de Anchieta,[71] or at the Duke of Najera's palace in Navarrete, or at all these places. He must have required great perseverance and assiduity before he could acquire sufficient skill to compose verses, for his style is so lacking in ease and color of diction.[72] Juan Velazquez' children or those of the Marquis de Santillana may have found their inspiration in some poem or other in "*Amadis*" or in the sequel "*Esplandian*"[73], but not the scion of Loyola, who was still struggling to master Castilian syntax.

We do not find the inspiration for Iñigo's poem to Saint Peter in the songs and ballads by Montesino. In his entire collection not one is dedicated to the Prince of the Apostles. It is true that from earliest childhood Iñigo was devoted to the patron of the shrine at Eguimendia, and that at Arevalo he may have visited the famous church of San Pedro.[74] Father Ospina informs us that "On a prominent site in the town of Arevalo there was an ancient church, an edifice of strange architecture, half temple, half fortress, which had been dedicated in Christian times to the Prince of the Apostles. Surely Velazquez' page must have visited it frequently. It would be quite plausible to conclude that its fusion of the heroic and the sacred would inspire in a naturally militant

---

[68]Boehmer, (I), p. 17.
[69]Astrain, I, p. 18.
[70]Henao-Villalta VII, pp. 227-228. This is also his opinion.
[71]Coster, pp. 76 ff. We may grant solid probability to his conjecture that at that time he was pastor at Azpeitia and that Ignatius probably knew him before these compositions. The probability is limited merely to his contact with him in learning music.
[72]*Scripta*, I, p. 358: Ribadeneira: "*Cum pater non esset eloquens ab heri et nudius tertius, sed imperitus sermone*".
[73]Gayangos, pp. 124-134, 463, etc. v.g.
[74]Gomez Rodriguez I, pp. 10-11. It was St. Ignatius' parish church. Only probable.

and pious young heart a special affection toward the Apostle who was equally noted for his militant spirit and his lordly primacy."[75]

There was an author who might well have inspired Iñigo to write his poem in honor of Saint Peter. He was the Andalusian poet, Juan de Padilla, the most famous composer of religious ballads in the new Renaissance style, as opposed to Montesino who belonged to the traditional school of short, popular verse of simple inspiration.[76] His two main works are: *"Retablo de la vida de Cristo,"* 1516, reprinted in 1518, and *"Los doce triunfos de los doce Apostolos,"* 1518, and followed by a new edition in 1521.[77] The poet stresses in the *"Retablo"* Saint Peter's decisive action on Pentecost.[78] It is in the *"Doce triunfos . . . "*, however, that he dedicates one of his most typical stanzas to the first Pope.[79] (Appendix I)

There is an element in Padilla's verses that is of great interest to the study of the Saint's youth. Padilla had retired at the age of thirty to the Carthusian monastery of Santa Maria de las Cuevas in Seville. Before that he had spent his youth composing mundane songs, as he tells us in his *"Retablo."*[80] Now he was famed as the Carthusian, for, not content with praising his profession in the Order he had embraced, and with singing of Saint John the Baptist as "the gentlest father of the Carthusians", he frequently celebrated the monastery where he wrote. He showed how the poverty in the life of each religious at Las Cuevas was joined to the external charm of its site, with its vineyards and olive groves opposite the Giralda in Seville.[81]

It is known that Ignatius, when he was pondering at the time of his conversion what he would do on returning from Palestine, thought seriously of entering the Carthusian monastery in Seville. To deduce from this, as Coster does, that Iñigo must have spent part of his youth in the Andalusian capital, and was even employed there in the *"Casa de Contratacion,"*[82] is to forge but one more of the many fantasies in which his work abounds. If the fame of the exterior magnificence and of the internal observ-

[75]Ospina, pp. 5-6.
[76]Menéndez Pelayo, *Antologia . . .*, VI, CCXL, CCXLII.
[77]Foulché-Delbosc, pp. 423 ff, 288 ff.: Texts.
[78]Foulché-Delbosc, p. 446.
[79]Foulché-Delbosc, p. 329; p. 330.
[80]Foulché-Delbosc, pp. 426, 431 ff.
[81]Foulché-Delbosc, p. 294. *"En una gran cueva feroz escondido aunque de fuera se muestre graciosa!"*
[82]Coster, pp. 76-77.

ance of that Carthusian monastery did not induce him to propose becoming a Carthusian, then at least we may rely on the antecedent of Padilla and his poems.

It would be absurd to exaggerate the influence of these and other works by Padilla and Montesino upon the youthful Iñigo. He had not become a devout, literary page who went about seeking the latest religious ballad, confining his love to Saint Peter and Our Lady, and collecting data about the Carthusian monastery in Seville.[83] Even prescinding from the reverse of the medal, "the shadows" which we shall shortly see, it should be kept in mind that his prayer to Our Lady was composed "when he was depressed", a state of mind not precisely that of an aspirant to the Carthusians. . . .

The value of this devout literature, which was so rich in Castile at that time, lies in the light it casts upon the background of Iñigo's youth, an aspect that has been neglected hitherto despite its importance. His affection for composing, and even for religious poetry, despite the imperfection of his language and the worldliness of his life, is explained by this background which influenced him indirectly and subconsciously rather than through formal reading. Here one touches upon the hidden vein of piety and devotion during his earliest formation.[84] This early piety and devotion, despite the errors of his years and the allurements of the world, made his passage to conversion so "natural". It was precisely by way of devout reading, coupled with recollections of Saint Peter and Saint Francis, and of "Las Cuevas," along with his diligent practice of copying in his fine hand, that a change to a new life was so easy.

4. Yet all these practical antecedents of devotion fell far short of producing at Arevalo and at the Court fruits of holiness or even of morality in the youthful Iñigo. Polanco writes: "Though he was ever loyal to the Faith, he did not live in conformity with it, nor did he preserve himself from sin. Especially did he

---

[83]Serrano y Sanz, pp. 144 ff. On *"Las Cuevas,"* despite a caricaturesque tone which is in his work. His data, however, is abundant and first-hand.

[84]Astrain, I, p. 10. We think the influence of Maria de Guevara has been neglected. It is true Father Henao's testimony about her importance during the first years at Arevalo (cf. VII, pp. 181-183, 226) is obscured by legendary details. But Father Tacchi-Venturi (II, pp. 9-10) is quite justified in insisting that Father Henao was working on the documents themselves and that "it is hard to believe there is no basis of truth in his statements."

indulge in gaming, duelling, and affairs with women."[85] Father
Nadal says: "There did not appear in him signs of a select spirit
or of piety. His Christianity was that of a run-of-the-mill
Catholic".[86] Those who are familiar with life in the sixteenth
century will recognize here an authentic son of his period in
Spain. He was whole and sincere in his faith, even devoted to
it, but he was lax in regard to its moral consequences, though
not with the refined perversion of other times and climes. Saint
Ignatius gives us an indirect clue to his worldly life in the "Autobiography" he dictated to Father Camara. He remarks on his
fondness for *"Amadis"* and similar books which he read to the
point of "having his head filled with them" (17, 46).

The revised *"Amadis"* of 1508, which was published at the
same time as Montesino's *"Cancionero"*, was not an irreligious
book, otherwise it would not have been tolerated by the Inquisition, nor would it have attained such lasting popularity on the
Catholic Peninsula.[87]

Within the vaporous and extravagant ambient of the novel,
King Lisuarte, Amadis, and his lady Oriana converse quite
naturally with priests and monks, strive for the exaltation of the
"holy Catholic Faith", assist at Mass and Vespers, listen to
exhortations "to serve Our Lord Jesus Christ", and "to follow
His holy doctrine and example."[88] Amadis and Oriana not only
go to confession for absolution from sin and to be advised in
moral problems, but one of the keys to the plot and the denoue-
ment is sacramental confession which ever retains its inviolability
and dignity.[89] Finally, advanced age and approaching death lead
the King and Queen to retire for a while to hermitages and
monasteries which, though magnificent and sumptuously furnished, are where Lisuarte and his wife "prayed and attended the
Hours every day in a beautiful chapel, engaging in nothing save
devout contemplation, gazing at the heavens and the stars, and
desiring that their merits would be of such worth that their souls
might be deserving of salvation."[90] Further, Amadis, in a

[85]*Pol. Sumario*, fol. 49 v.
[86]*Nat. Dial.*, fol. 29 r.: *"Nihil spiritus, nihil egregiae pietatis attigit; erat
quidem catholice sed populariter christianus."*
[87]Menendez Pelayo, pp. 213, 270.
[88]*Ed. Gayangos*, pp. 323, 326-327, Bk. IV, ch. xxxi, xxxii.
[89]*Ed. Gayangos*, pp. 118, 224, 327; Bk. II, ch. v; Bk. III, ch. ix; Bk. IV, ch.
xxxii.
[90]*Las Sergas*, ch. xliv, p. 119.

moment of disillusionment and despair, becomes a hermit, without, however, the least resignation or meekness: "Considering the strait and holy life of that holy man the anchoret of *"La Peña Pobre"* he resolved, with many tears and groans, not out of devotion, but rather out of deepest despair, to spend with him whatever of life might be left him to live, which he thought would be but little."[91]

Neither Iñigo nor those about him had any cause to object to the novel as far as the Faith was concerned.[92] Yet that very fact constituted its moral danger. For, apart from some loose-living characters, and a few scabrous incidents, such as those of don Galeor and Tristan and Iseult, there is in the work an atmosphere that renders it harmful especially to youths such as Iñigo during his stay are Arevalo. Menendez Pelayo describes it admirably:

He writes: "There predominates in *"Amadis"* the eternal feminine, for Oriana is equally or more important than Amadis. The constant and noble passion of these lovers is not absolutely pure, nor could that be expected of any chivalrous novel when we know the society that engendered it. But its gravest fault, and one which rendered *"Amadis"* and its numerous progeny suspect to moralists, was its false idealization of woman. She was converted into a fragile idol of a sacrilegious and absurd cult, rendered an extravagant amorous servitude, and imparted a certain effeminacy which pervades the work despite its relative chasteness. . . . Experience teaches that the most dangerous books for the young and inexperienced are usually those which are seemingly innocent. Few are attracted by brutal licentiousness; the greater peril for delicate souls is what might paradoxically be called sensual idealism.[93]

Such was the poisoned environment to which Iñigo would have been subjected. He would have succumbed the more readily inasmuch as the palaces of Velazquez and of Queen Germaine, as well as that of his excursions to the Castle at Azpeitia, would have been far from being a preservative. Even the atmosphere at Isabella's Court which, compared to that of Queen Germaine seemed austere, would have been no guarantee of his virtue.[94]

---

[91]Lib. II, ch. v. p. 119. *Ed. Gayangos.*
[92]Neither did Saint Teresa of Avila object on that ground a few decades later.
[93]Menendez Pelayo, pp. 213-214.
[94]*Ed. Sancha,* p. 427: poem by Montesino depicting the corruption of the Court.

(Appendix I.) This was so despite the seriousness with which Isabella strove to reform the morals of the Court, a reform that neither she nor her counsellors, Mendoza, Talavera, Cisneros, were ever able to accomplish. Whatever good was produced soon deteriorated in later reigns. The courts of the Archduke Philip, of Germaine de Foix, and of Charles V, which succeeded one after the other in a few years, imported foreign manners and customs. We have already mentioned the gay and festive behavior of Queen Germaine with the co-operation of Velazquez' wife before the eyes of, and shared in by Iñigo and the other pages.

The bookseller of Alcala, Miguel de Eguia,[95] in speaking of literature, said in 1526 that the most profitable books, despite the many editions of religious works, were "vulgar and at times obscene verses and inept rhymes."[96] This literature might have had a less injurious effect on the youth Iñigo had he had before his eyes the good example of the clergy. But he could see, even in his own remote Azpeitia, that, after Isabella's death, a scandalous litigation had broken out between two groups of the clergy, and nearer home, he knew of, and participated in the public scandals of his priest-brother, Pero Lopez de Loyola, of which we shall soon treat.[97]

The historical figure of Loyola stands out against this background. It is the figure of one whom the Saint later called "a man given over to the vanities of the world, delighting mainly in the exercise of arms with a great and vain ambition to win honor," "tempted," as Father Lainez adds, "and overcome by the lusts of the flesh."[98]

The records of the process brought against him in 1515 at Azpeitia and Pamplona depict for us his bearing and dress. But one or other touch supplied by Ribadeneira is needed to complete the picture.

The "gay and vain youth" wore a slashed suit of two bright colors, open cape, tight-fitting hose, and boots, sword and dagger at his waist, and upon his proud blond head, from which fell curls "reaching to his shoulders", a small scarlet cap, the insignia

[95]Miguel de Eguia, in later years Saint Ignatius' great friend and collaborator together with his brother Diego.
[96]Bataillon, p. 23.
[97]Tacchi-Venturi II, p. 9. Records that this unworthy priest had four children.
[98]Scripta, I, pp. 37, 101.

of the Oñaz, adorned with a jaunty waving feather.[99]   At times
he donned gleaming breast-plate, and wore, in addition to the
inseparable sword and dagger, a cross-bow with darts and other
weapons. Hernandez de la Gama, magistrate of Guipuzcoa, alluding to the tonsured Iñigo's character, finishes this disconcerting
portrait of the future founder of the Society of Jesus thus: "bereft
of every token of the heavenly militia, he bedecked himself in the
vain insignia of the secular soldiery."[100]

And his actions befitted his garb. He indulged in amorous and
sinful pursuits, in quarrels, and in delusions of worldly grandeur,
imitating Amadis with Oriana, or perhaps more exactly, the
gallant don Galaor of the scabrous episodes. If we judge from
his dreams in 1521, he aimed high, exceedingly high, although
during these first years before his departure for Navarre, those
dreams must have been projected far into the future.

A cruel blow brought him back for a few weeks to the harsh
realities of life. Ignatius confided the incident to Ribadeneira. It
is of peculiar interest because, due to the psychological state
produced by it in our disillusioned hero, there is a certain
similarity to Amadis' despair on *"La Peña Pobre."*[101]

When the gallant page least expected it, there formed on his
nose an ill-smelling pustule. The odor soon became unbearable
to those around him. He consulted all the doctors, tried every
remedy: *"omnibus medicis . . . omnia medicamenta",* but in vain.
We can picture the page's distress as a torturing image burned
itself into his imagination: the other pages and the Court ladies
holding their noses in his presence, and turning aside their heads.
. . . Those familiar with the "Exercises" will recognize the images
which they employ to bring the retreatant to humiliate himself
before God and others: "bodily ugliness", "suppurating sores",
and "most repellant poison . . . "[102]

Polanco testified in 1548 that, in his "affliction and trial, Iñigo
never blasphemed against God."[103]   Further, he wanted "to go off
into the desert and hide himself in some secret and inaccessible

[99]*Scripta,* I, pp. 595. ff.. Ospina, pp. 7-9.
[100]*Scripta,* p. 592: *"depositis infulis coelestis militiae, induens se infulis militae saecularis."*
[101]*Scripta,* I, p. 340, Cf. Ribadeniera: *"ego ex ipso."* We think that the episode belongs to this period at Arévalo, for it was when he was at the height of his youthful vigor: *"cum corporis rubore et aetatis flore gloriaretur."*
[102]*Ejercicios, no.* 58.
[103]Pol. *Sumario,* fol. 50 r.

place." But this was far from the perfect repentance of the convert. It was the effect of wounded, hounded pride, rather than the fruit of a mild and comforting grace. Ribadeneira concludes: "He thought that then men might not see him, or that he might no longer see them holding their noses, and turning their heads away, but had no desire or will to serve God."[104]

The poor youth finally overcame the crisis. Revelatory of his character, he did so without outside help, relying on himself. He stopped consulting doctors and taking medicines, but cured the infection with cold nasal douches. Then, with renewed health, he returned to his dreams and ambitions with fresh vigor. Once more he buried himself in his novels, in gaming, in amours, and in duelling, and stained anew the honor of his family during the visits he made to his native valley of Azpeitia between 1512 and 1515. For the details of the process brought against him and his brother, Pero Lopez de Loyola, in 1515, concern not only the Carnival of that year, but one or even more years before.[105] The reputation he left in his home town was deplorable: "*cum praefatus Enecus . . . in vestibus suis se habuerit inhoneste ac etiam in moribus suis deterius.*"[106]

As we pointed out before, conditions in Azpeitia after the death of Queen Isabella in 1504 were not very edifying for the young man from Arevalo. The clergy were engaged in a long and scandalous litigation with the nascent Franciscan convent and with the Franciscans who had been sent there to found and direct it. It was feared that their exemption would diminish the tithes and decrease the jurisdiction of the parish. In 1506 the clergy went to the extreme of excommunicating the "nuns," among whom was one of Iñigo's cousins, at the public High Mass, and overturned the improvised altar.[107] The situation had become even more complicated because of the antagonism between the pastor, Juan de Anchieta, and the Loyola family. The pastor wished at all costs that his nephew, Garcia Lopez de Anchieta, should succeed him in the rectorship. The Loyolas, on the other hand, as patrons, had decided that Pero Lopez should have the office. The

---

[104]*Scripta*, I, p. 340: "*Magis ea ratione ne aut videretur ab hominibus, aut ipse eos videret nares comprimentes et avertentes faciem, quam aut desiderio aut voluntate Deo serviendi.*"
[105]*Scripta*, I, p. 591.
[106]*Scripta*, I, p. 596: immodest in dress, and more immodest in his conduct.
[107]Lizarralde, (I), pp. 75 ff.

outcome was tragic. The young priest Anchieta was slain in 1519 near the House of Emparan by Juan Martinez de Lasao and Pedro de Oñaz. . . .[108]

Did the process of 1515 involve Iñigo in any of the antecedents of this crime which was perpetrated four years later? . . . That it did involve him is suggested by the fact that he is linked in the case with Pero Lopez, and that the indictment speaks of crimes "qualified as enormous, since they were committed by night, with malice aforethought, and after plotting ambuscade and treachery."[109]

However we cannot go beyond a not too well founded conjecture. For, even apart from the fact that this statement is in the indictment and the definitive sentence has been sought in vain,[110] the documents of the process do not specify persons and crimes. On the other hand, the "enormous crime" was committed four years later, and no one has adduced any document of 1514 or 1515 in which the Anchietas and the Loyolas are shown to have been involved in this tragic enmity. The documents which have been found are of 1518 and later.[111] Finally, the records suffice to conclude that no fatal wound was inflicted in 1515, otherwise the magistrate would have mentioned it, and asked for the death penalty, as he did in the case of the crime of 1519.[112]

Yet it is evident that Ignatius was compromised in an unworthy and dangerous action. Indicative of his guilt are the haste with which he exempted himself from secular jurisdiction by appealing to the tonsure, and his lawyer's, Martin de Cabaldica's, insistence on this point when he defended him at Pamplona.[113] A further confirmation may be found in the fact that when the Saint visited Azpeitia in 1535, his expressed purpose was "to give some edification there, where he had been a *cause of scandal* to many."[114]

Thus ends the tale of his sins during the most tempestuous period of his life. He himself when he was cleansed by the

---

[108]Lizarralde, (I), pp. 96-97; Dudon, pp. 29-30.
[109]*Scripta*, I, p. 587.
[110]Dudon, pp. 27-30; nor did Father Cros find them in 1883; my efforts to find fresh evidence in Azpeitia and in Pamplona were equally fruitless.
[111]Lizarralde, (I), pp. 93-97; Tacchi-Venturi, II, p. 10; Coster, pp. 93 ff. supplements documents with subtleties; we follow Perez Arregui (II), 1931, pp. 204 ff.; Dudon, pp. 29-30.
[112]Tacchi-Venturi, II, p. 11; Dudon, p. 30.
[113]*Scripta*, I, p. 585; Astrain, I, pp. 15-16.
[114]*Chron.*, I. p. 51; *Scripta*, I, p. 730.

most perfect contrition, the fruit of his "Exercises," found in
humble and sorrowful confession of his own sins the means to
infuse courage, and to arouse repentance in imperfect souls that
they might confess their sins.[115] He even employed this means
to avoid the heavy burden of Generalship of the Society in 1541.
When he submitted himself beforehand to whatever his confessor
of San Pedro Montorio should dictate, he began by confessing
to him "all his sins from the day he knew what sin was up to the
present moment", with the hope that he would deem him unworthy
of the office."[116]

Such humility and charity were not Iñigo's concern after the
events at Azpeitia. He returned precipitously to seek the protection of Velazquez and his wife, who in 1515 were still in favor
with Queen Germaine and King Ferdinand.[117] Some private
recommendation of theirs, together with the influence of the
Loyolas at the episcopal court in Pamplona,[118] apparently resulted
in the suppression of the indictment. There is no trace of any
sentence, and if there was one, it did not prevent Pero Lopez from
enjoying the charge of pastor of Azpeitia, or hinder Iñigo from
figuring prominently later on among the courtiers in the confidence of the Viceroy of Navarre.

5. Misfortune came from an unexpected quarter with radical consequences for Iñigo de Loyola's future.

King Ferdinand died at Madrigalejo on January twenty-third,
1516 with Juan Velazquez in attendance.[119] Spain was profoundly disturbed but was partially tranquillized under the
strong and prudent regency of Cisneros.[120] However, the event
indirectly brought about the ruin of the Treasurer and his family.

That same year Charles directed from Flanders that the pension
of thirty thousand ducats for life, and the five thousand for
widowhood which the deceased monarch had left to Queen
Germaine upon the revenue of Naples, should be transferred to
certain Castilian towns. Some of the towns thus designated were
governed by Juan Velazquez. As a consequence Arevalo, Madri-

[115]Scripta, I.
[116]Scripta, II, pp. 6, 193.
[117]Fita, (II), p. 502.
[118]Arch. de Navarra, "Papeles sueltos," 2a serie, Fondo Rena: letter by Don
Martin to Micer Juan Rena, Vicar General of the diocese, proves such influence.
[119]Fita, (II), p. 502.
[120]Cadillo, pp. 8-10.

gal, and Olmedo with their *lands and jurisdiction* were to be handed over *in seignory* to the Queen "that she might have them for life as her abode and residence." Juan Velazquez was to retain his office, but was now to govern in Queen Germaine's name. Charles decreed: "that Juan Velazquez should hold it for her and pay homage to the Queen."[121]

There was no additional financial burden laid upon the towns, nor was there any personal injury done the Treasurer. There was, however, a diminution and dismembering of the Royal Patrimony of Castile of which these fortresses were a part. Further there was a violation of the rights of the towns, for from the days of Ferdinand IV they had the often confirmed privilege of non-alienation from the Castilian Crown, a privilege they esteemed as their most prized glory.[122]

If Velazquez had consulted merely his own financial interests, which were untouched by Charles' decree, he would have obeyed without more ado. But he was concerned for the interests of the Crown and of the towns he loved, and felt they should be placed before his own benefit and that of his House. Also there had been a rumor in Court circles that María, his wife, had been too partial to the Queen, and had tried to obtain the right of succession to King Ferdinand for her. If he should now assent to the alienation of these places, and swear fealty to a foreign queen, these suspicions of disloyalty toward Castile would seem justified.[123]

Cisneros did not agree with the young King's action. He wrote his agent in Flanders, Ayala, on the twenty-second of September, 1516: "You will inform the King that in this (matter of Arevalo) he should say nothing, for it will not serve his Majesty. Rather, he who holds the fortress now should retain it, and no change should be made. Neither did I know until now that Queen Germaine intended to request such a thing, and even though she ask for it, do not let her have it, but let it remain in the hands of our King, our Sovereign."[124] Cisneros, however, despite his personal convictions, had to perform his

---

[121]Fita, (II), pp. 513-514; Gomez Rodriguez, (I), pp. 6 ff. Texts. A summary of the King's orders by Cisneros in letters of the third and twenty-second of September, 1516.
[122]Gomez Rodriguez, (II), pp. 387 ff: Texts.
[123]Gomez Rodriguez, (I), pp. 8-9.
[124]Fita (II), p. 514; Text.; Cedillo, pp. 166-167.

duties as Regent. So, while on the one hand he secretly dissuaded the King by letter, and even suspended the execution until Charles should confirm the order, he demanded that Velazquez, or whoever should govern in Arevalo, should prepare to obey at once the King's final decision, "so that His Highness may see that he is served in what he has done, for that will then be carried out."[125]

This is the core of the controversy. Velazquez and the Council of Arevalo held that the Royal Patrimony and the law were above all possible decrees of a distant and ill-informed young king. They felt they served him best by opposing him in the interests of his Crown. And in fact three years later, Charles solemnly admitted in Brussels on September 9, 1520, that, "the grant and favor we made of the said town of Arevalo and its lands to the said most serene lady, Queen Germaine, (Queen of Aragon,) was unlawful, and that it was against the laws of our said Kingdom and contrary to the privileges of said towns . . ."[126]

But that was in 1520. In 1516 the King insisted that the decree be carried out. Cisneros, who never handed over the towns to the widowed Queen as long as he was Regent, urged his friend to contribute along with the other towns to the payment of the charge laid on them for Queen Germaine. As for yielding them to the Queen, he advised him to postpone that until the King should make a definitive decision when he came to Spain.

The Treasurer refused to compromise, and in November of 1516 withdrew from Madrid to Arevalo to defend the town. When long negotiations were fruitless, the Regent acted energetically. He removed the Treasurer from his post, and sent the governor of Corte Cornejo to replace him, not in Queen Germaine's name, but in that of the King. After a stubborn resistance, not so much by lances and artillery as by legal proceedings and fulminations, Velazquez and the Council yielded.[127]

The old servitor of the Catholic Kings and the Patron of Iñigo de Loyola retired to Madrid. He was burdened with a debt of sixteen million maravedis, saddened by the death of his eldest

---

[125]Fita (II), p. 513: Letter of September 3; Cedillo, p. 167.
[126]Gomez Rodriguez, (II), p. 396: Complete text, Danvila, II, pp. 216-217.
[127]Fita, (II), pp. 514-516.

son the previous February, hated along with his wife by Queen Germaine, and bereft of favor at Court. He expired in Madrid on August twelfth, 1517 amid the ruins of his own interests. As Fita says: "He lost all save honor".

Iñigo de Loyola remained with him throughout his misfortunes. Alonso de Montalvo, his comrade in service at Velazquez' palace, and other contemporaries, who mentioned it to Father Alonso Esteban,[128] expressly testify to his loyalty. The scion of the Loyolas doubtless experienced profound bitterness in the course of the dramatic conflict of fidelities. We do not think, however, that he was ashamed of his benefactor's conduct, for he ever rejoiced that he had served Juan Velazquez and his house.

But now his ambitions were thwarted. His comrade Montalvo who was probably left in the same condition.[129] says: "The said Commander died leaving him (Iñigo) unprovided for". The times were propitious for advancement if only the misfortune of Arevalo had not happened. Iñigo wanted to "become a soldier" and it was precisely from 1516 on that Cisneros was organizing, with the King's approbation and in imitation of France, *La Gente de la Ordenanza*, i.e., the first permanent army of the Crown, independent of the nobility and of the towns.[130] Now, because of the ruin of his patron, Iñigo had to forego that promising career.

On the advice of the Treasurer's noble widow, he now turned to another powerful relative. This was the Duke of Najera, who, in addition to commanding a part of the royal army, was in high favor with the monarch. Montalvo relates: "The said Treasurer's wife gave him five hundred *escudos* and two horses. She advised him to go and visit the Duke of Najera, to whom he was related. From there he departed for Pamplona, the capital of the Kingdom of Navarre."[131] So the son of the Loyolas at last approached the frontiers where his lineage had won their first laurels, and where the actual political panorama showed prospects of becoming the stage on which he would perform deeds of loyalty.

At Arevalo from 1507 to 1517 he had led the life of a courtier

---

[128]*Scripta*, (II), p. 471; Fita (II), pp. 498-499; Dudon, p. 32 (questions their testimony.)
[129]Fita, (II), p. 498.
[130]Cedillo, pp. 74 ff. exact data.
[131]*Scripta*, II, p. 471.

and a sinner. In Navarre he would still lead a worldly life "with a great and vain desire to win honor" and with aspirations for the hand of a lady beyond his reach. But it would be a serious, disciplined and, humanly speaking, a fruitful life.

Chapter III

Navarre . . . In the Service of a Temporal King

1. Some understanding of the continental system of European politics during these critical decades is required to appreciate the role played by the Duke of Najera's courtier.[1]

France was the first nation to transform its still medieval institutions into a strong, united, and modern state. This she did toward the end of the fifteenth century. She had been strengthened by final victory in the Hundred Years War, and by Philip the Bold's and Charles the Bold's failure to realize their dreams of founding a Burgundian Kingdom. She had provided herself with the first permanent army in Europe. She could rely on a compact economy and reserves of sixteen million inhabitants against the seven to twelve million in Spain, and the three to five million in England. She boasted a glorious military and cultural past and universal diplomatic prestige. Under Louis and his counsellor she started out upon an imperialist career, and sought to extend her influence to her neighbors. On the pretext of a crusade she tried to expand her sway in Italy and in Palestine.[2]

A radical change took place when Charles VIII succeeded Louis XI in 1483. The idealistic son replaced the realistic, calculating father. The Crown of Jerusalem and rule over the universe would be the prize of a crusade against Italy. This was what Guilloche de Bordeaux and Jean Michel prophesied. This was what Etienne de Vesc, Briçonnet, and the Italian Lyonese bankers urged upon him. In vain Beaujeu and the practical statesmen of Louis XI's school bitterly opposed him. How bitter was their opposition may be seen in Comines' *"Memoirs."* The King sacrificed the certain advantages of a realistic policy to dreams of a "War of Glory." He embarked upon the Italian expedition of 1494 which involved France with the Empire and with Spain. His new policy resulted in the defeats of Gareglano, Gaeta, and the Pyrrhic victories of Ravenna and Marignano. The same policy continued by Louis XII and Francis I brought about the disaster of Pavia

[1]Fueter and Hauser: cf. works cited in Bibliography.
[2]Fueter, pp. 51-52; Hauser, pp. 14-16.

three decades later. The French historian, Henri Hauser, concludes: "Thus precious years were lost for the formation of
Modern France."[3]

The region to which Iñigo was going was one of the theaters of
that continental struggle. Of course it was not the main theater,
nor was it the center of action. That was Italy.

However, forces could not be concentrated in Italy if strategic
gateways on the frontiers were in the hands of rival powers.
Navarre was such a gateway. It was "the principal key to these
Kingdoms"[4] for from it led the direct road to Saragossa in
Aragon, and to Burgos in Castile.[5]

If Navarre had been united and compact, the crisis might
have been weathered or retarded. This the Duchy of Savoy had
managed to do on the Franco-Italian border. But in Navarre the
Agramontais and the Beaumontais had been opposing the authority of the Crown and threatening the unity of the nation in
Pamplona for more than a century after the decease of Charles
the Noble (+ 1425). They had converted the realm into a
plaything of foreign intrigue, jeopardizing its integrity by utiliz-
ing civil and international strife to gain their ends.[6] "It was of
no concern to them that they were injuring their country, so long
as their foes suffered. They sought or rejected foreign intervention according to their self-interest, and had lost all national
consciousness."[7] Because of them the Kingdom of Navarre ceased
to exist as an independent state.

When Iñigo arrived at Pamplona the destruction seemed complete. King Ferdinand had conquered the entire kingdom in
1512. In 1515 the Cortes of Burgos had incorporated it to the
Crown of Castile. Colonel Villalba routed the Franco-Agramon-
tese army under d'Albret. Francis I in August of the same year
apparently gave up all claim to Navarre in the treaty of Noyon
in return for Naples which was to be his daughter Louise's
dowry.[8] In contrast Guipuzcoa had remained loyal to its now
ancient Castilian traditions.[9]

[3]Hauser, pp. 71, 16.
[4]Expression employed by Cortes of Valladolid, 1518.
[5]Boissonade, p. 509; Fueter, p. 75.
[6]Boissonade, pp. 5-9; Fueter, pp. 75, 100-101.
[7]Campion, (I), p. 469.
[8]Hauser, pp. 93-94; Boissonade, pp. 481-482.
[9]Henao-Villalta, VII, pp. 8-12. (Martin Garcia de Oñaz in battle of Belate
(1512) captured French artillery.)

Cisneros, the Regent, and the King, Charles, were fully aware that Navarre was open to invasion. The Regent consequently restored the fortress of San Juan de Pie de Puerto and rebuilt the walls of Pamplona.[10] He ordered that a citadel be built at the latter city which would be near the Tejeria gate and which "would command the wall" from its highest point. It was probably constructed according to the plans of the engineer, Pedro de Malpaso. From Sojo, who has recently published them we learn: "It had a square base, several rounded turrets at the corners, and was built entirely of stone.[11] It also had a chapel dedicated to the Virgin of Pilar.[12] The work was so advanced by July of 1516 that Charles spoke of its proximate completion. The Duke of Najera, however, testified as late as 1521: "It was not finished and had neither a defensive nor offensive breast-work."[13] Cisneros was displeased by the appointment of Miguel de Herrera, an Aragonese, as governor. This is significant in view of Herrera's conduct in 1521.[14]

While the fortress, in defense of which Iñigo de Loyola was to shed his blood, was being constructed, Cisneros was negotiating with the Emperor for the appointment of a viceroy. Antonio Manrique de Lara, Duke of Najera, was chosen. He was a noble of distinction, brave and loyal to the Crown. An additional qualification, upon which Cisneros placed great weight, lay in the fact that the Duke's domains were located on the road between Navarre and Burgos. Besides this he could raise and put on a war footing some three thousand infantry and some seven hundred horses. His friendship with the Beaumontais in Navarre, and his relationship with the province of Guipuzcoa enabled him to call upon them in case of danger.[15]

There was but one obstacle; the hostility of the powerful Lord High Constable of Castile, Iñigo Fernandez de Velasco. Their rivalry explains many aspects of the situation in Navarre and in Guipuzcoa, and reveals the importance of the Loyolas in both. The underlying cause of the friction between these two nobles

---

[10]Cedillo, pp. 214-215.
[11]Sojo, pp. 270-271.
[12]Ascunce, p. 40.
[13]Perez Arregui (I): p. 84; Sojo, p. 271, note 1; Ascunce, pp. 33-37: description of walls as of 1520.
[14]Cedillo, p. 202; Sojo, pp. 271-272; Ascunce, p. 44; for details on Miguel de Herrera.
[15]Martyr, No. 507, p. 274; Sandoval I, p. 247.

is to be found in the ancient feud which their rival houses had waged in the Basque mountain country. There were two factions: the *Oñacinos* and the *Gamboinos*. The Burgos nobleman, Iñigo Fernandez de Velasco, was regarded as the chieftain of the Gamboinos. The nobleman of La Rioja, Antonio Manrique de Lara, was considered the head of the Oñacinos. The Loyolas, of course, were Oñacinos. In Navarre the Agramontais were ancient allies of the Gamboinos, the Beaumontais of the Oñacinos. This explains the following statement by the historian of the House of Lara: "The Lord High Constable, Iñigo de Velasco, took it ill that the Duke should be (the Viceroy of Navarre) and vigorously opposed his appointment. For he feared lest as head of the Oñacinos and their allies the Beaumontais, he would favor them against the Agramontais, his friends and the partisans of the Gamboinos."[16] In the light of these ramifications of the Oñaz among the highest Castilian nobility, Father Araoz scarcely exaggerates when he writes: "Oñaz, the most ancient house in Spain . . . which is divided among the partisans of Oñaz and of Gamboa, or the equivalent."[17]

Despite the Constable's opposition, Cisneros supported the Duke's candidacy. He was appointed by Charles and so on May twenty-second, 1516 the chief of the Oñacinos and the ally of the Beaumontais took the oath of fealty at Pamplona.[18]

Guipuzcoa was more closely affected by the Navarrese situation as a consequence of the Duke's appointment. It became even more straitly linked when its petition for independence from the jurisdiction of the diocese of Pamplona was rejected.[19] A further tie was the appointment of the illustrious Guipuzcoan, Rodrigo Mercado de Zuazola, as counsellor to the Viceroy. He was at that time Bishop of Majorca, and years later became Bishop of Avila, and founder of the University of Oñate. The "Annals of Navarre" relate: "The Bishop, being a native of Guipuzcoa and a man of great prestige, would be able to overcome obstacles, and bring prompt relief from that province to Navarre in case of need."[20] The Viceroy regarded Guipuzcoa as "the most important

---

[16]Salazar II, p. 171.
[17]*Scripta*, I, p. 725.
[18]Cedillo, pp. 216-217; Boissonade, pp. 457 ff.
[19]Cedillo, p. 471.
[20]Garibay, III, p. 593; Aleson, V, p. 363; *Ep. Mixt.*, V, p. 653; for friendship between Saint Ignatius and the Mercados.

and ready succour for the situation here."[21]   In a "memorial"
addressed to Francis I, one of his counsellors advised against a
direct attack upon Navarre lest "the Biscayans and the Guipuzcoans intervene and thwart the undertaking."[22]

2. From what has gone before we can see how suited this new
field was for the fulfillment of Iñigo's ambitions. A Guipuzcoan
relative belonging to the party of the Oñaz, a friend of the
Beaumontais, and coming from so important a family as the
Loyolas, he might well be of service to the Viceroy.

The noble Guipuzcoan had been on intimate terms with the
Duke's family from the end of 1517 on. Years later, in 1541,
Francisco Manrique de Lara, the Duke's brother, learned that
Father Fabre, one of Ignatius' first companions, was at Ratis-
bonne. Fabre writes: "He greatly desired to see me and to
speak to me. I went to see him, and first of all I related to him,
as he requested, all that had happened to Iñigo since his conversion. *He was well acquainted with his life before then, as one
who had known him for so long a time at his home.*"[23]   Saint
Ignatius in 1522 wrote to the Viceroy's son of "the favors and
affection for which he was under obligation to his forebears."[24]

It was Francisco Manrique, later Bishop of Salamanca, who
relates an incident which reveals Iñigo's character while at
Pamplona.

One day Iñigo was going up a steep street of that town.
Suddenly there came a "file of men" from the opposite direction.
They were, perhaps, annoyed by the haughty demeanor of the
Duke's new courtier, or they may have been Agramontais who
were disgruntled at the political situation. Whatever the reason,
trusting in their numbers, they "pushed him against the wall."
Francisco, who was present, testified forty years later to Iñigo's
reaction. "He drew his sword and chased them down the street.
If some one had not restrained him, either he would have killed
one of them, or they would have killed him."[25]   Boehmer and
Tacchi-Venturi remark that his action was more than that of a

---

[21]Boissonade, p. 667: text (1519-1520).
[22]Boissonade, p. 542.
[23]*Fabri Mon.*, p. 111
[24]*Ep. et Instruct.*, IV, p. 385. Letter of August 28, 1552.
[25]*Scripta*, I, p. 566.

punctilious "swordsman" for many in the city were still hostile to Castile and its authorities.[26]

Iñigo's first experiences in Navarre were not of a military nature. As is clear from the Arevalo chronology, he reached Navarre when there was fear in June of 1517 of a French invasion.[27] Other events, however, attracted attention throughout Navarre and Spain. The young Charles would arrive in September of 1517, and the Cortes were going to be held at Valladolid the following February. The Duke of Najera and his household were present at the new King's oath-taking. "He took part along with his soldiers in the tournaments which were celebrated on that occasion. The tournament was splendid. The young King in person entered the lists, and the white armor he wore on the field is the most remarkable that has come from the Royal Armory to the European Historical Exposition."

It is very probable that Iñigo was in the Duke's cortege, for his brother, Martin, the Lord of Loyola, was in Valladolid. He requested and obtained from the new monarch, on the Duke's recommendation, the confirmation of the honors and revenues of his house. He took advantage of the occasion to establish his right to the family estate on a new basis, March fifth, 1518.[28] There is another circumstance that inclines us to think that Iñigo was present. It was precisely during his career in Navarre that Iñigo aspired to the hand of a lady of royal birth. Since she could not have been Queen Germaine de Foix,[29] there only remained doña Catalina. How such an ambition could have arisen in his breast can be explained on the supposition that he witnessed her solemn introduction at the Court in Valladolid during these months.

When the King visited the unfortunate Juana at Tordesillas, he took pity on his beautiful young sister, Catalina, who shared her mother's wretched and secluded life, and whom he had seen for the first time. He determined to bring her to Valladolid unbeknownst to Juana. When she arrived the Court was overjoyed. Tournaments were held in her honor before the Royal Palace at which the gentle Princess appeared. She was dressed

---

[26]Boehmer, p. 23; Tacchi-Venturi II, p. 13.
[27]Cedillo, p. 218.
[28]Fita (I), p. 551.
[29]Leturia, (VII), pp. 86-87.

befitting her rank in "robes which enhanced her fresh beauty and
her natural charm." Lorenzo Vital writes: "I saw her enter
and leave her sister Leonor's chamber. She was walking along
a gallery while the Lord de Trazegnies and Madame de Chievres
held her by the hand, and Ana de Beamonte bore her train which
was of violet satin bordered in gold, and her head was adorned
in Castillian style."[30]

The festivities had a sequel which might well move a reader
of "*Amadis*". The Queen Mother missed her sole comfort. She
refused to eat or drink for two days, and apparently would have
starved herself to death if she had not got her way. Then the
King and the entire Court marvelled how the Princess, "dry-eyed
and without the least sign of anger", returned to the austere
Palace at Tordesillas. There for six years she lived a life of
abnegation and wisdom beyond her years. It was not until 1524
that she left to marry John III of Portugal.[31] As we said, Maria,
Juan Velazquez' widow, accompanied her.

The scenes at the new King's oath-taking, and the charming
apparition of the Princess, which were most likely witnessed by
Iñigo or at least described to him by the Duke and his familiars,
color his psychology from 1520 up to the time of his conversion.
The events at Arevalo had, perhaps, left some hesitancy in his
soul regarding the distant and semi-foreign King. This was now
completely dissipated. The young Charles, who had shown
such fondness for Catalina, had been sworn in solemnly by the
whole Kingdom represented in the Cortes. Then, too, he had
ratified all the privileges and favors granted the Loyolas in the
course of two centuries. . . . It was up to Iñigo, now, to win
honor in Navarre since the King, according to the plan of 1516,
relied on the loyalty of Guipuzcoa.

3. The uprising of the "*Comuneros*" in Castile tragically upset
that plan. Magnanimity, prudence and diplomacy were now as
necessary as the sword. Father Polanco gives us the most
complete picture of Ignatius' conduct in 1520-1521. He has
stressed not only his valor at Pamplona, but also his generosity
in Navarre and his prudent diplomacy in Guipuzcoa.[32] The data

---

[30]Rodriguez Villa, p. 274.
[31]Rodriguez Villa, p. 276; Danvila, II, pp. 70-71; III, pp. 112-115.
[32]Leturia, (I), pp. 9-10; *Chron.*, I, pp. 10-13.

he gives us, complemented by Nadal, has been somewhat neglected up to the present.[33] The details were related to Father Camara by Ignatius himself and suffice to give us some idea of the significance of Ignatius' wounding at Pamplona within the complex and tragic history of those days.

The "*Comunero*" uprising was originally a protest by the old Castilian communities against foreign influence in Charles' government. They objected to his preferring the interests of the Empire to those of the Kingdom. The uprising began at Toledo in May of 1520. It swept the realm even to Guipuzcoa and attracted to its cause many noblemen. The highest, however, remained loyal to Charles, but the movement soon assumed the nature of a struggle of quite dangerous proportions waged by the cities and towns against their lords.[34] In 1520 the conflict reached Najera and Guipuzcoa. The two cogs of Navarre's defense were thrown out of gear.

The Duke of Najera's reaction to the rebellion in his own city was swift. He wrote the Emperor on September 20, 1520 that to let it go unpunished "would seriously jeopardize his Kingdom of Navarre. Since (Najera) was a frontier town, irreparable damage might result to your royal estate and service."[35] As soon as he learned of the uprising of September fifteenth, he did not await the promised reinforcements, among others his "relatives" in Biscaya, Guipuzcoa and Alava, but marched at the head of some royal troops and others of the Count of Lerin and from his own domains.

All his efforts to avoid conflict were vain. He entered the city on the eighteenth "by force of arms". He tells us that "the greater part of the city was sacked according to the usage of war without his being able to prevent it". Polanco complements and confirms this account in 1548 when he writes that Iñigo was in the forefront during this attack,[36] but refused to take any part of the booty. "He displayed his great and generous spirit as one of the Duke of Najera's nobles. When Najera was taken and sacked, though he might have taken much booty, he deemed it unworthy and would have none of it."[37]

[33]Leturia, (I), pp. 55-56: texts.
[34]Danvila, III, p. 758; Hauser, pp. 362-365.
[35]Danvila, II, p. 155.
[36]*Chron.*, I, p. 13.
[37]*Fontes narrativi*, I, pp. 155-156.

The disturbances in Guipuzcoa were more complicated and prolonged. Two phases must be distinguished. The first was the Count of Salvatierra's rebellion at Alava. He had been appointed Captain General of the three Basque Provinces and of the *Merindades* in Castile by the Tordesillas Council. He had also made his influence felt in Guipuzcoa by seizing the artillery captured at Fuenterrabia which he brought to Burgos. Finally, however, he was defeated at la Puente de Durana by the Duke's son, Juan, on April twelfth, 1521.[38] These events do not directly concern Saint Ignatius' life for they were not centered around Guipuzcoa, nor do we think he participated in the suppression of the rebellion. He did participate, however, in the negotiations for the pacification of Guipuzcoa the terms of which the Viceroy dictated by decree of arbitration the very day of the battle.

The second phase of disturbances occurred in the very heart of the Province.[39] Though there is evidence of some connection, these disturbances were not properly a part of the *"Comunero"* uprising. The General Council at Lasarte had petitioned in September of 1520 that Charles' Regent, Cardinal Adrian, send the Licentiate Cristobal Vasquez de Acuña to be Governor of the Province. The towns which later accepted him, headed by San Sebastian, asserted that the accord had been unanimous and based on province privileges. They charged that subsequent resistance was due to the machinations of Nicolas de Insausti and other envoys from the *"Comuneros"* at Tordesillas. Tolosa, Azcoitia, Azpeitia, and most of the towns refused to accept the Governor "holding that he had been appointed contrary to ordinances which had been approved by past kings and by your Majesty."[40] They based their rejection on their own constitutions apart from the Castilian rebellion.

Civil war developed between the Council of San Sebastian and that of Hernani. The Regency decreed the suspension of statutory guarantees.[41] The Duke of Najera became alarmed at these latest developments, "because", as he wrote the Emperor on January seventeenth, 1521, "they may redound to your Majesty's dis-service and to the total destruction of this Province which is so

---

[38]Danvila, II, pp. 222-223, 581; III, pp. 706-710.
[39]Perez Arregui, (I), pp. 73 ff.; Mujica (III), p. 436 ff.
[40]Danvila, II, p. 187: text; of the Duke of Najera; p. 186: text of the Council of Hernani; of San Sebastian, II, pp. 600 ff.
[41]Danvila, II, p. 599.

important to your royal estate. Out of this situation may come irreparable harm to the defense of the Kingdom of Navarre . . . etc."[42] Although Guipuzcoa was outside his jurisdiction he decided to take the initiative.

He dispatched some "persons of his household" to conduct negotiations. While the negotiations were under way, the San Sebastían faction seized some messengers from Hernani. The Hernani party retaliated. Hostilities broke out again with greater violence. Again the Viceroy sent representatives "with measures of agreement". The Duke did not mention Iñigo de Loyola, but we learn from Father Polanco that he was one of the envoys. In 1548 the secretary wrote: "On several occasions he proved himself a man of great prudence and ingenuity in worldly affairs, especially in settling disputes. He was particularly successful in this when the Viceroy of Navarre sent him to settle a serious conflict in the Province of Guipuzcoa. By his tact he brought about an agreement that was satisfactory to all parties."[43]

The Duke's report gives the details of the agreement. Due to Ignatius, his negotiators recognized that the faction of Hernani and Azpeitia would never consent to Acuña's appointment. They claimed it violated their privileges. Their party was the more powerful, for it could muster an army of six thousand men and there was inter-communication between their towns. When Ignatius gave them some hope that their objections would be sustained, they accepted the Viceroy as arbiter. The San Sebastian faction also agreed to arbitrate "for their adversaries had a large army and could bring still more men against them and, as a result, they were in dire straits. . . .[44] After that "the matter was on the way to a settlement", as the Constable wrote the Emperor,[45] and the Duke was able to conclude an agreement.

When the Duke arrived at San Sebastian in January of 1521 he promised that Acuña's appointment would be withdrawn, and actually induced the Regency to do so.[46] The basic issue was now settled. It was agreed that the Viceroy should settle the other differences within a term of three months and that meanwhile no Councils should be convoked. Subsequent memorials of March

[42]Danvila, III, p. 187.
[43]*Fontes narrativi*, I, p. 156.
[44]Danvila, III, p. 188.
[45]Danvila, III, p. 153; Pérez Arregui, (I), p. 77.
[46]Danvila, pp. 135, 189.

second and of May twenty-seventh, 1521[47] to the King show that the San Sebastian faction was not entirely satisfied. The Duke, however, could report on January twenty-first "that the region is quiet", and issued his final decree of arbitration at Pamplona April twelfth. This decree impartially annulled the ordinances and sentences of both Councils.[48]   A new governor, Pedro Sarmiento,[49] was not appointed until May twenty-third, 1521. Meantime the Duke had written: "since they hold that they have rights according to which the governor appointed over them must be petitioned for by them and must have certain qualities, which privilege is based on ordinances which have been confirmed by past kings and by your Majesty, I have charged them to petition you according to said ordinances. . . ."[50]

That "tact" which Polanco admired in Ignatius' activity in Guipuzcoa is discernible in this concern and respect for "ordinances" and insistence on "these certain qualities." He was probably the one entrusted with promulgating and enforcing the decrees. It is certain from Nadal's testimony that Iñigo was in Guipuzcoa when the French invasion began a month later. It was from there he hastened to Pamplona with Martín and the auxiliary troops of the Province. Assuredly the defendant in the trial of 1515 had made great strides in a few years. He could now avail himself of his prestige and sound judgment in the defense of Navarre. The French invasion was imminent.

4. The fear of such an invasion had been used to bolster accusations of disloyalty against the *Comuneros* from the beginning of the disturbances in the Basque country. The Basque leader of the *Comuneros*, the Count of Salvatierra, ridiculed such fears as late as September twenty-second, 1520. He asserted: "There is no more likelihood that the French will invade Navarre than that they will go off to Turkey. All the French King's men are in Italy and in distant parts."[51]

We would say that the Count from Alava had been deceived if there were not such strong evidence that the *"Comuneros"* had

---

[47]Danvila, III, p. 494; IV, p. 131.
[48]Danvila, III, p. 719: texts.
[49]Danvila, IV, p. 132.
[50]Danvila, III, p. 190.
[51]Danvila, II, p. 223.

an understanding with Francis I.[52]   It is true that Charles, following the policy of his Chancellor Chièvres, was inclined toward
friendship and alliance with the King of France.   But a misunder-
standing arose after the former was elected Emperor in June of
1519.   One after another a series of incidents occurred from
February, 1519 to December, 1520.   The Montpellier Conference
failed.   There proposals had been made to settle the issue of
Navarre.   Now Francis intimated he would restore the d'Albret
family to its throne.   He appointed André de Foix commander
of the invading forces.   He was taking advantage of the oppor-
tunity to invade Navarre while the *Comuneros* were striking at
the Emperor in the very heart of Castile.[53]

Fortunately for Charles, his rival did not execute his plans at
once.   Andre de Foix had not even begun to concentrate his
troops at Toulouse and Bordeaux from December, 1520 to March,
1521.[54]   This left the Duke's eldest son free to take part in the
attack on Tordesillas with forces from Navarre, and even employ-
ing artillery from its fortress.[55]   The Duke himself was also able
to pass into Castile with the cream of the royal forces.[56]

After February the situation deteriorated.   Henri d'Albret
arrived at Bearn and with French help prepared for war.   He
gathered twelve thousand infantry, eight hundred lances, twenty-
nine artillery pieces.   The Viceroy, alarmed, reported "the great
insurrection" this event produced in the interior of the
kingdom."[57]

By March twenty-fourth the Duke's position was critical.   Two
years before his brilliant army of ten thousand men had made
the French hesitate.   Their ambassador, La Rochebeaucourt, had
urged caution.   Now, of the three hundred royal guards whom
he had described as "dressed in the fashion of the soldiers who
crucified Our Lord",[58] the Viceroy had only two hundred and
fifty veterans who were mutinous because of ten months arrears
in their pay.   He could rely only on the "mounted personnel of
his household" along with some auxiliaries and the decimated,
discontented garrisons of Maya, Pamplona, and Estella.

---

[52]Boissonade, p. 545.
[53]Boissonade, pp. 526 ff. 546 ff. for full explanation.
[54]Boissonade, p. 546.
[55]Danvila, II, p. 630; VI, p. 187; Boissonade, p. 544.
[56]Danvila, II, p. 673.
[57]Pérez Arregui (I), p. 80: text.
[58]Boissonade, p. 527. Text.

Two fresh worries disturbed the Duke. He wrote the Emperor on March twenty-fifth: "The Province of Guipuzcoa on which we rely most for assistance, responded to my request even before the insurrection *that they too were on the frontier* and had to defend themselves." He could expect little help from that quarter. He said in the same letter referring to Pamplona: "Although I regard it as most faithful to your Majesty, I do not know what would be the effect of the appearance of King John's son, Henri d'Albret".[59]

The Viceroy's fears were justified. Not only the Agramontais but many Beaumontais, carried away by the enthusiasm of the moment, welcomed the King when de Foix's army invaded Navarre. A letter, first published by Father Cros, vividly depicts the state of mind of the populace. "A countless multitude of men advances through the valley of Roncal, through Maya and through San Juan. Sangüesa (where the letter was written), Caseda, Gallipienzo have gone over to Henri. At their head was the Marshall's son, Pedro de Navarra. The Duke has fled Pamplona. The city is now its own master. The French army is expected to reach there tomorrow and it is said it will be able to ride into the fortress. The entire Kingdom and all the mountain region have gone over to Henri d'Albret and I think the Duke will be lucky if he reaches Castile."[60]

This letter is a good description of the situation and explains the discouragement felt by many at Iñigo's side during that critical moment. The Viceroy left Pamplona on the seventeenth. He sent more than ten couriers to the Regency for help. His efforts were fruitless for the Constable's opinion prevailed: "The loss of Navarre is of no importance (*no vale ni una castaña*), for the King will be able to recover it at will."[61] All the Duke could obtain was that Governor Herrera undertook the defense of the castle.[62] He left for Segovia on the seventeenth to obtain reinforcements[63] on the advice of the Admiral, who had counselled him: "The Captain was better off free so that he could help, than tied down able to do nothing."[64]

---

[59]Boissonade, p. 665-666: text.
[60]Cros, I, p. 84.
[61]Danvila, IV, pp. 190, 201. The Admiral's letter of June twenty-first.
[62]Ibid., p. 47.
[63]Perez Arregui, (I), pp. 82-83. The Duke's letter to the Emperor May twentieth.
[64]Danvila, p. 204.

Before his departure for Segovia, the Viceroy had taken two important measures. He had armed the citadel with nineteen large cannon and numerous small pieces, supplied five hundred corselets and many cross-bows, and in addition laid in a supply of provisions and munitions.[65] He had then stationed some one thousand militia in the city under the command of Francis de Beaumont.[66] Francis was the Count of Lerin's brother, one of the most distinguished leaders of the Beaumont party. He it was who had captured the *Comunero* Juan Bravo in the battle at Villalar.[67] Finally the Viceroy ordered Iñigo de Loyola to bring whatever help he could from Guipuzcoa, and to put himself under Francis' command in Pamplona.[68]

Ignatius obeyed these orders. Before the French had entered the capital between the seventeenth and nineteenth of March, he and Martín, by forced marches, arrived with a corps of Guipuzcoan troops. Father Nadal later called it "an army". It was quite large and experienced enough to warrant the brothers' belief that they could hold the city alone. In addition to the Loyola troops there was also the Province militia. Otherwise Nadal's observation that Martín "had been appointed their leader", (*copiis illis fuerat praefectus*), would be meaningless.

The sending of the Guipuzcoan troops accords admirably with the situation in that Province. When it was learned that the French had broken through to Pamplona, the authorities sent a protestation of loyalty[69] to the Cardinal Regent on the sixteenth. The auxiliary force, however, was not the bulk of the Guipuzcoan army. That delayed several days concentrating at Villafranca. Only after the fall of Pamplona was it mobilized at La Guardia and Logroño to the strength of some three thousand, five hundred men. It was commanded by Juan Perez de Anciondo of Tolosa, under the superior orders of the young Juan Manrique de Lara, the Duke of Najera's son. The "Municipal Archives of Azpeitia" seem to indicate that Martín's auxiliary expedition was drawn

———————
[65]Bordenave, pp. 6-7; account of booty taken by French; cf. also Ascunce, pp. 40-42.
[66]Tacchi-Venturi, II, p. 142; *Chron.*, I, p. 12; Cros as well as Polanco consulted the Dukes memorial to the Emperor.
[67]Danvila, II, pp. 629-630, 754.
[68]Leturia, (I), p. 56 Iñigo's mission to Guipúzcoa deduced from Nadal; *Fontes narrativi*, I, pp. 154-155: under the orders of Francis.
[69]Dudon, p. 48: says the Governor of the Province, but the new Governor, Pedro Sarmiento was not appointed until May twenty-third.

from a previous "recruitment" or concentration at Oyarzun which
had Pamplona as its objective.[70]

The Loyolas and their Guipuzcoans were about to encounter an
adversary quite different from the Franco-Agramontais. By the
eighteenth the storm had swept over Pamplona, as the Duke
reported on the twentieth. Of the inhabitants, some feared for
the destruction of the city; others were in sympathy with the new
movement. The Duke reported: "They stirred up great opposition
to the presence in the city of the soldiery I had left there, in
order to have some pretext for permitting the enemy to enter. . . .
Since there was no judge present to decide the issue, the troops
were forced to leave."[71] Through their Council the inhabitants
contended that the entire civil and military administration be
turned over to them. This Francis and his men resolutely refused to do.[72]

During this impasse, the Loyolas arrived with their troops.
Nadal relates that Martín and his men remained outside the walls
and from there negotiated with the authorities the manner of their
entry and the question of subordination of command. He does
not say that Iñigo was entrusted with the negotiations. The
situation, however, would seem to demand this, for he was a
Guipuzcoan and the Viceroy's courtier.

The gist of the negotiations is contained in Nadal's statement:
"Since the situation was desperate, they insistently demanded
("contendunt enixe") of the authorities that they yield the command. In return they promised to defend (the city)." Since
"neither the Council nor Francis reached an agreement, (Ignatius'
brother) became so enraged that he rode off with his troops."

Ignatius remained. He felt it would be ignominious to leave,
and was filled with the desire to win glory. It must not be forgotten, however, that military discipline kept him there too. The
Viceroy had ordered him to place himself at the orders of his
immediate commander, Francis.

Followed by a handful of brave volunteers, Iñigo entered the
city at a gallop: ("incitato equo"). Once more he had to make
a choice. Polanco writes in 1548: "The said Francis wished to

---

[70]Leturia, (II), pp. 23-24.
[71]Perez Arregui, (I), p. 83: Text.
[72]Leturia, (I), p. 56: Gravi dissensio orta inter milites et cives, cum illi con-
tenderent sibi tradi totam urbis et belli administrationem, hi constanter negarent.

abandon the city. He did not think he could oppose the French, nor could he trust the populace of Pamplona. Iñigo refused to follow for he was ashamed lest departure be regarded as flight, but put himself at the head of those willing to defend the fortress along with its garrison."[73]

With visor lowered, shield on arm, and sword flashing he galloped through the streets of Pamplona. This is the culmination of his military career. His brother had withdrawn to Guipuzcoa. His commander had retired to La Rioja. Iñigo chose his own road to honor and imperturbably followed it. He did not ride alone. Those "desirous of signalizing themselves in every service of their King" accompanied him: a handful of knights, among them one of his rivals.[74] As they drew near the fortress they could see the populace rioting and sacking the Viceroy's palace.[75]

On the night of the eighteenth and nineteenth, the citadal looked down upon a spectacle that might well have daunted the bravest heart. Below, the city was preparing to welcome the army of de Foix and d'Albret which was encamped at Villalba. Down beneath in the obscure castle Herrera and his captains, probably the Master of Artillery, Alonso de San Pedro, too, were holding council. All were in favor of surrendering since they were so weak and so few. Though Iñigo did not belong to the garrison and should have been with Francis on the road to Logroño, out of courtesy they consulted the Viceroy's courtier. Polanco gives us his answer: "They should defend the citadel or die." Then Iñigo gave his reasons. As he tells us himself in 1553: "He gave so many reasons that he finally persuaded the Governor to defend the citadel even though it was against the judgment of all the knights. He then inspired them all with his own courage and zeal." (1.38) Besides appealing to their loyalty and ambition for glory, he undoubtedly stressed the imminence of reinforcements which might come from La Rioja and Guipuzcoa in a matter of hours.

The effect of his intervention was soon felt. Before the representatives of Pamplona left for Villalba on the nineteenth to capitulate and surrender the citadel, they sent messengers to

[73]*Fontes narrativi*, I. p. 155.
[74]*Chron.*, I, p. 12: Polanco.
[75]Perez Arregui, (I), p. 83: shortly after Francis' departure.

Herrera.[76]   The Council was prudently looking out for the interests of the populace.   If the citadel resisted, it was possible the French might attack from within the city and then the besieged would fire toward the interior, i.e., upon Pamplona, and destroy its houses.   For, as we mentioned, the citadel commanded the wall, presenting three of its four sides to the exterior, while the fourth with its gateway faced the interior.   The Council proposed that Herrera should pledge not to fire on the city, if he should decide to defend the citadel.   The Council, through its representatives, would try to obtain from the French a pledge to attack only from the outside. . . . Since the Governor had already determined on resistance, he informed them that he was ready to defend himself and that he would respect the city if the French abided by the condition.[77]

Shortly thereafter Pamplona capitulated at Villalba.   The French general refused to grant the condition although he acceded to almost all the other requests made by the Council.   The Council willingly accepted the terms.   For the general was acting not only in the name of France, but also in that of King Henri d'Albret, who was designated in the capitulation as "our natural and sovereign Lord.[78]   That very day the populace enthusiastically welcomed the three hundred French veterans who entered Pamplona under their commander, Sieur de Sainte Colombe.[79]

Within fifteen days enthusiasm had changed to disillusionment and despair.   Day after day the French general put off Henri's entrance into Navarre.   The emblem of France flew over the fallen fortress.   Instead of organizing and protecting the cities of the Kingdom, he despatched his troops to Logroño and to Burgos with the cry: "Long live the *Fleur de Lis* and the *Comuneros* of Castile."[80]

That was after the nineteenth.   Before that the defenders observed only the enthusiasm that reigned in Pamplona, as they looked down from their breastworks.   They could see the French troops entering, and could observe where they set up their

[76]Aleson, V, p. 363. No. 18: Carlos de Artieda, lord of Orcoyen, commanded in Pamplona these days.
[77]Boissonade, p. 519; Dudon, pp. 618-619: Text recently published of capitulation at Villalba.
[78]Dudon, pp. 618: cf. text on preamble.
[79]Bordenave, pp. 7-8; Boissonade, p. 549.
[80]Boissonade, pp. 551, 553.

artillery, and how they were deployed to encircle the citadel. Evidently they were not going to observe the previous day's agreement. The Duke of Najera reported a few days later that: "Herrera demanded the city expel the enemy; otherwise he would inflict upon them all the damage he could. This he did, causing much destruction with his artillery"[81]

On the twentieth the French cannon, the best in Europe,[82] were already set up before the walls and André de Foix entered with the bulk of his army. We learn from French sources that both Sainte Colombe and de Foix demanded the surrender of the citadel before opening fire.[83] Father Araoz, a relative and contemporary of Ignatius, tells us that this demand resulted in a conference with de l'Esparre. He promised them honorable terms. (*"de honesto aliquo pacto tractaret"*).[84] The sources do not say what these terms were. Perhaps they reduced themselves to surrendering the fortress to the authorities of Pamplona instead of to the French. Araoz says that André de Foix particularly requested Iñigo not to return to the citadel.[85] He may have known he did not pertain to the garrison, or that he had served Queen Germaine de Foix at Juan Velazquez's house. . . .

Loyola was adamant. Polanco relates that after Herrera and his three captains had spoken, "he persuaded them not to accept the terms which appeared disgraceful to him. Thus he induced them to arm themselves and defend the citadel."[86]

The voice of the cannon was to be decisive. The son of the mountains and shrines of Loyola, the future founder of the Society of Jesus, had prepared himself for death. He reviewed his stormy life and humbly confessed his sins. There was no chaplain present,[87] so he confessed to one of his comrades. This was a customary practice in the Middle Ages and had been expressly permitted in Fray Hernando de Talavera's "Manual of Confession". This work was current during Iñigo's youth, and so now he took advantage of one of its counsels to satisfy God for his sins and to move himself to perfect contrition.[88] Then he

[81]Perez Arregui, (I), p. 84: Text Auñes, confirmed in Cros, I, p. 85.
[82]Fueter, pp. 60 ff.; Hauser, pp. 16, 69.
[83]Boissonade, p. 519.
[84]*Chron.*, p. 12.
[85]*Scripta*, I, p. 726.
[86]*Pol. Sum.*, in *Fontes narrativi* I, p. 155.
[87]Bordenave, pp. 6-7.
[88]*Scripta*, I, p. 38; Talavera, in Mir. I, p. 32.

took his post on the breastworks, recalling the laurels of Beotíbar
and of Belate and thinking of his King and of his Lady.

Miguel de Auñes, an eye-witness, states that the bombardment
lasted six hours.[89] Despite serious technical defects of which the
Inspector General Diego de Vera[90] had complained several years
before, Herrera's artillery replied effectively. As we shall see,
the enemy's losses were so great that they were angered and only
reluctantly gave quarter to those responsible. At the end of six
hours a part of the wall crumbled, the Master of Artillery was
wounded, the gates breached,[91] and the infantry prepared for the
assault.[92]

At this moment Iñigo fell wounded. Since he was not an
artillerist, before the breaching of the wall, he must have accompanied the Governor who was observing the effect of the artillery
on the enemy, and endeavoring to repair the havoc wrought by
their fire. When the wall crumbled his post was at the breach.
There he went with drawn sword to meet the assailants. It was
then that the providential missile struck him down. In 1548
Polanco relates: "The gunfire was so heavy that the walls soon
crumbled, for they were not very strong at that time. While he
was fighting bravely a ball struck him full in the leg, shattering
the bone, and inflicting a flesh wound on the other without, however, fracturing it." In his revision of 1574 he adds that the
broken leg was the right one, and that the wound in the left was
probably due not to the ball but to a piece of the wall broken off
when the ball ricocheted."[93]

In 1553 Ignatius tells us: "As soon as he fell, the garrison
surrendered to the French." (2, 38). The fate of the survivors
was tragic. According to Miguel de Auñes, the French did not
wish to spare their lives. It may have been because they had fired
upon the city. Whatever the cause, Pedro de Peralta, the son of
the Marshall of Navarre, had to intercede for them.[94] Even his
intercession did not entirely protect them. Bordenave relates that
when they emerged from the citadel the French infantry fired
upon them wounding some and killing others. Only the swift

---

[89]Cros., I, p. 85.
[90]Creixell, I, p. 5; texts.
[91]This proves that the French were firing from within the city.
[92]Boissonade, p. 549: concerning the gates; Bordenave, p. 8, and Polanco, *Chron.*,
I, p. 12: concerning the breach in the wall.
[93]*Chron.*, I, p. 12; Ribadeneira, *Vita, Lib. I, cap. I.*
[94]Cros, I, p. 85.

intervention of de l'Esparre's cavalry prevented all from being slain.[95] A letter of the Bishop of Burgos, Fonseca, written June ninth, indicates that they re-entered the fortress where they were held two or three days.[96]

Iñigo did not undergo these risks. His own report and the accounts by Polanco and Nadal have only praise for the chivalry and courtesy with which the French treated him from the very first. The anonymous author of an early unpublished biography adds a revealing detail. The victors "on entering the citadel searched for him.[97] This fits in with de l'Esparre's offer before the bombardment. Polanco relates in 1548: "Finding him stretched out on the ground they bore him to the city, for he was well known. His very enemies attended him caring for his wounds and providing doctors and the rest." The noble Basque responded to their chivalry. "While he was being cared for at Pamplona by the doctors in the French camp, he gave them affectionately and generously whatever gifts he could. On one he bestowed his shield, on another his dagger, and still another his corselet."[98] This chivalrous rivalry reached such a point that, if we take Ignatius' words in their obvious sense, it was French and not Navarrese or Guipuzcoan soldiers who bore him on their shoulders to Loyola.[99]

Before we accompany the wounded man to Loyola, a word about the Governor Herrera. The French had kept their promise, so he was able to appear before the Regents at Burgos and make his excuse to the Constable of Castile. As is clear from the latter's report to the Emperor, Herrera told his story in his own way. He completely omitted the role played by Iñigo.[100] The Constable reported on June eleventh: *"The French artillery had not yet opened fire* when the defenders lost courage. *Against the Governor's will* they shouted: "France! France!" and thrice raised the flag of surrender. Then they rushed to the gates to let the French enter. They wanted to kill the Governor, for he *alone* was doing all he could to resist. He has managed to escape and give a report of the defeat."[101]

[95]Bordenave, p. 8; Boissonade, p. 550.
[96]Cros in Tacchi-Venturi, II, p. 5, and Danvila, IV, p. 228.
[97]Anonymous, fol. 2.
[98]*Pol. Sum.*, in *Fontes narrativi*, I, p. 156.
[99]*Scripta*, I, p. 38, note the advertance by the editors, note 4. It is not certain, however, as the *Fontes narrativi*, I, p. 365, note 7, warn.
[100]Pérez Arregui, (I), p. 87.
[101]Danvila, IV, p. 183. First used by Pérez Arregui, (I), p. 87.

The underlined phrases are false, as first hand and impartial sources prove. But the Constable, the Duke's persistent rival, lent a ready ear to whatever might discredit the latter's administration of Pamplona. His colleague, the Admiral of Castile, wrote more sincerely to the Emperor on June twenty-first: "I report to your Majesty . . . that no assistance was given the Duke, and that the entire Kingdom (of Navarre) rose in rebellion. We have clearly lost it by default."[102] His judgment of Herrera is extreme. He was convinced that Herrera had committed "the greatest possible treason. Yet not only have we not beheaded him, but he and others are supported as loyal, and go about here defended and protected, and, I should not be surprised, if some should even beg your Majesty's favor for these governors. The proper thing to do would be to behead them."[103]

5. While the Duke, the Constable, and the Admiral were indulging in these disputes at Burgos, Iñigo was enduring excruciating pain as he was borne on a litter through the valleys and hills.

The wounded man and his attendants left Pamplona between the first and fifth of June (2.366) They did not go to the Duke of Najera's house which was the patient's abode at that time. The palace was in the war-zone and further, the French chivalrously thought his native air would be beneficial. Polanco says in 1548: "His very enemies attended him, providing him with doctors and the rest, until it should be safe to send him home to Loyola."

Before they set out they most likely contacted his brother, Martín. He had probably gone first to Segura, where the Provincial Council was assembled, on his return from Pamplona.[104] Thence he went to Loyola to raise militia in Azcoitia and Azpeitia. For "when it was reported that the French had taken Pamplona" between the twentieth and twenty-second of May, the Council of Azpeitia sent Pedro Perez de Zabala "to the Loyola bridge" and to Azcoitia four or five times "to investigate what should be done."[105]

Some time before Iñigo's arrival Martin went off again to the war in Navarre. He did not return until after the victory of

[102]Danvila, IV, p. 204.
[103]Danvila, IV, p. 202; Pérez Arregui, (I), p. 86: text used first time.
[104]*Repartimientos*, Azpeitia, fol. 117 r.
[105]*Repartimientos*, Azpeitia, fol. 118.

Noain, when the crisis of Iñigo's illness had passed. Magdalena de Araoz, his wife, Magdalena and Maria, his young daughters, and his young heir, Bernal, cared for the wounded man. Juan Perez and Catalina were little children, and Martinchu, the future hero of Peru and of Chile, was still but an infant.[106]

Father Lizarralde describes the road the caravan probably followed. "Undoubtedly they carried the wounded soldier through territory still unoccupied by the French. They took the pass from Val de Ollo toward Goñe. Then they crossed the heights of Lizarraga, proceeded to Urbasa, Olazgutia, near Alsasua, thence to Ozaeta, and skirted the port of San Juan, traversed the sierra of Elguea, and finally reached Azpeitia by way of Oñate." He adds that Ozaeta may well have been the hamlet where, according to Father Nadal,[107] the caravan stopped a week to rest the patient.[108] This is quite plausible for two reasons. Ozaeta is on the road from Guipuzcoa to the Ebro and to Saragossa. Later Nadal followed it when he passed through the town where Saint Ignatius had rested. Then, too, Teresa Ibañez, the lady of Vergara, had a house and an estate there. She was a relative and an intimate friend of Ignatius' sister, Magdalena de Loyola, and in 1525 left her estate at Ozaeta to Beltran, Magdalena's son.[109] However, there is a serious objection to the rest having been made at Ozaeta. The town mentioned by Nadal was in the diocese of Pamplona, while Ozaeta belonged to that of Calahorra. We do know for certain, however, that Iñigo spent a night in Anzuola, a town near Vergara. There his sister, Magdalena, was living in a house called *Echandia.*[110]

The week's rest and the patient's condition prevented the caravan from reaching Loyola before the sixteenth or eighteenth of June. It may be that Pero Lopez, the priest,and Martín de Iztiola, the doctor of Azpeitia, met him at Anzuola, or at least at Azcoitia,[111] at the old Loyola bridge which is still standing. We may be sure that Magdalena, her daughters, and the young Beltran, of whom the founder of the Society of Jesus was so fond in later years, would have been awaiting him in the arched gateway of the family house.

[106]Cros in Tacchi-Venturi, II, p. 16, note 2.
[107]Nat., II, p. 28.
[108]Lizarralde (II), 10, p. 180.
[109]Henao-Villalta, V. p. 116.
[110]*Fontes narrativi,* I, p. 366 no. 7.
[111]Cros in Tacchi-Venturi, II, p. 16.

Their welcome had to be brief for the patient was exhausted. The jouncing of the litter, as it was passed through the narrow gateway and carried up the steep stairway to the top floor, was extremely painful. Tradition derived from contemporaries informs us that Magdalena put the wounded man in the highest room in the castle. The plan of the house as it was in Iñigo's lifetime confirms this. The ground floor was used for the wine-cellar and farm equipment and may also have contained a trough for kneading dough. It is not true, as has been stated, that the stables were there. The first floor consisted of a common armory, a spacious kitchen with pantry, and a couple of rooms for the servants. The second floor was set aside for the lord and lady of the castle. It contained a luxurious salon of arms and reception, an ample dining room, an adjoining chapel and adjacent to these, the nuptial chamber of the Loyolas, Ignatius' birthplace, and corresponding alcoves. On the third floor were the children's bed rooms and guest rooms.[112]

They installed the wounded man in the largest and brightest room. It was a spacious room with two windows, one on the north overlooking Izarraitz and its marble quarries and oak trees; the other on the east, with a view of the valley and the gardens of Azpeitia, the shrine of Our Lady of Olaz, and the parish church. At this season, however, all that was quite hidden by the verdant foliage of a giant oak.

There was a canopied bed in the center of the room.[113] That room still retains its low ceiling with its enormous, austere beams which witnessed the agony and struggles of the convalescent-convert. Little windows of Moorish brick let into the wall shed upon his bed the summer light which was tinted with green from the nearby ash groves and the sweet-smelling apple trees encircling the house.

Ignatius mentions nothing of all this in 1553. Naturally he was unaware of it, since he was spent from the journey and his wound. He does tell Father Camara of the diligence of the family to summon "doctors and surgeons from all over." He recalls the fresh "butchery" they perpetrated on his leg and his impassivity in enduring it and the tortures of the journey. "He never uttered

---

[112]We intend to document this data in a later study.
[113]The room now contains the main altar.

a word, and showed no sign of suffering save to clench his fists",
(2, 366) the only concession to pain permitted by the code of
chivalry.

The warrior lay moribund during the feasts of the patron
saints of the shrines at Loyola and Oñaz. He may have but
vaguely heard the bells of the shrines, yet he recalled their dates
in his "Autobiography." The feast of Saint John the Baptist,
patron saint of Oñaz, fell on the twenty-fourth, that of Saint Peter,
patron saint of the Loyola shrine, on the twenty-ninth. On the
feast of Saint John the doctors advised him to receive the last
sacraments. He did so with the piety and simplicity of an "old
Christian." They told him on the eve of Saint Peter that should
he not improve by mid-night, "death was certain." (3,368)

He had been devoted to Saint Peter from early childhood. His
devotion had increased at Arevalo, at the church of San Pedro,
and in the pious environment of the Duke's household.[114] It now
burst forth in an ardent prayer. There was no thought of a
change in his worldly manner of life. There was no question of
a vow to make a pilgrimage or to do penance. That was to come
later. There was merely a dying man's plea for the protection of
the Saint to whom he would devote his prowess as a Knight and
his skill as a poet. . . .

"And so Our Lord willed that he begin to recover that very
night. So rapidly did he improve that he judged himself out of
danger of death a few days later." (3, 368). There is no trace
here of an apparition strictly so-called.[115] There is, however, a
strong conviction of his patron's special intervention. It was the
dawning of that joyous day which was to grow ever brighter until
the day of his conversion.

The echoes of victory were his first impressions as he emerged
from semi-consciousness "as one brought back to life." The bells
of the church and shrines of Azpeitia rang out jubilee throughout
the valley in early July, probably the first or second. The
Azpeitian, Pedro de Zabala, reported that on June thirtieth the
Basque-Castilian army of the Duke of Najera had routed the bulk
of André de Foix' forces on the heights of Noain. All Navarre

---

[114]Creixell, I, p. 21: chapel built by Pedro Manrique, the Duke of Najera's father
for family burial place, in Benedictine Abbey of Navarrete, was dedicated to St.
Peter.
[115]Astrain, I, p. 40.

was being recovered. The Guipuzcoans had distinguished themselves in the vanguard. Foremost among them was the brilliant
company of one hundred and two Azpeitians commanded by their
Captain Juan Lopez de Ugarte. André de Foix had been blinded
and crippled in the fight and had been forced to surrender. At
that very hour the Viceroy was entering Pamplona in triumph.[116]

We may be sure Pedro de Zabala visited the Castle to bring the
wounded hero such joyous news.[117] Soon, however, actual par-
ticipants in the struggle brought him further details. First Martín
de Oyarzabel and Pero Fernandez de Idiacaiz[118] came to visit him.
Then his brother, Martin, who arrived before the second opera-
tion on his younger brother's leg.

Martín related to the convalescent details which the ordinary
person would not know and which would interest Iñigo. The
French Captain General had surrendered at Noain to Francis de
Beaumont, who received ten thousand ducats in ransom. He
admitted his error in attacking Logroño instead of remaining in
Navarre. He confessed he had done this "at the repeated
insistence of the Comuneros.[119] The fortress of Pamplona had
surrendered without firing a shot. Tolet, its Governor,[120] at first
refused to yield, even after the Viceroy's army had entered the
city. However, when he was informed of the capture of de
l'Esparre, his lord, he capitulated with his captains on the fifth
of July and received payment for so doing.[121] Herrera was again
in command of the fortress,[122] and both the Constable and the
Admiral were loud in their praises of the loyalty shown by the
Guipuzcoans.[123]

These tidings opened up wide vistas of glory before Iñigo's
eyes. His own deeds would pave his way. As soon as his leg
healed, he could appear proudly in the Duke's presence. He
might have an audience with the Emperor himself. He might

---

[116]Repartimientos, fols. 116, 118, v.; Gorosabel, V, pp. 81, 88-89; Danvila, IV,
pp. 214-215: Gomez de Buytron's letter of July fourth, 1621. Danvila slightly
varies the number of Guipuzcoans "of Biscayans we were twenty-five hundred men,
and of Guipuzcoans two thousand under Manrique.
[117]Dudon, p. 55.
[118]Repartimientos, fol. 115 v.
[119]Danvila, IV, pp. 212, 216.
[120]Bordenave, p. 9; Ascunce, p. 51.
[121]Danvila, IV, pp. 218, 216, 215: Francis' account, Sept. 5, 1521.
[122]Danvila, IV, p. 216.
[123]Danvila, IV, p. 206 (The Admiral to King Charles) "The Lepuzcoans have
served your Majesty well. All the mountains come to serve Your Highness in the
matter of Navarre. I trust in God that your Majesty will continue to be well
served". (The Constable to the Emperor) (p. 184). "After the battle both wrote
thanking the Province", Henao-Villalta, V, p. 288.

even embark upon a fresh career of heroism in France, in
Flanders, in Italy, in the Indies. . . . His brother may have
reminded him, as he did later, "what expectations everyone had
of him now, and what great honor he might win in the future."
Surely the Duke would promise him "some good lieutenancy . . .
due to the credit he had gained by the past." Such hope of
reward for past deeds and expectations of the future consoled him
as he lay there alone with his thoughts.

Other comforting memories welled up in his mind. His old
friend of Arevalo days, Alonso de Montalvo, had come from
Castile to visit him and to marvel at his fortitude.[124] He
recounted dramatic incidents of the *Comunero* uprising. He told
him that all the Court and the army was talking of the Princess
Catalina. She was just fifteen and remained in the gloomy palace
at Tordesillas. Fray Lope de Hurtado had written the year before: "She is the gentlest lady . . . the most beautiful creature on
earth." The Admiral wrote:[125] "Now that she has reached
woman's estate she feels what they are doing to her. . . . Her
common sense and wisdom is a wonder to behold." When the
Comuneros seized Tordesillas they proposed to set up a Court for
her, and to betroth her in Portugal. In September 1520 the
Marquis of Denia wrote: "In what concerns Your Majesty's
service, as well as in our expenditure, her conduct has been
beyond her years."[126] He wrote again a year later: "Her Highness, may God protect her, is now a woman. It is but right that
your Majesty accord her greater favor and assistance."[127]

Despite the report of her discretion during the *Comunero* disturbances, a rumor was now circulated that was not entirely
without foundation. So the Cardinal Regent and the Marquis
and Marchioness of Denia proposed to transfer her to Arevalo.
This city was more suitable than Tordesillas for her and for her
mother. Furthermore, her presence would serve as a reward for
its loyalty during the *Comunero* uprising. For there had been an
insurrection at Arevalo. Its purpose had been to shake off Queen
Germaine's rule, and to reintegrate the city to the Crown of
Castile.[128] Among the ladies whom the Marquis of Denia con-

[124]*Scripta*, II, p. 471.
[125]Llanos y Torriglia, pp. 21-22: these and other texts.
[126]Danvila, II, p. 71; IV, p. 298.
[127]Danvila, IV, p. 293; V., p. 18 etc.; July 28, 1521 and Jan. 25, 1522.
[128]Rodriguez Villa, p. 380; Danvila, IV, 393; V., p. 15.

sidered for serving the Princess was Maria de Velasco, Juan Velazquez' widow. She too had suffered much through the *Comuneros*.[129] As we have mentioned, three years later she was actually chosen as head lady in waiting to the future Queen of Portugal.[130]

If we keep all these facts in mind and recall his days at Arevalo and at Vallodolid, Loyola's dreams of love and glory during his long inactivity in 1521 will seem less strange.[131] He sat up in bed with dreaming eyes fixed on the marble slopes of Izarraitz which could be glimpsed above the fruit trees through the Moorish arches of his alcove. There he gave free rein to his fancy converting his customary realism into a chimaera of chivalry.

"Of the many vanities that came to him one so obsessed his heart that he was absorbed in thinking about it for two, three, even four hours, oblivious of the passage of time. He envisioned what he must do to serve his lady. How he might go to the region where she dwelt. What verses, what words he should address to her. What deeds of arms perform in her service. His vanity was so great that he disregarded how impossible she was of attainment, for the lady was not of the lesser nobility, a countess or a duchess, but of a rank higher than any of these." (6, 370).

This obsession, this vanity led him to subject his leg once more to the "butchery" of the surgeon. He had noticed how deformed his leg had become after the wound healed. "When the bones had already begun to knit, there remained on the knee-cap a lump caused by the over-lapping of the reset bones. One leg remained shorter than the other. The lump was so large that it was unsightly." . . . (4, 368) We may infer the horror this deformity caused him from the importance he gave, even as a Saint during the last days of his life, to showing his wounded leg. As a proof that he was then completely detached from the world, he confessed to Father Lainez that he would not mind in the least "even going about with his bad leg exposed."[132]

---

[129]Danvila, II, p. 307; III, pp. 120, 287, 292, 457, etc.
[130]Fita, (III), p. 78; cf. his sources.
[131]Fita's opinon; cf. Llanos, p. 74; Leturia, VII, pp. 8 ff. Ignatius indulged in these dreams when the conflict between good and evil thoughts had already begun; but in regard to the lady, he was thinking "about worldly things he was *formerly* wont to think of." The Princess' age was not necessarily an obstacle. Juan de Zuñiga, future tutor of Philip II, became enamoured in 1519 of Estefania de Requesens when she was but ten, and obtained permission for the marriage, which due to her years, was postponed until 1526. Cf. March, (II), I, pp. 270-275.
[132]*Scripta*, I, p. 127; *Fontes narrativi*, I, p. 140.

The very thought of such a thing was unbearable in 1521. How could he appear at the imperial tournaments with that absurd lump showing under the tight hose? How could he ever present himself with such a deformity at the Castle wherein dwelt the lady of his heart. . . . At the first examination by the surgeons he asked them coolly and laconically if it could be removed. They answered that it could, but the pain would be greater than any he had suffered. The bone was now sound, and they would have to reopen the wound to cut the lump off. . . . They did not add that he would remain conscious throughout, for in those days there were no anesthetics. Ignatius does not mention that his sister-in-law and his nieces wept and begged him not to permit the "butchery". He does, however, tell of his brother's protests. "His elder brother was astounded. He said he would not dare submit to such pain." The outcome was quite simple. "He determined to undergo martyrdom for his personal satisfaction." Then the surgeons cut "the superfluous flesh and bone" from his living body. As a commentary Ignatius adds: "the wounded man suffered with his usual patience." (4, 368)

That was but the beginning of the torture. In order to stretch the shrunken tendons of the leg they placed him in an ingenious device "where they kept him many days stretched out so that he could not stir, with his leg fixed in an apparatus which exerted a pull on it, causing him excruciating pain". The good surgeon of Azpeitia received ten ducats for these exquisite refinements of his art. The patient's brother paid seven at that time. Magdalena de Araoz, Iñigo's sister-in-law, paid the remainder in 1539.[133]

He cared naught for these torments. Now, despite the enemies' missile and the surgeons' ineptitude, he could once more don tight-fitting hose and the polished boots of other days. He tried them on as soon as his feet touched the ground. The deformity was no longer noticeable. Ribadeneira says[134] there was only a slight difference in the length of the right and left leg. Garibay tells us: "His lameness was hardly visible. If one did not know of it before, or did not observe him closely, no one would guess he was lame."[135] The gallant courtier was content. If he wore a slightly higher heel on the right foot, or an inner sole, as he did

[133]Cros, _Sección Doc. Azpeitia; Fontes narrativi_, I, p. 369, note 9.
[134]Leturia, (II), p. 105; cf; this and other texts of his.
[135]Garibay, III, p. 594.

years later in Rome,[136] the difference would not be apparent nor unsightly, and there would remain but the record of his glorious wound.

He imagined himself once again in the tournaments at Court performing feats of arms for his lady. No longer would he have to fear lest the weakness of his leg prevent the attainment of his illusory ambitions. "He resolved to follow the world", and pondered again and again "these mundane deeds he yearned to perform." (4, 366; 7, 372). That is why he asked for those books of chivalry with which to foment his illusions, and while away the forced idleness of his convalescence.

This is the psychological state depicted by the "Autobiography" and all other immediate sources on the eve of his conversion. To picture him as sunken in deep melancholy, discouraged at the prospect of failure and the perspective of an ordinary old age, oppressed even to the point of despair "by the lowering skies of the Cantabrian countryside and the limited horizon",[137] is to make a novel out of history, and to forget that the horizons were those of Iñigo's childhood.

Not the pessimism of failure, but the dawning of the most transcendant spiritualism, was to impel him toward other shores. Simply, yet profoundly, Polanco said the same in 1548: "In his accomplishments and endeavors he ever proved himself a man of great worth. Though due to ignorance of spiritual things and to bad habits, he at times made poor use of his ability and natural talent, there was still to be seen in him one whom God had created for a great destiny".[138]

---

[136]*Scripta*, I, p. 490: Lancicius' testimony.
[137]Leturia (II), p., 104 ff: criticism on this point of *"Loyola"* by José M. de Salaverria.
[138]*Pol. Sum., Fontes Narrativi*, I, p. 156.

CHAPTER IV

THE KNIGHT OF CHRIST AND OF THE VIRGIN

1. The convalescent wanted to while away the hours of enforced inactivity by reading. He knew there was no point asking his brother, Martin, for novels of chivalry. Martin apparently had little liking for books despite the smattering of Latin he had acquired in his youth. In his will he enumerates all the effects of the Castle, not even omitting to mention "a jug and two silver salt-cellars . . . three plain basins and two ordinary cups."[1] There is not a word about a library. He does speak fondly and frequently of one book. It is not a scientific or literary work but an account book which, to be sure, is bound "in red leather." Its contents are carefully written in his own hand: "What I owe to so and so, and what so and so owes to me." There were "additional trifling matters which there was no need to make public" that reflected certain quirks of conduct from which the lord of Loyola was not exempt. His will sufficiently shows that.

So Iñigo turned to the lady of the house, Magdalena de Araoz. Possibly the richly bound volumes he wanted belonged to her. She was more given to literature and piety than her husband, for she had been reared at Isabella's Court.[2] Iñigo may have vaguely remembered some collection of books kept in a closet, and asked one of his nurses, Magdalena or one of her daughters, Magdalena or María to bring him a copy of *"Amadis,"* or of *"Sergas de Esplandian."*

Instead, the good ladies brought him the *"Vita Christi"*, and a life of the saints, the *"Flos Sanctorum"* in Spanish.[3] When Ignatius recounts this in his "Autobiography" of 1553, he makes no mention of the comments, the jokes passed, perhaps, in apology for the substitution. No one could have realized the result of the exchange upon the patient's life and even on the history of the Church. He merely stated: "There were no books of the kind he was accustomed to read, so they gave him a life of Christ and a

---

[1]*Chron.* I, pp. 507-508. Text.
[2]Codina, p. 222; Dudon, p. 56.
[3]Codina, pp. 220 ff. proves that the *Vita Christi* which Montesino translated was by the Carthusian. Further details on the *Life of the Saints*, called by Ribadeneira *"Flos Sanctorum,"* will be given later.

83

book on the lives of the saints in Spanish. As a result of reading
and re-reading them he was drawn to what he found written in
them." (6,370)

These words in no way indicate an aversion toward the type of
literature they so unexpectedly handed him. Doubtless he had
seen similar illuminated tomes at Juan Velazquez' house, especially Maria de Guevara's retreat. At Cisneros' request Montesino's translation of the "*Vita Christi*" was published, 1502-1503.
It was the first work printed by the Alcala printing-press, and
was dedicated to Ferdinand and Isabella since they had desired it.
There is a magnificent cut at the beginning of the first volume,
in which the translator is depicted on his knees offering the book
to their Majesties who are seated on their thrones. A large shield
of a united Spain is portrayed at the foot of the page. It is
symbolical of the reception the Court gave the complete work,
which is a classic in the literature of devotion, as its influence
upon Saint Ignatius, Blessed Juan de Avila and Saint Teresa of
Avila shows.[4]

As a page at Arevalo Iñigo might well have preferred the
winged stanzas of the "*Cancionero*" to these beautifully illuminated but heavy tomes. If he read it at all it was because his
aunt obliged him to. But when the dull task was over, he would
at once bury his nose in the other books "he used to read." But
now at Loyola the work was interesting enough to make a virtue
of his necessity. The translator was his favorite author, and his
very name brought to his mind some of the songs and verses he
had read as a youth. He was impressed, too, by its fine Gothic
lettering in black and red as in a Missal. Later in his spiritual
notes he was to use three different colored inks. He was struck
most of all by the "Epistolary prelude by the translator" in the
first volume, which was addressed "to their most Christian and
powerful Majesties, King Ferdinand and Queen Isabella . . . at
whose command he translated it".[5]

His interest was aroused by Montesino's panegyric to their
Majesties. He praised their piety, zeal for justice, and the peace
and order which they had brought to Spain. He recalled their
great triumphs on land and sea, the discovery and settlement of

---

[4]Cejador, p. 241. Unfortunately he does not mention its effect on Ignatius.
[5]It extends from fol. 1 r to 3 r, and is of interest for the history of the period
from more than one viewpoint.

new islands overseas. Iñigo could remember these events which had happened when he was a child, and could contrast with that golden era the disturbances and malaise which followed upon the Queen's death. The brave soldier's attention was perhaps drawn to Montesino's description of their courage and constancy "in having wrested the Kingdom of Granada from the Saracens who were wont to die rather than surrender, thirsted for Christian blood, and defended their wicked, foolish, profane and most abominable sect, and all their cities, towns and castles, which were so powerful and impregnable, that it was beyond belief they could ever be taken. Montesino praised his sovereigns "for having resisted time and again the fierce and bloody hand of the Turks and infidels who waged cruel war by land and sea with mighty armadas and numerous armies." Nor were they less praiseworthy "for the excellence and virtue of their persons, as well as fortunate and blessed by glorious victories, and by discoveries of various lands and islands in distant seas, in the Indies as well as among other barbarous peoples. . . ."[6]

The convalescent read of the zeal these sovereigns had shown for religion and the reform of the churches. The panegyric continues: "You provided all the churches of your kingdoms with proper and very excellent prelates for their administration, having more concern for their spirituality, virtue, and learning than for the nobility and influence of their lineage. For you regarded conformity to the will of the Most High and to Canon Law more important than the affection of ambitious and importunate men. You considered that *the prelates should serve the churches, and not the churches the prelates.* You also have reformed most of the religious orders in Spain which had lost most of their founders' primitive spirit. Not without fierce opposition, you have succeeded in bringing them back to their original observance and have generously endowed them with revenues and privileges. . . . Your Majesties have advanced and reformed learning in the schools and universities of these kingdoms, so that their students might be no less proficient in divine and human studies than these same kingdoms are fertile and abound in temporal blessings. You have constructed throughout Spain, and even at Rome and in *the holy city of Jerusalem,* temples of re-

---

[6]Ibid. fol. 2 v.

ligious and magnificent splendor for the service of God, endowing them with wondrous riches and ornaments of gold, silver and precious stones. You have erected castles and fortresses for the greater ennoblement and defense of your lands and domains."[7]

The convalescent soldier and noble of Spain must have re-read this passage over and over again, as is evidenced by his desire to go on pilgrimage to Palestine.

However, if we attentively study his Autobiography we find that the influence of the second book mentioned, the "Lives of the Saints," is the one that seems to have affected him most. He refers more directly to Saint Francis and Saint Dominic than to Christ and His Mother when he first speaks of his inner conflicts. In fact the "Life of Our Lord", spoken of along with that of the saints (7, 41) may be the life contained in the *"Flos Sanctorum"*. For in that work, in addition to biographies of heroes of virtue, there was likewise an account of the principal mysteries of Our Saviour and of Our Lady which was arranged according to their feasts.[8]

The wounded hero naturally preferred the *"Flos Sanctorum."* It was a two-toned illuminated volume adorned with pictures, some devotional, others quite bizarre.[9] It contained a gallery of heroes and heroines whose lives were told in a rich picturesque style. Its extravagant and chivalresque episodes particularly appealed to the Iñigo of 1521.[10] The copy which divine Providence had so unexpectedly placed in his hands, and which was to open up new vistas before the future founder of the Society of Jesus, was a translation of a work which was enormously popular throughout western Europe. It was a translation or revision of the *"Legenda aurea"* of the Dominican, Jacopo da Varazze (Voragine). Though this book had serious critical and linguistic defects, and at times was marred by grotesque elements,

---

[7]Ibid. fol. 2 r.
[8]This observation may well confirm Father Codina's view which seems certain to us, that the work read by Saint Ignatius was not Father Vega's. The *Flos Sanctorum* might also be called "The Life of Christ and of the Saints."
[9]In the copy at Loyola they greatly resemble in regard to the mysteries of Our Saviour others of the period, for instance that reproduced in Salcedo, II, pp. 56-57; others resemble those in books of chivalry.
[10]*Flos Sanctorum*, fols. 67-72: St. Amarus' adventures in search of the earthly paradise, and his encounter with Leonatis and the duenna St. Baralides. The resemblance of such books to the novels of chivalry resulted in translations of "The Pious Allegories of Chivalry" long extant in France: "The Human Pilgrimage," translated into Spanish by Fray Vicente de Mazuelo, printed at Tolosa in 1490; and shortly after, *"Le Chevalier délibére"* by Olivier de la Marche, which Charles himself translated. Cf. Menendez Pelayo, p. 270; Langlois, pp. 199 ff.

it also possessed a remarkably correct historical basis for most of its stories as well as an ingenuous and profound piety.[11] (Appendix I)

From this work of Voragine, whose name Ignatian sources do not mention since they assume it is known, most of the Castilian lives of the Saints current at the time derived. The copy used by Ignatius was probably edited by Fray Gauberto Maria Vagad, or a reprint at Toledo in 1511. Vagad, a Cistercian, had written a prologue to his edition, and had been a well known personage at Ferdinand's Court where Iñigo was reared.[12] (Appendix I) So his name was quite familiar to the convalescent of Loyola, who during his long service at Court must have seen or heard of its chief chronicler who was a satirical as well as a religious poet.

This would explain his readiness in accepting the books Magdalena brought him. It would also explain how the literary and historical environment in which he was reared at Arevalo later gave way to his total interest in reading novels of chivalry.

2. Let us now see how Iñigo read these books at Loyola. At first he probably did not read any one life in its entirety but passed from one to another, as one reading for distraction. Even then he noticed a certain inner attraction. "By reading passages over and over again he was drawn somewhat to what was written in them." In 1533 he explained the nature of this attraction: "while reading the life of Our Lord and of the saints . . . he pondered over many things which he found good, always proposing to himself difficult and serious things, at which times, he seemed to experience in himself an ease to put them into effect." (7, 41)

He had accustomed himself during the last few months to propose all sorts of difficulties to himself and to overcome them. Father Kreiten observes[13] that Ignatius intended to stress in his "Autobiography" his constancy at Pamplona and his fortitude during his cure at Loyola. This is shown by the very details he selected and emphasized. The practical and heroic side of the saints, then, would impress him most, along with the divine assistance of inner movements. No longer did he set himself to compose poems in honor of Saint Peter, or prayers to the Virgin,

---

[11]*Acta SS. Januarii*, I, pp. xix ff: the authoritative judgment of the Bolandists.
[12]Antonio Nicolas, II, p. 347; Latassa, III, pp. 301-304; Gallardo, I. p. 742.
[13]Kreiten, p. 42.

as he had done at Arevalo. Now he strove to act, to signalize
himself among the heroes, to carve out a future for himself by
his deeds. He kept asking himself "were not the saints heroes? . . .
Why, then, should not he who had yielded to no one in prowess,
why should he not do what they had done?   Would the lash of
the discipline cut deeper than the teeth of the saw that bit into
his deformed leg?   He had resolved to die of hunger and thirst
in the citadel. Could he not fast in a cave?   He had fought his
way through swords and bolts for arquebuses. Could he not go
about barefoot, a beggar braving the jeers of men?   He had done
so much and ambitioned so much for the world. They had done
it for God and eternity.   He realized in a flash that he had
reached a turning point, and "found within himself an ease" to
effect all these things.

These probings had reached to the quick. His worldly habits
reacted vigorously. "But when he stopped reading them," he continues, "sometimes he no longer thought of what he had read; at
other times he turned his mind to the worldly things about which
he used to dream. Of the many vanities that came to his mind,
one so obsessed his heart that he was absorbed in thinking of it
for two, three and four hours without realizing it." (6, 370) Then
follows the passage about his royal lady, for that was the goal
Iñigo the courtier had set before him.

The emulator of the saints was once more changed into a
gallant knight.   He pictured himself raising his shield and
brandishing his lance as he rode by the castle wherein dwelt the
Princess Catalina, the lady of his dreams. But how was he to get
there? And once there, what verses, what words address to her?
He thought back over the journeys he had made as a youth. He
imagined the road to Tordesillas and pictured himself among the
cortege that conducted the Queen and the Princess to Arevalo.
He composed, corrected and re-wrote, only to correct again his
imaginary discourses, interweaving discreet items from *"Amadis"*
with others of his own invention. We see him there as he lay on
his couch dreaming and smiling to himself. Two, three, four
hours without realizing it.

This marvellous psychological analysis continues. "But Our
Lord *came to his aid,* causing other ideas to follow upon these
imaginings, ideas that rose from the books he was reading."

(7, 372)   Without this special assistance the undertaking was impossible. But the spontaneity with which the worldly hero from the very first breathes in that superatural atmosphere proves once more the depth and naturalness of his faith. This is the fundamental phenomenon which caused us to insist on the influence of the shrines of Loyola, of the poetry of Montesino, and of the Catholic tone of Amadis and Oriana. In the actual conflict that went on in Iñigo's soul there was no question of his faith, or of fulfilling the essential duties of a Christian before death, as there was at Pamplona and during his first days at Loyola. He had no thought of retiring from the world, discouraged and a failure, as he proposed during the days he was afflicted by that "ugly" ulcer. Now it was a matter of bidding farewell to the customs of almost twenty years of worldly life, at the very moment his imagination was painting for him smiling prospects of glory and greatness.

That divine "assistance" brought about a greater concentration in Iñigo's reading. He read fewer lives and was more selective in those he read.

The first specific name mentioned in his "Autobiography" is that of Saint Francis (7, 372)   This is not surprising.   For, though there is no justification for the opinion held by some that he belonged to the Third Order at Arevalo,[14] it is true that, after Saint Peter, the *"poverello"* was the saint with whom he was most acquainted. The influence of Saint Francis runs throughout his early life. Maria de Emparan y Loyola, on his paternal side, had founded the convent of the Third Order at Azpeitia. Maria de Guevara, on his maternal side, a member of the Third Order, had founded the Poor Clares at Arevalo. Juan Velazquez de Cuellar, his patron there, had endowed that Franciscan establishment. The Duke of Najera, his present patron, was a generous benefactor of the Reformed Franciscans.[15]   At Court he had known or heard of Ambrosio Montesino, the Cistercian, who was favorite court poet, and of Cardinal Cisneros, who was the Queen's confessor and Regent of the Kingdom. That was why he read and re-read the life of the patriarch who after three centuries still exercised so

---

[14]Rohr, p. 80, has asserted this recently.
[15]Salazar, II, p. 174, records how the Duke assisted at the General Chapter of the Reform at Burgos in 1522 (1523) where it is said he paid the expenses of eighteen hundred friars attending.

remarkable an influence upon the spiritual and even upon the political world.

We can divine Ignatius' feeling as he read over the ancient tale in the *"Flos Sanctorum"*.

"He was a merchant up to the age of twenty, which time he spent in vanity by thus living. So God punished him with an illness, and changed him all at once into another man, so that he came to be a prophet."[16] Was there not some similarity here? Hadn't he too lived a life of vanity, been punished by illness, and was he not now moved to reform his life?

Then he would go on reading: "Once when he came to Rome on pilgrimage he exchanged garments with a poor man, and stood before the church of Saint Peter among[17] the poor and begged and ate quite willingly as they did." Here Iñigo must have stopped reading and asked himself: "What if I were to do what Saint Francis did?" Later we shall see him exchange his soldier's garb for pilgrim's sack-cloth and beg his way among the poor at the hospital of Santa Lucia. For the moment, however, he must have shuddered at the thought of such filthy beggary, as he lay there on the comfortable couch at Loyola. But when he picked up the book once more he found an answer to his qualms:

"And he did this often without permitting shame in the presence of his acquaintances, or the devil who kept after him, to draw him away from the good road he had begun to follow. . . . And then there came a man with a claw hand (a leper), and though naturally he felt some repugnance, yet remembering what that voice had said to him: *Francis, take the bitter as sweet and despise yourself if you desire to know Me,*[18] he ran after that man and began to kiss him. And straightway after that the leper vanished. So he went at once to a lazar and embraced and kissed the hands and feet of the lepers very devoutly and gave them of his money."[19]

Now instead of asking himself as he did before: "What if I were to do what Saint Francis did?" his whole reasoning was to say to himself: . . . Saint Francis did this, then I must do it." (7, 41) His progress is evident.

---

[16]*Flos Sanctorum*, fol. 119, col. II.
[17]The text says *'ante'* (before).
[18]The words italicized are several lines before in the text.
[19]*Flos Sanct.*, fol. 141 v., col. II.

In both of the above citations Ignatius associated Saint Dominic with Saint Francis. We know of no special bond in Iñigo's earlier life that would have made him especially devoted to the founder of the Dominicans or to his Order.[20] Of course he had lived many years at Arevalo which is near Caleruega, the Castilian founder's birthplace. He had visited San Pablo and San Gregorio in Valladolid with the Court when Charles took the oath at the Cortes in 1518. That may have been why he associated Saint Dominic and Saint Francis. If we judge from his words, Saint Ignatius was attracted to both because of their dynamism. He admired their apostolic zeal, their austerities, their poverty rather than the delicacy of their inner life.

That is precisely how the *"Flos Sanctorum"* depicts Saint Dominic. As Iñigo turned the pages to his life he would read:

"And each night he disciplined himself three times with an iron chain: the first time for himself; the second for the sinners in the world; and the third time for the souls in purgatory."[21] Ignatius was to imitate him at Manresa.[22] He was also to copy Saint Dominic in another trait: his utter contempt for money and a limitless trust in divine Providence, as he showed during his pilgrimages and journeys throughout Spain, Italy, and Palestine. That resolve must have been prompted by Dominic's life which related: "Once in the region of Tolosa, when Saint Dominic was embarking on a ship, a sailor demanded his passage money. The Saint answered that he was a disciple of Christ and carried neither gold nor silver nor money of any kind. The sailor then took hold of his cloak and said: "Either give me the money or your cloak." The Saint then raised his eyes to Heaven, prayed a moment and then looked on the ground and saw a coin lying there. Thinking it was sent by God he said to the sailor: "Brother, there is your money. Now leave me in peace."[23]

No other saint is mentioned by name in the "Autobiography." But Ignatius must have made other confidences to Father Nadal for in a sermon in 1561 at Alcala the latter says that at Loyola Iñigo desired "to do great deeds in the Lord's service, as did Saint Onuphrius and other saints who dedicated themselves to

---

[20]Constant, pp. 2 ff. He finds none either. His study was made in 1931.
[21]*Flos Sanct.*, fol. 120 r, col. II.
[22]*Chron.*, I, p. 19: "Severely disciplining himself three times daily."
[23]*Flos Sanct.*, fol. 119 v., col. II.

Him."[24] Saint Onuphrius (St. Humphrey) was an anchoret of the East who was said to have been of princely origin, either an Ethiopian or a Persian. Thus Iñigo in his reading interests passed from the modern, popular saints to those of distant climes and far off times, to saints formerly unknown to him.

The extreme austerity of Ignatius' life for some time after Montserrat and Manresa shows how he was affected by this Saint's life and how determined he was to imitate him. In medieval art and literature Saint Onuphrius was known as the "savage saint". For he lived in the solitude of the Thebaid a life bordering on the savage. The monk Paphnutius, who assisted at his death, describes the spiritual gentleness that lodged within his abject and uncouth body. (Appendix I) His cult became popular in the West at the time of the Crusades and rapidly spread to Italy, France, Germany and Spain.[25] Latin translations of his life date from about that period.[26] The Castilian version of the "Flos Sanctorum," which Saint Ignatius was reading, drew on one of these translations for his life.[27]

As the future penitent of Montserrat and Manresa lay on his couch, the extraordinary life led by this Saint furnished material for his resolves to do "those difficult and serious things" he mentions in his "Autobiography." He decided at Loyola "to eat nothing but herbs". (8, 41; 12, 43) After his "retreat" at Montserrat he rigorously chastized his former excesses in regard to "his personal appearance" by neither combing his hair nor cutting it, by letting his nails grow and by wearing rough and mean sack-cloth. (19, 48) In the caves at Manresa and on the neighboring cliffs and rocks of Montserrat he led the life of a penitential hermit of the desert.[28] He, too, had there his inner conflicts with the "enemy of human nature", as Saint Onuphrius had called the devil, a conflict that has left so deep an impression on the "Exercises" and on the Ignatian letters.[29] When the

---

[24]Leturia, (IV), p. 229. Text first published in 1925.
[25]Acta Sanctorum, Junii, II, pp. 520-523; Leturia, (IV), p. 330: notes and bibliography.
[26]Migne, P. L. 73, pp. 213-222: text.
[27]Flos Sanct., pp. ccxxx-ccxxxiii.
[28]Scripta, I, pp. 731-736; Albareda, (I) p. 80 ff., although we think that sound criticism requires that we attend before all else to the autobiography of Saint Ignatius. We do not think, however, that they exclude the substance of the account by Araoz and other witness concerning the saints which influenced Ignatius while he lived among the cliffs near Montserrat after he had already entered Manresa.
[29]Exercitia, No. 325; Epist. et Instruct., XII, pp. 638, 642-643; "Manresa," 12 (1936), pp. 153-167 (Leturia).

temptation came to turn back from the goal he had set, it took a form that reveals the effect this Saint's life had upon him. He asked "How will you be able to endure such a life as you propose for seventy years?" The desert Saint had lived such a life for precisely seventy years. This and the other details find a natural and at the same time a providential explanation in the light of Nadal's testimony that Ignatius had read the life of Saint Onuphrius.[30]

3. Many other saints influenced him, for he was continually immersing himself in their biographies. In his later actions and in the "Exercises" there are more or less clear traces of Saint Andrew, Saint Joseph of Arimathea, Saint Joachim and Saint Anne, and of Saint Bernard.[31] The "Autobiography" speaks in rather general terms of "the rigors *the saints* had undergone" and employ the expressions, "to imitate *the saints*", and "to do what *they* had done." Clearly, then, Iñigo did not confine his reading to the few saints named above, but rather all of them passed in review before his eyes in triumphal procession, as in Fray Gauberto's prologue where they are called the "knights of God."

There the saints appear in their brilliant and diverse hierarchy: "the true prophets, and the more than true patriarchs . . ., the apostles in wondrous wise made perfect, the unconquered ever triumphant martyrs, the celestial and heroic fathers of the desert, the luminous array of divine doctors, the angelic and most pious virgins, the holy confessors, and the illustrious and marvellously holy founders of such exalted and mighty Orders" . . .[32]

Fray Gauberto, when he comes to this company of the holy founders, gives free rein to his admiration as a monk and medieval chronicler. "The holy founders of such exalted and mighty Orders; Paul in Egypt, in Syria Sts. Anthony and Pachomius, Hilary and Josaphat in the Indies, Basil in Greece, who established the first approved rule; Patrick in Ireland, then Conchello and even more Luno who founded a hundred monasteries among the barbarians, a greater achievement than if he had founded a thousand in Italy, in Africa Augustine, Benedict in Italy, Bruno

---

[30]Obviously it is not our concern to establish the authenticity of St. Onuphrius' Life, but only to consider its influence on St. Ignatius.
[31]Creixell, I, p. 39. Additions and corrections by Codina, pp. 258-259; *Fontes Narr.*, I, p. 397, Note 12, re St. Andrew.
[32]*Flos Sanct.*, fol. A, 2 v.

in Germany, who established the Grand Chartreuse in the Alps of
Savoy, Bernard of France, but why do I say France? rather
throughout Europe where he founded a hundred and seventy
monasteries so large that many were the equivalent of two
counties, so that it was as if he had founded two Castiles and
peopled them with angels; Dominic in Spain, Francis in Asia, in
Catalonia Ramon de Peñafort, Pero Melendez in Guadalajara in
Castile, a monastery begun by the Jeronomites counselled by Saint
Bridget who had founded four monasteries in Sweden, and insti-
tuted a new order in Rome, and countless others in other regions
which, to be brief, I shall not mention."

The former Lieutenant of Saragossa had opened Ignatius'
eyes to a new world of prowess and revealed to him a hitherto
undreamed of source of glory. These were the *knights of God*"
and in their center stood *"the eternal Prince Jesus Christ"*. Such
expressions as these, which would be so pregnant with meaning
for a soldier-courtier, are not mere embellishments, but the sum
and substance of Vagad's entire work.[33]

The directive idea which inspired him was to preface the lives
and sufferings of the saints by "a harmonious history of all the
wonders of the *eternal Prince Christ Jesu*, and particularly the
story of that more than seraphic and divine Passion and death
which He suffered for us."[34] With this in mind, Fray Gauberto
translated into Castilian the story of the Passion as related
in the four Gospels which were harmonized as in Gerson's
"Monotessaron."[35] The *Principle* and *Foundation* of his work is
the Passion and death of Christ. That the reader may realize it
the more, he depicts Jesus Crucified[36] on the very first page, and
on the next explains:

"It was decided that at the main entrance to all holiness and as
an introduction to the heroic lives of all the saints there should be
placed[37] at the very beginning of the work which contains them . . .
the most perfect, the unsurpassed, the most exalted and the most
sovereign example of magnanimity which was manifested in the

---

[33]As we indicated above this is found not only in the first edition by Vagad but
also in the reprint of Toledo in 1511. The description of the latter in Gallardo, II,
519, agrees exactly with the copy at Loyola we are using.
[34]*Flos Sanct.*, fol. A, 2 v.
[35]Gersonii, *Opera Omnia* (Antwerp, 1706), IV, pp. 163-202; Cornely, I, p. 688;
its value in the history of textual and biblical exegesis.
[36]Salcedo, II, p. 56: contains a picture similar to that in the *Flos Sanctorum.*
[37]Errata in text: *'pudiese.'*

Passion and death of the *King of Kings,* the Lord of all virtues, *Christ Jesus.* The picture of the (Crucified) was put on the very first page to portray the sovereign and wondrous *summit of all virtue.* The reader should place it in his right hand, as a living, propitious, magnanimous and ever *victorious royal symbol of the Knights of God* who are His saints, by whose special strength, help, light and favor they were enabled so mightily, wondrously and virtuously to overcome not only the world, the Flesh and the Devil, but even the greatest princes on earth: surpassing the august Caesars in authority and power, the philosophers in wisdom, and the sovereign pontiffs in devotion, and even the mightiest princes of Hell, the wiliest and cleverest of the damned spirits."[38]

This was no new concept in the ascetical literature of the Middle Ages. However, the force and conviction of the former Lieutenant of Prince Juan were admirably adapted to impress Iñigo and give a solid basis and peculiar tone to his thoughts of holiness. Another book he was reading reinforced that impression. It was the *"Vita Christi",* for in its pages, too, he read of the King of the Saints:

"Hence our Sovereign and *benign Leader* Jesus wishes that they walk ever alert and with their eyes and faces, as holy Knights, raised toward his saving wounds, thereby lifting up their hearts to Heaven, and by thus gazing in the mirror of His Passion they are made stronger to suffer the hardships of the combat."[39] (fol. 4 r.)

Father Kreiten, although he was unaware of these texts, came to the conclusion in 1882 that the first movements of the Saint's conversion constitute the germ of the exercises on the *"Kingdom of Christ"* and on the *"Two Standards."*[40] When Ignatius reached in his "Autobiography" the culminating passage of this first phase of his conversion, i.e., his changing his rich military dress for his "longed for pilgrim's sack-cloth" at Montserrat, (18, 388) he summed up the whole process by saying he had determined "to put on the armor of Christ." (17, 386) Thenceforth he calls himself "the new soldier of Christ." (21, 392)

Ribadeneira confirms this and bases his conclusions on the

---

[38]*Flos Sanct.,* fol. A, I v.   Italics ours.
[39]*Flos Sanctorum,* fol. 4 r.
[40]Kreiten, pp. 42-51.

above statement, or, perhaps, on disclosures made to him by the Saint.[41]   In his first *"Life"* he writes of the initial movements in Iñigo's soul: "Further, he was gathering strength and courage to fight and to achieve, and *to imitate the good Jesus Our Captain and Lord* and the other Saints, who *by having imitated Him* merit to be imitated by us." It is noteworthy that Ignatius, in the contemplation on the *"Kingdom"*, recommends only the *"Lives of the Saints"*,[42] omitting the *"Vita Christi"*, a fact of ascetical, autobiographical, and critical interest. Again, during the first days at Manresa Ignatius tells us: "He usually read the Passion at Mass", which he attended daily. (20, 390)   This is another trait characteristic of Vagad's *"Flos Sanctorum"*, namely, the central place given the Passion in ascetical practices.

There is still another confirmation. We shall soon see how Ignatius derived the "election" in his "Exercises" from these inner movements at Loyola. The "Kingdom" and the "Standards" are substantial elements of the Ignatian "election". So we see that the substratum of the first movements and the fruit of his early readings are, in germ, the concept derived from Vagad: the eternal King, as Captain of His Knights, the saints, and the combat between that King against "the mightiest princes of Hell, the wiliest and cleverest of the damned souls."[43]

Ignatius had now attained to the central idea of Christ the King, of the saints His knights, and of the soul as the battleground of a conflict nobler and far more "adventurous" than that of earthly warfare.[44] Though there would now be greater orderliness and consistency in his reading, Iñigo's disturbed spirit was still far from emitting an efficacious *"I will"*. During this first phase of his inner motions, his will was still the plaything of his thoughts, now of holiness, then the very next moment of the world. Polanco shrewdly notes that "With the same ease he permitted himself to be drawn about in these first stages by the current of the vainest ideas."[45]

The inspirations to holiness had managed to creep in and even to fortify themselves in his spirit on an equal footing with his worldly illusions. He had made some progress. But the irrevoc-

---

[41]Ribadeneira, *Vida*, Lib. I, cap. II, p. 14.
[42]Exercitia, no. 100.
[43]Cf. other instructive passages in *Flos Sanctorum*, fol. 9, A. 2 v.
[44]*Flos Sanct.*, fol. ccxxxii.
[45]*Chron.* I, p. 15.

able and efficacious *"I will"*, the embrace of God within the recesses of his soul, had neither been consummated nor would be consummated through mere chivalrous impulse. His union with God was to be more intimate, more conscious, more "modern".

4. The psychic activity of the unreflective soul has been compared to the instability and disorder of a throng hustling and bustling along a public thoroughfare. The way is closed to no one. Amid the whirl of people going in opposite directions and to diverse destinations there is no distinction of hierarchies, no regulation of tendencies, no fixed orientation in the multi-colored and noisy flow of traffic. So in the dissipated soul it is impossible to find a stable synthesis of ideas and sentiments which may serve as a basis for character or for the strengthening of the will. The picture changes kaleidoscopically as does the appearance of these city streets during rush hour.

How different is the picture of the inward-looking soul where reflection rules. In the penumbra of the unconscious the affections and frivolous ideas yield to its influence as multitudes marching along the street on parade. The ideas, accompanied by their cortege of affections and resolves, file along in ordered array, rapidly and fascinatingly if a passion moves them, with measured discipline if a profound thought informs them.

Saint Ignatius might well have had such a picture in mind when he described to Father Camara the psychological motions produced in his soul by the first touch of grace. There began at once a conflict between his thoughts of sanctity and the world. This struggle was not one of intermingling and confused elements, but rather a procession of two opposed yet parallel series, each of which advanced, organized and compact, toward its destination.

Here is how the Saint describes this curious phenomenon:

"Of the many vain things that presented themselves to him, one had so possessed his heart that *he was absorbed in thinking of it for two, three and four hours without realizing it. . . .* The holy thoughts, too, lasted a rather long time, and after other things interposed, the above-mentioned worldly thoughts succeeded, and in them *he delayed a long time.* And this sequence of such diverse thoughts lasted quite a while, *during which he continued to dwell on the thought which obsessed him, whether of those worldly deeds he yearned to perform, or those others of God which came before his imagination,* until, *exhausted,* he left them and attended to other matters." (6-7, 370, 372)

We have already said that one of the most salient traits of Saint Ignatius' *Basque character* was his inner concentration and reflective individualism. Perhaps there is no situation in his whole life which portrays this more faithfully and forcibly. An enemy of inanity and divagation, he puts his whole soul into his ideas and pursues and diagnoses them *by himself* until he has extracted the last vital sap from them. The key phrase is *"by himself"*. There was no other witness, no other counsellor, save his own conscience and the spirit prompting him during the strange and formative conflicts throughout the spiritual process that went on from Loyola to Montserrat. He writes of his confessor at Montserrat: "He was the first to whom he had revealed his resolve, for till then he had told it to no confessor." (17, 368) Or in the words of his confidences to Father Lainez: "without any other interior guide and without communicating his resolve to another, he determined . . . to go away, etc. . . ."[46]

A wealth and intensity in his soul was revealed at the crisis of his conversion, a crisis that revealed the wealth and intensity of his spiritual life. This revelation was never to be dimmed throughout a long and complex life. Its existence had been quite unsuspected in the amorous page, or in the gallant and ambitious courtier, even if we consider his skill in arbitrating disputes in Guipuzcoa and his insistence on going his own way at Pamplona, a way counter to that of his brother, Martín and to Francis de Beaumont.

A man of spirit so attached to his own ideas had to end up by reflecting on his own thoughts. He had to harmonize the two conflicting worlds which had made a battleground of his soul. Perhaps it has not been sufficiently observed that the "divine assistance" of which the convalescent speaks made this reflection the central clue to his victory. There was thus imprinted on Ignatian sanctity and asceticism its characteristic stamp, as much if not more characteristic than loyalty and chivalrous impulse.

Saint Ignatius reveals to Father Camara his discovery by himself of the art of discerning spirits. He says: "There was still another difference, that while he was thinking of worldly things

---

[46]*Scripta,* I, p. 131.

he felt great pleasure; but when later on, exhausted, he left them, he found in himself dryness and discontent. Yet while he was thinking about going barefoot to Jerusalem, eating naught but herbs, performing all the other austerities he had seen the saints doing, not only did he feel consolation while engaged in such thoughts but even after he had left them he remained contented and happy. At first he paid no attention to this, nor did he stop to consider this difference, until one day his eyes were opened a little, and he began to wonder at this difference, and to reflect on it, learning by experience that from some thoughts he remained sad, from others contented." (8, 372, 374)

Later in life the Saint wrote in his "Exercises" that "not great knowledge but to feel and taste things interiorly satisfies the soul;" and that to find this inner taste one is helped not so much by lengthy instructions by directors and by books, as by experience and the savor one acquires "by himself . . . whether through one's own reasoning, or through divine illumination."[47]

It is remarkable he should have learned this at Loyola. This discovery, which was followed by personal introspection without outside help, was a sure stroke of grace. He had come to equate worldly ambition and the desire of sanctity through military and knightly ardor. Now this equation was no longer an impossibility for him. By way of interior pleasure and joy he realized that for his soul sanctity alone remained, and in its train, and along with it, God alone filled his soul. The "Autobiography" concludes: "He began to wonder about this difference and to reflect on it, learning by experience that from some thoughts he remained sad and from others contented. And gradually he learned to *discern the diversity of the spirits that moved him, the one from the devil, and the other from God."* That hidden struggle between God and the enemy of human nature of which his books had spoken, was now being waged within himself. *Of himself* he became aware how the devil acted by momentarily delighting his senses and then leaving his spirit empty; and how God worked by satisfying and rejoicing the permanent depths of the soul.

The effects of this experience were definitive, but not theatrical. He did not rise from his couch and swear fealty to the new standard, but rather, touched by grace, the hidalgo withdrew into

---

[47]*Exercitia,* no. 2, anot. 2 a.

the secret recesses of his spirit to initiate therein a radical and silent transformation. He tells us: "This was the first reasoning he made on the things of God. Afterwards when he composed the 'Exercises' he drew upon the illumination he had received concerning the diversity of spirits. After he had *acquired no little light from that lesson* he began to think more seriously about his past life and about his need to do penance. At this point there came to him the desire to imitate the saints, disregarding all else save to promise to himself by God's grace to do as they had done." (9, 374)

After he had taken this efficacious resolve, his attitude toward the *"Flos Sanctorum"* changed. Formerly a spirit of rivalry had impelled him. He could not allow himself to be surpassed in the will or desire to signalize himself by anyone, not even by the saints. Now in the presence of those saints, and under the influence of divine motions, he began to feel shame for his sinful life: the vain duels, the sins of the flesh, the scandals and escapades at Azpeitia. His imitation of Saint Francis would no longer be staged in public where he would prove the strength of his indomitable will. Its setting would be in the hidden recesses of his soul where he would avenge before God his past sins without express thought of pardon.[48] This is the explanation of his anxiety later on to hide himself in a corner where no one would recognize him, and of his eagerness to avoid throngs. (12, 375; 18, 388)

And all this he would do *"by God's grace."* The expression appears for the first time, never to leave Ignatius, either in his life or in the "Exercises." This phrase he used during the very months when Luther was penning at Wartburg his indictment *"De votis monasticis"*, charging that Roman Catholic piety trusted in the human will and denied grace.

"And now he was forgetting his past thoughts with these holy desires that he had." (10, 374) Ignatius relinquished his former ideals, even his aspirations toward his lady which were enwrapped in so chivalrous an aura, abandoned them without a sigh or a tear of farewell, in contrast to the rending and variable velleities Saint Augustine describes in his own conversion. Ignatius tells

---

[48]He specifically mentions this detail in no. 14, of *Exerc.*, p. 382; Leturia, (II), pp. 40-41.

us that from the making of that efficacious "I will" at Loyola up
to the third or fourth month at Manresa "he had *always* maintained himself in the same interior state with great equality of
joy." (20, 390)

How can so striking a phenomenon, which was perpetuated in
the later resolves of sanctity throughout his life, be explained?
It was doubtless due to the intensity and intimacy of his experiences in interior consolation and desolation. He sums them up
in one of the most expressive formulas of the "Exercises" by
saying "that in those who proceed from good to better the good
spirit touches such a soul gently and softly as when water drops
upon a sponge; and the devil spirit strikes it sharply and noisily
causing disquiet as when water drops upon a stone."[49] The
penetrating and diffusive consolation of virtue now caused the
former diabolical and worldly suggestion to remain and sound
outside.

Polanco writes: "(Ignatius) was ever magnanimous and ambitioned great things."[50] This magnanimity and ambition is fundamental to Iñigo's character. Even in his worldly dreams, he
did not compromise with his own frailty or pursue the lure of
low passions. He was attracted by the brilliance of what he
conceived to be noble and heroic. Yet he was always naturally
disciplined, rational and integral. Once analytical and reflective
grace had revealed to him that there was a finer savor and a
deeper satisfaction of his own dignity in the humble and loving
service of his Eternal King, he enlisted in that service, never to
feel in the depths of his will the desire to turn back. Grace had
not annihilated nature. The fountain rose higher under divine
pressure and purified itself as it mounted. It did not suppress
or distort the innate nobility of his former impulses.

Now the conversion was consummated. The only resorts that
functioned in that noble and rational soul had been transformed
into instruments of virtue. As Father Frusio said of him in his
last years: "He has so accustomed his natural passions to virtue
that apparently of themselves they serve for no other purpose
seemingly than good."[51]

---

[49]*Exercitia*, no. 335.
[50]*Chron.* I, p. 14: "*ut enim erat animo magno, in ultravis parte semper ad magna
propendebat.*"
[51]*Memorial* of F. Camara, no. 207, in *Scripta*, I, p. 256.

5. The convert confided to Father Camara two immediate fruits of his conversion: a resolve to go on pilgrimage to Palestine, and Our Lady's appearance which was followed by a wondrous result.

He had determined to make this pilgrimage to Jerusalem when he first began to read during his convalescence. He was going to undertake it in imitation of the saints, and as a mark of his special love for their King. Now that the transformation is complete, his resolve is clothed with his new ideal. He reveals: "But all that he wanted to do was to go to Jerusalem, as was said above, and this desire was coupled with frequent disciplinings and mortification such as a generous soul burning with love for God is wont to desire to perform." (9, 42)

The devotion to the Holy Places which was traditional in Guipuzcoa and throughout Spain is the remote explanation of Iñigo's resolve.

According to Gorosabel the "*collection*" for its churches was made there from time immemorial.[52] The charters of some of its cities, for instance of San Sebastian,[53] speak of going on pilgrimage to Jerusalem as a current practice. This was not a mere survival from the Middle Ages. The pilgrimage to Jerusalem lived on in the aspirations and customs of Guipuzcoa and Castile at the beginning of the sixteenth century. We find it mentioned in the poems of the Azpeitian, Juan de Anchieta and of the Castilian, Ambrosio Montesino.[54] Pedro Velez de Guevara and the Marquis de Tarifa, Maria's nephew, went on the pilgrimage [55] which was made in Spain even during the most unfavorable years, such as 1523. Of the nine pilgrims including Iñigo who sailed for Jerusalem that year on the Venetian ship "*Negrona*", three were German-speaking Swiss, one a Tyrolese and five were Spaniards.[56]

Ferdinand and Isabella were to a large extent responsible for this revival. It will be recalled that the prologue to the "*Vita Christi*" mentions the temples they erected in the Holy City. They set aside revenues of some two thousand ducats at the in-

---

[52]Gorosabel IV, p. 131.
[53]Echegaray (I), p. 345: Text of San Sebastian charter: "having rented a house should go on pilgrimage to Jerusalem or to another place."
[54]Sancha, p. 432: for Montesino; for Anchiela cf. Appendix I.
[55]Lopez de Haro, I, p. 502.
[56]Boehmer, (I), pp. 79-80 for names and rank.

stance of Fray Antonio de Millan in 1489 and of Fray Mauro de
San Bernardino in 1504 "for the repair of the holy mount of
Sion" and of other churches such as those of Saint James and
of the Nativity at Bethlehem.[57] Since Queen Isabella could not
personally go there, she sent "along with other precious gifts
a veil she herself had made, which was of great worth",[58] and had
established the *"Obra Pia"* which existed for centuries and collected annually approximately six hundred and seventy thousand
silver reales up to the seventeenth century.

This background remotely explains the Loyola convert's resolution. It explains too the wholly Jerusalemite vocation of one
of his most intimate Basque friends of later years. This was
Pedro de Zarate, a native of Bermeo, the "Knight of Jerusalem",[59]
who founded an arch-confraternity for the protection and main-
tenance of divine service at the Holy Sepulcher.

The immediate preparation for Iñigo's resolve to go on pilgrimage to Jerusalem is to be found in his reading. Not only the
lives of the various saints in the *"Flos Sanctorum"*, but the very
pictures it contains, readily awaken the desire to accompany Our
Lord in the land He walked and in which He died. There is, for
instance, a reproduction of the footprints, which, according to
pious belief, the Saviour left upon a rock on Olivet when He
ascended to Heaven, a detail which aroused tremendous interest
in Ignatius during his pilgrimage in 1523.[60] The fundamental
passage is in the *"Vita Christi"*.

"It is indeed a holy and pious exercise to contemplate the holy
land of Jerusalem where all the churches of Our Saviour are
never empty. For that sovereign King of ours, Christ, dwelling
therein and enlightening it by His word and doctrine, at last
consecrated it with His precious Blood. And since this is so, it is
even more pleasing to behold it with bodily eyes and meditate
upon it with the mind, for in each of its places Our Lord wrought
our salvation. Who can number the devout who visit each place
therein and ardently kiss the earth, reverence and embrace the
places in which they know or hear that Our Lord visited, taught,
or performed some work? And these at times strike their breasts,

[57]Eijan, pp. 241-242.
[57]Eijan, (II), p. 375 for the gift; Lejarza, pp. 73 ff, for the *"Obra Pia."*
[59]Granero, pp. 108 ff: re *Zarate.*
[60]*Flos Sanct.,* fol. 89; *Fontes narrativi,* I, p. 425 for passage on visit to Olivet
in *Acta.*

at times shed tears and groan, at times sigh to Heaven with sorrowful gestures and yearning devotion. Often their outward
manifestation of their inner contrition moves even the Moor.
What shall I say of the patriarchs Jacob, Joseph and his brethren?
For, whereas they were unable to look upon that land in life, they
chose and desired to die there and have there their tombs. Is there
need to say more? Surely we ought to groan and bewail the
idleness and indifference of the Christian princes of our day who,
having before them so many examples, are so weak and uncon-
cerned for its conquest out of the hands of the enemy, for Our
Lord consecrated it with His precious Blood."[61]

In the state of soul in which Iñigo found himself after he had
been touched by grace, this passage would undoubtedly have
directed his desires of penance, and devotion, of loyalty and of
love. And quite naturally his early devotion to our Lady now
burgeoned into a new life transformed by grace. The Carthusian,
too, had predisposed him for Our Lady's visit to her wounded
Knight at Loyola. The devout Carthusian had written:

"This 'Life' reveals that the saints of God are well disposed,
interested and benign to those who honor them. And this they
do out of love for that Lord who is a joy common to them and to
us. Of this let us take for an example the glorious Virgin Mary.
By any chance could or would this Blessed Lady, Mother of
Mercy, of Piety and of Grace, wish to despise or turn away Her
Eyes from you even though you be a sinner when She sees that
not once a day but many times Her Son, more beloved of Her
than all things, dwells in spirit or by contemplation in your arms
and heart? Will She, perchance, abandon you when She beholds
you in His arms, and when She sees you accompanying everywhere the Fruit of Her Womb? For, when She sees that you contemplate and serve Him every day, and that you do Him devout
service by works of piety, I well believe She will in no wise be
unmindful of you."[62]

If these passages were not the ones that moved the knight
Loyola, he must have been inspired by similar thoughts of his
own. Perhaps he thought of the shrines at Olaz and at Elosiaga,
or recalled the prayers he had addressed to Our Lady during his

---

[61]*Vita Christi C.*, I, fol. 9, 5, 9, v. Taken from Burhardt of Monte Sion, a
Dominican of the twelfth century; Grausem, p. 271.
[62]*Vita Sanct.*, fol. 5.

sinful life. We do know, however, that at this point he bade
farewell once for all to worldly vanities, motivated by love of the
Virgin and of purity. He tells us:

"And now his past thoughts were vanishing, dissipated by these
holy desires he had which were confirmed by a visit of the following nature. One night while he was wide-awake, he clearly
saw a figure of Our Lady holding the Child Jesus. For a long
space he felt exceeding great consolation at the sight, and was
left with such a horror of his past life and especially of his sins
of the flesh, that it seemed to him that all the images of them
which had previously been imprinted therein, were obliterated
from his soul. And so from that hour up to the August of 1553[63]
when this is written, never more did he give the least consent in
carnal matters, and from this effect one may judge that it was
from God, although he did not dare to affirm it or say anything
more than state what was said above." (10, 42)

And that was sufficient. The shrines at Loyola, Montesino's
pious hymns, his reading at the Castle, his analysis of his own
reflections, as many antecedents and concomitant as the historian can register concerning Saint Ignatius' conversion, vanish
into thin air before these two facts to which the Saint so firmly
testified thirty two years later; an interior consolation that was
"very excessive" which arose from the figure of the Virgin and
the God-Child; and a radical and irrevocable renovation of his
imagination and of his hitherto sinful flesh. He was not concerned whether the vision he saw through bodily eyes or with
the eyes of his mind was a product of his ardent love or a
species miraculously sent by God. He inclined to the latter but
"dared not affirm it."[64] What did concern him and concerns history was the effect of that vision: it was the supernatural seal
stamped on his conversion, the unction that changed the Castle
of Loyola into the "Santa Casa" of Guipuzcoa and of the Society
of Jesus.

The convalescent apparently received this wondrous grace while

---

[63]*Fontes narrativi*, I, p. 375, note 18, *Praefatio*, pp. 17-18. In the principal copy
of the autobiographical autobiography "53" was changed to "55." This was erroneous
as Saint Ignatius dictated this first part in 1553.

[64]*Exercitia*, nos. 332-333; *Epist. et Instruct*, XII, pp. 633 ff. In this he conformed
to the rules for the discernment of spirits: to regard the process of the movements
and especially their effects.

lying on the couch in his alcove at Loyola. The "Autobiography" relates that only after his renewed concentration on his reading "did he begin to get up and go about the house a little." But as soon as he could he rose, and knelt before a picture of the Blessed Virgin, and offered himself entirely to God.[65] This picture was probably in the "old Oratory" which Magdalena de Araoz had had built many years before and was the Annunciation we have already mentioned. It was commonly reported in Azpeitia and known of also in Valencia and Pamplona around the end of the sixteenth century, that at that moment a strong earth tremor shook the house, and a stained glass window, depicting Christ bearing His Cross, was shattered. [66] This quake is not mentioned by the Saint, or Polanco, or Nadal. Ribadeneira does not speak of it in the first Latin or Castilian edition of his "*Life*." He does, however, admit it into the succeeding versions of his work. In this case, too, the external fact is of lesser importance than the inner effects of this secret and irrevocable oblation.

The mainspring of that perseverance is glimpsed in what Polanco relates of the Saint in later life. Ignatius had decided to leave Rome in order to go to the town of Alvito on November 2, 1552. There he intended to reconcile Juana de Aragon with her husband Ascanio Colonna. On that very day a heavy rain fell. The secretary feared lest the trip might be injurious to the infirm General's health, and asked whether he was still determined to go. Ignatius answered: "For more than thirty years I have never failed to carry out despite any difficulty whatsoever what I have once determined upon for the glory of God."[67] This incident brings us back to the very days of the efficacious "*I will*" emitted at Loyola.

---

[65]Astrain, I, p. 26: on this and what follows. But we think this oblation was made after the visit by the Virgin.
[66]Astrain, I, p. 26, note 2: texts; *Scripta*, II, pp. 250-257: account by eye-witnesses in Azpeitia.
[67]Huonder, p. 16, 330: for the whole story with annotations from Polanco, Ribadeneira and Fluvia; *Fontes Narrativi*, I, p. 51.

CHAPTER V

THE FIRST RETREATANT AT LOYOLA

1. January 1522 is the earliest date proposed for Saint Ignatius' departure from his home.[1] From the Virgin's visit the preceding August or September, three months, October, November and December, had transmuted before the convalescent's eyes the summer verdure of mountain and valley into the golden tints of autumn, and into the white snows of a rigorous winter.[2] What was Ignatius doing in those three months?

Above all he was edifying, by his example and conversations, the immediate family and neighboring friends who came to congratulate him. Ignatius writes in his "Autobiography": "And thus his brother, as well as the other members of the family, became aware from his external attitude of the interior change that had taken place within his soul. He remained unperturbed, and persevered in his reading and in his holy resolves. Whenever he conversed with the members of the family, he treated wholly of the things of God and brought great benefit to their souls." (11-12, 376)

A select share in these first manifestations of change fell, doubtless, to his nurses, Magdalena and her daughters. Potenciana de Loyola, apparently referring to this period, relates a curious episode which reveals that admiration was not the sole reaction.[3]

One day a messenger came from a relative in Iraeta.[4] He had been sent to ask for the loan of the Castle hounds, that his masters might hunt with them. Magdalena who, perhaps, had had enough of such borrowing, "told him that the hounds were out, though they were not." Ignatius, precisely at this time, "had great scruple" in regard to telling the truth. (12, 378) Potenciana says that when he learned of his sister-in-law's answer, "he rebuked

---

[1]Usually the latest date is put in February or March. Father Lizarralde, as we shall see in the next chapter, puts it at the beginning of January.
[2]Lizarralde, (II), 9, (1929), p. 154. Blas Ortiz records a heavy snowfall in 1522. (1546).
[3]*Scripta*, II, p. 193. The 5th question in the processes at Azpeitia does not refer as do the former, to the Saint's stay there in 1535, but is general. His reply may be better understood if we place it at the period Iñigo lived at the Castle: in 1535 he spent one night there.
[4]Henao-Villalta, VI, p. 325: St. Ignatius' paternal grandmother was Sancha Perez de Iraeta, an estate in Cestona; VII, p. 41: during the Saint's life the lord of Loyola dealt with the lord of Iraeta, Nic. Mart. de Eguia.

her sharply, refused to sit at the same table with her, and even refused to speak to her for a few days."

The good lady along with her husband and daughters was quite bewildered. What an unexpected preacher his pious books had made of the vain and gallant captain! But she did not hold it against him.[5] It must not be thought from this and other incidents of his severity that he was ungrateful to the good ladies who had so solicitously tended him in his illness. Ignatius confided to Father Baldoino d'Angelis a curious incident which probably concerns his sister-in-law, Magdalena, or one of his other relatives.[6]

During his noviceship Father d'Angelis felt a strong inner conflict because of his affection for his parents and relatives. This conflict had been strengthened by the urging of one of his nephews that he give up his vocation. Saint Ignatius learned of this, and summoned him kindly to his room. He had him sit beside him and then told him quite frankly of his own struggle against a similar affection toward his relations. He told him he had overcome this feeling at the beginning of his conversion, *"initio conversionis suae a saeculo ad Deum"*, i.e. during either the months at Loyola or at Manresa. The Saint confided to him that the book of Hours he used at prayer contained a picture of the Virgin which resembled one of his sisters-in-law. Every day, when he came to that page, he felt a "human affection toward the person, which disturbed his devotion."[7] The Saint continued, to remedy this, he "very reverently" covered the picture with a clean piece of paper and was able to pray without further distraction. He thus removed the distracting effects of his affection without, however, crushing legitimate feeling.

The Belgian Provincial adds that the founder then embraced him and sent him away without another word. This so moved him to tears that, he moderated his feelings and subjected them to the divine service, and so persevered in his vocation.

Let us now return to the days at Loyola. The researches of Fathers Lizarralde, Cros, and Dudon on life at Azpeitia and on

---

[5]Pérez Arregui, (I), pp. 135-136. She was ever friendly toward him. It was she who paid the 3 ducats still owed in 1538 to the Loyola doctor who had attended Iñigo.

[6]A novice at Rome in 1551, later became Provincial and champion of the ancient faith in Flanders.

[7]*Scripta*, II, 435: *Sentiebat affectu quodam humano in cognatom perturbari cursum devotionis suae.*

its clergy during those summer and autumn months of 1521 enable us to reconstruct another subject of conversation at Loyola Castle.

In speaking of the process brought against Iñigo in 1515, we mentioned the dissension provoked in the town by one of his relatives. It was caused by his cousin, Maria Lopez de Emparan y Loyola, and the Franciscans of the Sasiola monastery who were supporting her in establishing the Isabellite convent. The religious and the Franciscan friars were able to uphold their rights and even construct a new house and church. This they had done despite the excommunication which had been fulminated against the poor nuns at the public High Mass in 1506. The lord of Loyola, despite his interest as patron of the parish, had thus far observed a benevolent neutrality. He had allowed the nuns to inter his cousin, Sister Maria de Emparan, deceased in 1518, next to his own tomb. He had also attended the opening of the main portal of the new church in 1519.[8]

The opposition of the clergy and of their Rector, Juan de Anchieta, was vehement. In 1518 Fray Felipe de Valdivielso had appealed against him and his vicar, Pedro de Izaguirre, to the Bulls of exemption, "*Aurea*" and "*Mare Magnum*", and called attention to the censures therein contained.[9] This action had been futile, and it seemed as if the affair would be prolonged. So it turned out, for that very year the old pastor ceded his rectorship to his nephew, Garcia Lopez de Anchieta, thereby thwarting the Loyola's plans that the family cleric, Pero Lopez, should have the post.

When the young Anchieta was assassinated in 1519 the situation changed completely. Pero Lopez became rector, but only after he had gone to Rome to regularize matters.[10] Anchieta, in reaction, became the most generous benefactor of the Isabellites. He determined to erect in their church the tomb he had first intended to build in the parish church.[11] Then he assigned to the convent a rich benefice he held in Vilarino, in the diocese of Salamanca, stipulating that its income should maintain three, or at least two, chaplains who would be appointed for their spiritual care. They in return were to have two anniversary Masses or

---

[8]Lizarralde, (I), p. 91, 80.
[9]Lizarralde, pp. 93-94.
[10]Lizarralde, (I), p. 80.
[11]Lizarralde, pp. 96-97.

Offices of the dead celebrated annually at the convent: one for
their Catholic Majesties, the other for the repose of the donor's
soul. The documents of this agreement were signed at the convent
August twenty-fifth and twenty-sixth, 1521, i.e. in the middle
period of Ignatius' conversion.[12]

The Loyolas no longer maintained their benevolent neutrality.
The change began in 1519-1520 before Iñigo's illness, and manifested itself violently in 1523 after his departure from Loyola.
During the first period Pero Lopez obtained from Rome a Bull
containing censures which prescribed that the belfry and other
public signs be removed from the nuns' church.[13] During the
second period both Loyolas, pastor and patron, forcibly removed
one of their nieces, Nicolasa Perez de Ojanguren,[14] from the
convent under threat of burning it down. They also prevented
by force the burial in the Franciscan church of Juan de Anchieta,
who died on July thirtieth, 1523.[15]

The parenthesis between these two periods coincides with the
months of Ignatius' convalescence and conversion. There was a
truce, even an agreement, and the Loyolas sent one of their servants to Burgos to conduct the Franciscan Provincial from Castile.
According to Father Dudon,[16] both parties held a conference at
the Castle on August twenty-seventh, 1521. As a result, the
Loyolas not only consented to the donations which Anchieta had
made to the convent, but added on their part a terrain that they
possessed in the neighborhood. Father Lizarralde is justly
amazed at this conduct: "Even their former adversaries, the
patron and the parish clergy, had ceased their obstinate opposition, at least apparently."[17]

There is a logical explanation. The converted captain must
have joined his pleas for harmony to the need for union and
concord which the military expeditions to Noain and Fuenterrabia
in June and October of 1521 had imposed on the Loyolas and
the Azpeitians. At mealtime Martin and Pero Lopez may have
spoken of the conflict, and then the transformed captain of Pamplona would reveal signs of his conversion by his remarks. Father

---

[12]Lizarralde, (I), pp. 102-103; documents.
[13]Dudon, p. 61.
[14]Lizarralde, (I), p. 109.
[15]Lizarralde, (I), pp. 115 ff.
[16]Dudon, pp. 60-61.
[17]Lizarralde, (I), p. 107.

Dudon has well said, "the first fruits of Iñigo's domestic apostolate" was the truce in the matter of the Isabellites in 1521.[18]

Father Lizarralde thinks, with equal plausibility, that on this occasion some of the Franciscans of Sasiola who took part in the litigation, for instance, Fray Martin de Segura, may have visited the convalescent.[19] There is no warrant to presume that Ignatius confided his conversion and plans to him. This he did not do, in our opinion, until his confession at Montserrat. None the less he would have had abundant material for conversation with a Franciscan. For it was precisely during those months that the example of the seraphic patriarch was fostering his conversion and fomenting his spiritual fervor. What more natural than that Iñigo should make use of his mediation to assuage the bitterness between the Loyolas and his Order?

2. Such conversation, however, was but incidental. His real occupation those months was the development of a new phase of his interior life. The "Autobiography" gives quite a few details which are supplemented and interpreted by a note appended to them.

It is strange that Ignatius, though he mentions the "Exercises"[20] at least fifteen times in the "Autobiography" never speaks of their origin. Since he did not regard them as a literary work or even for reading, but as a practical directory which summarized the fruit of his own spiritual experiences,[21] he undoubtedly believed the origin of the "Exercises" would be clear from the very account of his inner life. Father Camara, his confidant, was not satisfied to rely on indirect deductions, so on October twentieth, 1555 when the "Autobiography" was completed, he asked Ignatius "how he had composed them?" The Saint's answer is, and will always be, the basic historical source for all research on the origin of the celebrated work.

Father Camara says: "He told me that the "Exercises" had not been composed all at once, but that some things he had observed in his soul and had found helpful he thought might be of use to others also. So he wrote them down, for instance, the *"Examen"*

---

[18]Dudon, p. 61. No direct document has as yet been found that proves it as there is for 1535.
[19]Lizarralde, (I), p. 9 (June 1929), pp. 181-182.
[20]Codina, p. 14.
[21]This may de deduced from Ignatius' answer which follows.

with its method of lines, etc. He told me that he had derived *espècially* the *"Elections"* from that diversity of spirits and thoughts which he had *while at Loyola* when he was still suffering from his leg." (99, 504)

This precise confession places the remote origin of the 'Exercises" at Loyola, the only place he mentioned. The Saint did not say that he wrote his book at the Castle, or even drew up there the "Rules for the discernment of spirits." He did not say that he personally meditated and practiced his devotion in the order and form in which they later appear in the book. We know that he ascribed the latter to Manresa.[22] But he did attribute to Loyola the profound and penetrating self-analysis of the movements which influenced his conversion, and his detailed and tenacious memory of them.[23]

Another curious fact has been unearthed by research into the origin of the "Exercises." No passages, or perhaps, not a single passage, has passed in *its literal text* and with certainty[24] into the "Exercises" from the "Exercitatory" of Garcia de Cisneros, or from the "Spiritual Ascensions" of Gerard of Zutphen, or from the "Meditations on the Life of Christ" by Saint Bonaventure, or from the "Rosetum" by Mauburno, or from other works more or less probably read after Loyola. The same cannot be said of the "Imitation of Christ" with which Ignatius first became acquainted at Manresa. There are several passages from the *"Flos Sanctorum"* and from the *"Vita Christi"* which the critic recognizes in the definitive Ignatian text. They find, for instance, Montesino's influence in the account of the creation of our First Parents in the expression "in the Damascene field;"[25] in the triple, gradated call of the Apostles;[26] in the typical manner in which Saint Anne and Saint Joachim divide their goods.[27] Literary traces of the *"Flos Sanctorum"* may be found in Our Lord's appearance to Joseph of Armimathea "according to the Gospel of Nicodemus,"[28] and in Saint Bernard's expression, which has vainly been sought in other books; "Neither for you did I begin, nor for you will I stop."[29]

[22]Beguiristain, pp. 5-7. We think there is some exaggeration.
[23]Casanovas, pp. 60-72.
[24]We shall prove later that there was a psychological and indirect influence. It can hardly be proved their influence was literary.
[25]Codina, p. 147.
[26]Codina, pp. 142-143.
[27]Codina, pp. 144-145.
[28]Codina, p. 144.
[29]Codina, p. 151.

This should not lead us to conclude that Ignatius wrote the book itself at Loyola. None the less, it was there that he jotted down the notes that later, except for the "Imitation of Christ", were the only *literary* material that influenced its reaction. The Saint mentions these notes in his "Autobiography" when he tells of what he did during these months at the Castle.

"When he was savoring (*gustando*) many points he had come across in those books, it occurred to him to note down briefly some of the essentials in the 'Life of Christ and of the Saints.' He decided to write them very carefully *in a note book*, for he could now go about the house a little. He wrote Christ's words in red ink, Our Lady's in blue, on shiny, lined paper in a good hand for he was a fine writer. He spent part of the time writing, part in *prayer*. His greatest consolation was to look at the heavens and the stars. He did this frequently and for a long time, because he felt within himself great strength to *serve Our Lord*. He thought much about his resolve, and yearned to be entirely well soon so that he might put it into execution." (11, 375)

Ignatius was engaged, then, in a renewed and deeper concentration on "those books" during these months, and not on others, and still less on Latin books, as one authority suggests.[30] He was re-reading the same works which had inspired and fostered his conversion while he was isolated from the outside world, even from directors and confessors. His was a solitude that may well be called "domestic".

There was a change in his attitude. He no longer tried merely to pass the time or to reform but rather to *taste* (*gustar*)[31] in their fullness the books that had wrought so great a change in him. He was selective. He distinguished the essential from the accessory. He briefly summarized the most important passages, arranging them in hierarchical order according to whether the words are spoken by Christ, the Virgin or the Saints. This note-taking was not mechanical. Prayer now occupies habitually part of his day; during the other part he copies his resumés or extracts into his note-book. Then there are preludes before the mysterious silence of the stars, and the practical confirmation of his firm resolution to practice poverty and make a pilgrimage to

---

[30]Van Ortroy, p. 289. Suggests that the Saint read Abbot Werner's Latin homily at Loyola.
[31]Montesino employs the word "*gustar*" more frequently than the original.

Palestine. That resolution crowned the first "retreat" at Loyola, the first of the endless series continuing throughout the centuries in that sanctified corner of Guipuzcoa.

The prologue of the *"Vita Christi"* directed Iñigo to these pious practices during his "retreat." Ludolph's introduction to the work, which Montesino had translated and given a Franciscan tone, is a moving exhortation, not merely to read Our Saviour's life, but to contemplate it, and to take notes where one finds fruit. The Carthusian urges this in a passage which is a mosaic of the counsels of the Carthusian Guido de Ponte, Saint Bernard, and Saint Bonaventure in his "Meditations on the Life of Christ".[32]

"Take heed that you do not hurriedly read such a life, but taste some part of it each day. You will then hold high festival with Christ by your contemplation, affections, and *prayers* and all your praises and all the works of God. Then you may rejoice in Him, withdrawing from worldly hindrances, and may delight and contemplate Him with all sweetness. . . . The virgin, Saint Cecilia, led such an evangelical life. We read of her that, she always carried the Gospel of Christ hidden in her bosom, which is to say, that she took from the life of Our Lord Jesus Christ which was written in the Gospel, *some of the most devout points* on which she meditated day and night with pure and entire heart. She went over them time and again from beginning to end, and *tasted them to the full.* Then she restored them to the secret of her bosom with a sublime and prudent discretion. *I advise you to do likewise,* for I believe this is more necessary than all endeavor of spiritual exercise. And in such wise read this holy life that you strive to *imitate* its divine example as best you can. For it will avail you little to read the Redeemer's life, if you do not follow Him in His actions".[33]

These excellent counsels fully illuminate Iñigo's conduct during his "closed retreat" at Loyola. Their influence is to be found in some expressions of the "Autobiography": "and savoring (*"gustando"*) many points he had come across in those books, it occurred to him *to note down briefly some of the essentials* in the 'Life of Christ and of the Saints' . . ." He spent part of the time

---

[32]Grausem, pp. 270, 264: analysis of the prologue showing it to be such a mosaic; Boehmer, (II), pp. 8-14, 16-20, 25-30; Codina, pp. 140 ff.; Zarncke, pp. 46-73; on the Carthusian's work and its influence on the "Exercises."
[33]*Vita Christi,* fol. 4 r.

in writing, part in *prayer*. . . . "He thought much about *his resolve*, and yearned to be entirely well soon so that he might put it into execution."

His devout practice of contemplating the heavens seems an echo from the life of Saint Francis in the *"Flos Sanctorum"*: "And Saint Francis, filled with simplicity, draws all creatures to the love of God. When he saw the sun, moon and stars he felt ineffable joy in the love of God."[34]

According to the tradition of the valley of Iraurgui, the only relaxation Iñigo permitted himself during that period of profound concentration of spirit was occasional walks. We can see him as he limped through the meadows where he had once run as a child, meadows which extend from Loyola to the farm settlement at Eguíbar, where he was nurtured, to Azpeitia. Here we can imagine that the novice knight of the Virgin checked the swing of his crutches to salute the Virgin of Olaz, whose hermitage on the slopes of Izarraitz dominates the valley. Those who have visited Ignatius' country will recall the stone that commemorates that prayer made by the father and fellow-countryman of the farm-lands of Azpeitia.

3. The convalescent was not content with reading, meditating, taking notes, and contemplating. Even then he was *concerned over the election he should make*. Upon his conversion he had decided to make a pilgrimage of poverty and penance to Palestine. That decision was irrevocable. But when he returned? . . . What would he do then? . . . He sought to determine this now, in the presence of God and his conscience, thereby directing all his exercises spontaneously toward one final purpose.

"He thought much about his resolve, yearning to be entirely well soon so that he might put it into execution. And having *decided* what he would do after he had returned from Jerusalem, that he might thereafter live a life of penance, he proposed to immure himself in the Carthusian monastery in Seville. He would tell no one there who he was lest they esteem him, and he would eat nothing but herbs. But, when he again came to consider the austerities he intended to perform in the world, the desire to enter the Carthusian monastery *passed*, for he feared he

---

[34]*Flos Sanct.*, fol. 152.

would not be able to exercise the hatred he had conceived against himself. He ordered, however, that a house servant who was going to Burgos, (apparently to conduct the Franciscan Provincial), should find out about the Carthusian rule. (When the servant told him) he was satisfied with the information, but, because of the above-mentioned reason, and *because he was entirely absorbed in planning for his proposed journey,* he did not concern himself overmuch since there was no need to come to a definitive decision until after his return". (12, 376-377)

There is to be noted in this passage the absence of any idea of an apostolate. The spiritual conversations he had with the members of the family, the earliest indications of his new piety, do not as yet spring from a conscious vocation to the apostolate. He thinks only of himself: self-hatred, denial of a formerly haughty ego, unrestrained austerity throughout life, that is the ideal he had before the great revelations of Manresa. Consequently his note-book at Loyola is not yet the book of the "Exercises." The latter was written to help others, the former to help himself.

The choice Iñigo set before him was not Jerusalem or Rome. Jerusalem will be the goal of his life only after Manresa; at Loyola it is but the beginning of a life of penance. Rome does not as yet appear on his horizon.[35] The real choice lay between two kinds of penitential life: that of religious living in community under rule; or that of a penitent living alone and unrestrained by any rule save hatred of self. Saint Onuphrius had made his election. He had abandoned the monastery for a life of austerity in the desert. Ignatius was clearly inclined toward the same choice. The religious rules that seem to attract him are precisely those which offer a minimum of monastic discipline and a maximum of isolation and austerity. This partly explains his preference for the Carthusian rule.

According to John Mayr, a theologian at Paris in 1519, "The Carthusian was considered the best and most rigorous of the Orders, not only mendicant but non-mendicant,"[36] even in that century when so many Orders were lax. Their observance was

---

[35]Leturia, (II), pp. 58-91; for the Jerusalem-Rome disjunctive in Ignatius' later plans.
[36]Joannes Major, in 2a ed. of *Comm. in IV Sent. Disp.* 38, Q. 23 (Paris, 1519), fol. 315.

especially esteemed in Castile. The Priors of Las Cuevas in Seville, Fray Juan de Bonilla, and Fray Miguel de Villareal, as well as their poet, Fray Juan de Padilla, had made that monastery famous in devout circles and even at the Court of the Catholic Kings."[37]

Ignatius sought information concerning their rule at the Carthusian monastery of Miraflores in Burgos since it was the nearest. Isabella herself had founded a pantheon for Juan II, and for her brother Alonso.[38] Ignatius may have become acquainted with Miraflores during his service at King Ferdinand's Court. Also, the fact that the author of the *"Vita Christi"*, a book to which he was so indebted, was a Carthusian, may have made him incline to that Order.[39] This inclination revived at Manresa during the first months of his new elections and lasted until he conceived his ideal of the apostolic life.[40] The privileges in the Pontifical Bulls establishing the Society of Jesus[41] are concrete evidence of this sympathy toward the Carthusians.

However, he did not limit his election at Loyola to deliberating on whether to adopt the Carthusian rule, or lead a life of autonomous penance. Another problem *"obsessed"* (*embebido*) him. This is the very word he used to express his state of mind when thinking of his royal lady. He was obsessed with the problem of how he was to begin his new way of life.

He was presented with a dilemma. He wanted to begin as soon as possible his life of austerity, and at the same time conceal his intention to go on pilgrimage to Jerusalem, and the radical change that had taken place. He feared his acquaintances might look on him as a saint, a fear that tormented him throughout the first years of his conversion.

While he was struggling amidst this perplexity, he saw the solution shine out as a guiding star: Montserrat!

Ignatius had never visited the famous shrine, but he had heard of it, since it was well known among the Guipuzcoans of the period, and throughout Spain. (Appendix I). During his service with the Duke of Najera he witnessed the devotion of this

---

[37]Serrano y Sanz, pp. 156 ff.
[38]Tarin, pp. 20 ff.
[39]Watrigant, (I), p. 519: holds the same opinion.
[40]*Scripta*, II, pp. 75-76: reference by Lainez in 1558. Of Manresa: "He tells me he was tempted and was given much to contemplation and intended becoming a Carthusian. But since he was aware that he was called to aid souls, etc."
[41]Edit. Crit. Constitutionum, I, p. 361.

family to Montserrat, and must have known of his sovereigns'
devotion to the famous shrine. There he would find the solution
of his problem. He would not don penitential sack-cloth until he
reached the distant and frequented sanctuary by which he would
have to pass if he was going to embark at Barcelona for the
Holy Land. He devised his plans well. He would leave Loyola
under pretense of paying a visit to the Duke of Najera in Navarrete; then he would leave there to go on pilgrimage to Montserrat, as one of the many pilgrims who fulfilled vows of gratitude to the Virgin. He would not mention Jerusalem. (36, 410)
He could change his clothing unnoticed at Montserrat among the
crowds of pilgrims. That very character of pilgrim would give
him the chance to essay his first austerities.

Iñigo reached this decision in his election at Loyola. He
testified to Lainez in 1547: "He resolved to leave his country and
home under pretense of visiting the Duke of Najera's Court.
and to renounce his share of the family estate . . . and to enter
upon a life of austerity. For this purpose, he decided to go to
Catalonia to Our Lady of Montserrat."[42] The "Autobiography"
supplies additional details: We learn that certain incidents of
the journey were not contemplated at Loyola: the vigil of arms
at the Virgin's shrine was due to a chivalrous impulse which
came to him on the way, (17, 386) and the lengthy retreat at
Manresa, which came between Montserrat and Barcelona, arose
unexpectedly during his stay at the sanctuary. (18, 386-388) The
main project, however, namely that of changing his garments
and of beginning life anew at Montserrat, was decided upon at
Loyola. He had previously *determined* on it, and it was one
of those resolves which "according to his custom" he pondered
on the way. (17,386)

During his *"absorption"* at the Castle he must have decided to
visit the shrine of Our Lady at Aranzazu. On the road which
would bring him to Navarrete in La Rioja was Oñate, and near it
the shrine dedicated to Our Lady. It was not as ancient or as
sumptuous as that of Montserrat, but intimate and familiar to
every Guipuzcoan. The church was but recently established in
1469 and by 1522 was little more than a Basque shrine which was

---

[42]*Scripta*, I, p. 101.

somewhat more elegantly and solidly built than others but of the same general style. In 1514 the Reformed Franciscans, who preserve it lovingly to this day, had taken it over from the Mercedarians, the Cloistered Franciscans, and the Dominicans who had precariously maintained it for some time.[43] (Appendix I)

The convert of the Urola once more accommodated his resolves to the pious environment of his country and century. According to the "Autobiography" (13,380), before leaving the Castle he proposed to visit the sanctuary of Aranzazu, not merely as an act of devotion, but rather as an introduction to his new way of life. He prayed there "to gain fresh strength for his journey." Later the Saint explained this phrase to Father Lainez from whom Father Ribadeneira learned it: "When he left his country to go to Montserrat, since he feared lest he be overcome by carnal vice by which he had formerly been assaulted and conquered more than by any others, he made a vow of chastity to Our Lady, imploring Her to take him under Her protection.[44] This is the "fresh strength" the pilgrim wished to gain for his journey,[45] and helps us to a better understanding of his "absorption" at Loyola.

An effect of the Virgin's visit to the former gallant and proud soldier was a deep seated hatred of carnal vice. But, due to his absorption during the autumn that followed, he could not foresee that he would not give the least consent in matters of the flesh as a result of that sublime gift. Hence his pre-occupation as the day drew near to renew contact with the world of his recent vanities, as he paid his visit of respect to the Duke of Najera, and as he traversed the region along the banks of the Navarre. His favorite book, the *"Vita Christi"* must have inspired him to take the most efficacious means. It relates of the child Mary: *"She was most pure in chastity* and perfect in all other virtues, constant and unchangeable in her highest resolves. *She was the first of all women to make a vow of chastity,* provided God not demand otherwise of her, and no one from the beginning of the world until her

---

[43]Gorosabel, IV, pp. 216-217.
[44]*Scripta,* I, p. 379, no. 85. He concludes with *"ex P. Laynez."* Mention is also made in a letter of 1547, *Scripta,* I, p. 101.
[45]Iriarte, pp. 8 ff.: monograph treating the critical problem as to whether the vow was taken at Aranzazu. Solid reasons confirm the opinion of Michel Drive and the editors of the *Monumenta.;* Huonder, p. 24 and note 71: defends the same view. It is still not certain.

time ever offered such a vow to God." Then comes a colloquy: "Virgin of Virgins, glorious Mary . . . Thou who first of all women *made a vow to observe virginity and offered so glorious a gift*, though untaught by word or example of any mortal to do this new thing. And Thou who wast pleasing to God, adorned with this virtue and all others, and hast left all an example to live, I beg of Thy immense bounty, direct Thou all my life and obtain for me from *Thy Son the grace to imitate all Thy virtues and example as far as in me lies*, and, Lady, grant me that Thy grace may ever be present. Amen."[46]

The plans which Iñigo had been maturing at Loyola were now complete. He reviewed them in his mind: the vow of chastity at Aranzazu at the outset of the journey; the exchange of clothing at Montserrat transforming the captain into a beggar; the pilgrimage of poverty and devotion to Palestine; the postponement of a new "election" for the return. Lending color and warmth to all were the thorns of the severest austerity, and the Rose among the thorns, the Basque and Catalan Virgin, and enthroned in the center, the King and Lord of the Saints Who left his loving foot-prints in the Holy Land. This is the fruit of Iñigo's "election" at Loyola.

4. There remained for him to put the plant into execution. He began by taking leave of his brother Martin's household.

During the months of Iñigo's convalescence, Martin had not remained at Loyola. The fluctuations of the war with France had taken him away from the Castle to serve his King and country on the frontiers of Guipuzcoa. For the victory of Noain, which coincided with Iñigo's crisis on June thirtieth, 1521, though decisive for the fate of Navarre, did not end the European war of which Navarre was but an episode.

As early as August 1521, it was reported in Guipuzcoa and Castile that another French army under Admiral Bonivet was concentrated on the Pyrenees frontier. Its strength was estimated at twenty-five thousand men and was especially formidable because of its artillery: twenty-two heavy pieces and many small cannon.[47] Bonivet feinted at Pamplona through Roncal, left the

[46]*Vita Christi, Lib. I, cap. II,* p. 7, fol. 12, col. b.
[47]Danvila, IV, pp. 435, 457, 539.

Agramontais of Navarre to defend the fortress of Maya or Amayur, and then hurled himself upon Fuenterrabia which is on the road to San Sebastian.[48]

The Regency dispatched the veteran master of artillery, Diego de Vera, as Governor, with pieces seized from the French in Navarre and with infantry and cavalry reinforcements.[49] The militia men of Guipuzcoa were again called to arms in September. A corps of fifteen hundred men was formed. The company of Vergara which was commanded by Juan Lopez de Ugarte, the former captain of the men from Azpeitia, was especially prominent. Juan de Eguibar, an intimate friend of Ignatius, was captain of the company from that town, some eighty-three men, who represented a whole list of Loyolas: the lieutenant and corporal of the squadron, Pero y Lope Garcia de Loyola, respectively, down to the shoemaker, Miguel de Oñaz.[50] Martín, personally active in the expedition, marched among the first to garrison Fuenterabia with the men from his household and farms. They were to defend the fortress at all costs. The *Parientes Mayores*, Juan Ortiz de Gamboa, of the house and estate of Zarauz, and Juan Perez, lord of Lizaur, accompanied him.[51]

It must have been during the preparations for, and at the departure on this expedition that the lord of Loyola noticed most the change that had come over his younger brother. It is probable that the expedition was ready by the end of September.[52] At a time so critical for the loyalty and glory of his line and of his Province, the defender of Pamplona, whose zeal none knew better than Martin, was living in another world. "The time he spent conversing with those of the household, he spent entirely on things of God." . . . What could be the reason for such strange conduct?

A month and a half later Martin wondered the more when he saw how little effect his report of the outcome of the expedition had upon Iñigo.

---

[48]Campion, (I), p. 509; Danvila, IV, p. 457; Francis Xavier's brothers were there.
[49]Danvila, IV, p. 471.
[50]Danvila, IV, p. 616; *Arch. de Azp., Report.*, p. 140, v.
[51]Henoa-Villalta, VII, pp. 8-10.
[52]Dudon, p. 60: suggests, reasonably, that the Virgin's visit took place around 15-30 August. We would not put it later than the end of September. Creixell (I, p. 13), would postpone it to December or January to allow for his view that Iñigo was reading Vega's book published in September at Saragossa.

The French had begun the bombardment of Fuenterrabia from the fortress of Gasteluzar on the Bidasoa October sixth.[53] The lord of Loyola had signalized himself in the defense when, six days later, the garrison valorously repelled a general assault.[54] But they had brought too many troops into the beseiged fortress "there was not enough bread for so many," and above all water was so scarce that to economize on the little that remained "they had to cook the meat in cider."[55] The courage and morale of the militiamen began to fail as a result. They had been trained for open mountain fighting, to choose favorable terrain for attack. There within the confines of the fort, among the debris of walls crushed by the most powerful artillery in Europe, they were unable to act in concert and were faced with the prospect of starvation.[56]

The situation was critical. Diego de Vera held a council of the *Parientes Mayores*. We can imagine Martin proudly repeating to Iñigo what he stated before he returned to the Castle in the presence of His Majesty's scribe, Juan Ibañez de la Plaza, at San Sebastian: "That they along with their men, would die with him in defense of that town, even though all the others should fail him. For they had not entered said town to lose honor but to win it.[57]

Vera, however, did not think he could resist longer because of the militia,[58] and surrendered the fortress on the sixteenth. He and his troops marched out "bearing their arms and with banners flying.[59] The Regency was then transferred to Vitoria, San Sebastian was fortified, and Beltran de la Cueva, the Duke of Albuquerque, took over the command as General of the frontier.[60] Thus the military and political center had been removed from Burgos to Guipuzcoa. The Province was resolved to defend itself and he, Martin, was waiting orders to march.

The lord of Loyola could hardly overcome his amazement when he observed how his younger brother failed to react to that dramatic narrative. Of course Iñigo admired his brother's valor,[61]

---

[55]Danvila, IV, pp. 688-699.
[54]Henao-Villalta, VII, p. 8.
[53]Danvila, IV, p. 617; O'Reilly y Moret: citations.
[56]Danvila, IV, pp. 689, 539: 616-617.
[57]Henao-Villalta, VII, p. 10.
[58]Danvila, IV, p. 689: the Regent Adrian states this in cipher Dec. 7, 1521. The matter is not clear.
[59]Henao-Villalta, VII, p. 8.
[60]Danvila, IV, p. 489.
[61]In the dialogue we shall cite there is no sign of personal rancor on Martin's part.

and showed he was still loyal to the Crown, for he maintained that loyalty even as a Saint.[62] But his eyes did not gleam with that earlier spark of ambition and glory. It was clear that his ideals revolved in new orbits. As Ignatius told Beltran, Martin's heir in 1539: "As our forefathers have endeavored to signalize themselves in other things, and God grant they have not done so in vain, you should strive to distinguish yourself in that which will endure forever.[63]

Martin, however, knew nothing of these new ideals which his brother concealed beneath that apparent enfeeblement and destruction of his personality and character. His behaviour seemed to him a sign of the ruin of the man, and a threat of infamy to the line. Pero Lopez, his priest-brother, must have felt the same. For the "Autobiography" seems to refer to him when it associates with Martin's "suspicions" those of *"some of the household."*

At this juncture Iñigo mentions his proposed journey to the head of the family. The style of the "Autobiography" becomes rapid and broken when this scene is described. The narrative turns into dialogue and the details which are recounted thirty-one years later bear the impress of recent events.

"Since he found himself quite recuperated, he thought it was time for him to leave. So he told his brother: Sir, as you know the Duke of Najera is aware that I am well. I ought to go to Navarrete." (The Duke was there at the time.) His brother, and some of the household also, suspected he was about to make a great change. He led him to one room and then to another,[64] and somewhat puzzled, began to exhort him not to ruin himself. He should consider the great hopes people had of him, and what the future had in store for him, and many like considerations, all intended to deter him from carrying out his high resolves." (12,378)

Father Ribadeneira in his paraphrase of these words explains that the people of whose expectations Martin spoke were chiefly

---

[62]*Ep. P. Natalis*, I, p. 424. Nadal wrote in 1562 to Lainez that he had said in an audience with Philip II: "We of the Society are sincerely devoted to Your Majesty in all our ministries . . . due to the affection which from childhood our Father Master Ignatius had toward him, in which he reared us all".
[63]*Ep. et Instruct.*, I, p. 148.
[64]This conversation may have begun in the dining room on the main floor, and then Martin brought him to his suite in an alcove facing the former oratory.

in Guipuzcoa, "the good will toward you in all this region."[65]
The head of the Loyolas alluded to the favorable circumstances
which were present that very moment for devoting his sword in
an enterprise at once for the glory of the King and of his
Province. It was all very well for him to reform his life and
imitate the saints. But could he not do so in the Emperor's service and in that of his country as so many saintly kings and
captains had done?[66] Ignatius concludes: "His answer was such
that, without departing from the truth, for he was now quite scrupulous in that regard, he managed to *throw his brother off the
track.*"

This was neither a gesture of apathy or of disdain, nor was it
an open defense of his own ideal, for he preferred to keep it
secret within his soul. It was the tactic of a firm will which,
when the adversary attacks, triumphs by avoiding combat.

Ignatius did not communicate with his brother for many
years. He explained this apparently harsh and unkind behaviour
in June of 1532 when he thought he was secure in his new mode
of life and in a position to benefit his soul and his family. He
wrote him: "Do not be surprised. To heal a serious wound one
ointment is to be applied at once, another when the wound is
half healed, and still another when the wound is closed. So in
the beginning of my new way of life I required one remedy, a
little later another was suitable. . . . The truth is, the measure
of my love for a person in this life must be how it helps in
serving and praising God Our Lord. I desire greatly, and more
than greatly, if I may so say, that this love made true, and
this strength made strong in the service and praise of God Our
Lord, may be exercised toward your person, relatives, and friends,
for then I should love you the more and serve you better." He
concludes, referring to Martin and in him to all his line: "He
toward whom God Our Lord has been so generous, ought not be
niggardly."[67]

By then the Lord of Loyola had begun to realize that Iñigo's departure in 1522 had not meant ruin for him and infamy for the
family name. He would have acquired the correct perspective

[65] *Vita,* lib. I, cap. III.
[66] Perez Arregui, (II), 1931, pp. 211 ff.: Coster's absurd supposition is that the
Loyolas feared lest Iñigo become a reformer in the Lutheran sense.
[67] *Epist. et Instruct.,* I, pp. 79, 81.

when the nine years had run the full course appointed by divine Providence. For from that departure derives the immortal fame of the obscure Guipuzcoan castle: the glory of one of the most sublime saints that adorn the Catholic Church, and the most potent and fertile force of true Christian universalism the sixteenth century knew.

CHAPTER VI

OUR LADY'S PILGRIM

1. When did Iñigo leave Loyola on pilgrimage to Montserrat? The "Autobiography" does not give the exact date. We do know, however, that he made the vigil of arms before Our Lady's altar on the night of March 24, 1522. This was the Monday which followed the third Sunday in Lent, and the eve of the Annunciation. We know, too, that the triduum of confession came before the vigil, and that the vigil followed the prayer at the shrine and the interview with his confessor. Father Camara states that when he began the triduum he had already "arranged for" the interview. (nn. 17-18) This brings us at the latest to March twenty-first. We say "at the latest", because several authorities advance his arrival a few days. Father Tacchi-Venturi, for instance, bases this opinion on Father Nadal's reference to a series of meditations and note-taking prior to the confession.[1] Father Lizarralde finds warrant for an earlier date around the fifteenth of March, in a statement made by Garibay in the sixteenth century that, "the *novena* of penance, confession and communion" was made in preparation for the vigil.[2]

The principal and primary source is the text of the "Autobiography." This demands a prompt arrangement for the interview as soon as Iñigo reached the sanctuary and immediately before he made the triduum of confession. "When he came to Montserrat, had prayed and had made arrangements with the confessor, he confessed as a rule in writing, and that confession lasted three days. . . ." (17,386). We agree, then, with Astrain, Dudon and Albareda that, he probably entered Montserrat early on the morning of March twenty-first, for the monastery usually granted the pilgrims only three nights' lodging in its hostelry.[3]

We can now approximate the time of Iñigo's departure from Navarrete for Montserrat. He must have left around the sixth or eighth of the same month. He travelled by mule along the road

---

[1]Tacchi-Venturi, II, p. 23, note 2.
[2]Lizarralde, (II), p. 9 (1929), p. 218, note 2.
[3]Albareda, pp. 93, 120; Dudon, p. 72.

126

which connects La Rioja with Catalonia by way of Saragossa.[4] He carefully avoided throngs and, although his leg became swollen each night, (16,386) hastened to reach his goal, Our Lady's altar.[5] The Emperor, Charles V, had made the same trip travelling. in the opposite direction in 1520. Despite rests and leisurely stopovers made by the royal cortege, he had taken only twenty-one days. Our Pilgrim may well have covered the same road in fifteen or even in twelve days.[6]

How long did it take Iñigo to journey from Loyola to La Rioja? It may well have taken him about a week due to delays at Oñate and Navarrete. That is why most authorities think he left the Castle around the end of February or the beginning of March. Father Lizarralde alone advanced it to January fifth. He holds that the vigil the Saint held at Aranzasu was popular and public. As a general rule, public vigils were celebrated in wintertime only on the eve of the Epiphany.[7] We prefer the traditional opinion which places the journey between the beginning and the twenty-first of March. First, there might have been an exemption from the general rule on account of special petitions due to the war and to the election of a new Pope. Further, it is not certain that the vigil Iñigo made was public.

2. What had happened in the world while Iñigo was convalescent? What was the situation in the regions through which he was now passing?

We mentioned that the French attack in September and October of 1521 had forced the transfer of the Regency to Vitoria and that the Basque country had become the military and political center of the Peninsula. The Regency was still at Vitoria when Ignatius left home around the end of February. Everywhere on his way from Guipuzcoa to Alava the Pilgrim would encounter the attractions of his former military and courtly life.

A number of events that had occurred on the international and national scene would have made a return to this life especially attractive. In the international sphere the French had halted their offensive without attacking San Sebastian. The Emperor's alliance with England on August twenty-eighth, 1521, and Pes-

[4]Creixell, I, pp. 45-46.
[5]Father Lizarralde neglected to account for his desire to avoid crowds.
[6]Foronda, pp. 158-160; Lizarralde, (II), p. 8, (1928), 123.
[7]Lizarralde, (II), pp. 16, 54.

cara's reconquest of Milan on November eighteenth, had checked Francis I. He had been forced to concentrate his armies on more vital fronts, and so withdrew his best troops under Admiral Bonivet from the Pyrenees.[8] Though Cardinal Adrian was somewhat discouraged,[9] his colleagues in the Regency, the Admiral and the Constable of Castile, with the military and political leaders of Guipuzcoa and Alava, were optimistic. Diego Martinez of Alava, the Deputy General of that Province, wrote the Emperor on December thirty-first: "Your authorities are in this city awaiting spring to retake Fuenterrabia with God's help, and later avenge ourselves on the French."[10] The General of the Frontier, Beltran de la Cueva, had already written him on December eighteenth: "It would be well for Your Majesty to command, as all of us believe you will, that another army be formed here (at San Sebastian). Then the *Lepuzcoans* may avenge themselves in Bayonne for the harm inflicted on them at Fuenterrabia."[11]

On the national scene there were hardly any disturbances within the Kingdom. On May twenty-fourth, 1521 Perrote, one of the Duke of Najera's lieutenants, had captured near Navarrete the fiery leader of the *Comuneros*, Antonio de Acuña, Bishop of Zamora. He was attempting to flee to the French camp "disguised as a Biscayan wearing hose and a long white cloak."[12] On October twenty-fifth the surrender of Padilla's widow at Toledo brought the *Comunero* uprising practically to an end. Bands still roamed the country-side, and quarrels broke out among the victors and vanquished and even among the loyal leaders. An unexpected event, however, brought a ray of light and hope even to this somber sector of the Peninsula.

A new Pope had been elected. On the twenty-fourth of January, 1522, Blas Ortiz, Vicar General of Calahorra, brought the news to Vitoria. He informed the Cardinal Regent, Adrian of Utrecht, that he had been chosen Supreme Pontiff on the ninth of the same month. He announced that Cardinal Carvajal's envoy, Antonio de Astudillo, would arrive soon with the official notification of the Conclave. On February ninth the envoy reached

---

[8]Hauser, p. 384; Fueter, p. 286; Danvila, IV, p. 698.
[9]Danvila, IV, pp. 677 ff: his letters of December 1521.
[10]Danvila, IV, p. 715: text.
[11]Danvila, IV, p. 716.
[12]Lizarralde, (II), p. 9 (1929), pp. 5-52. Additional details.

Vitoria, received Adrian's assent on the tenth, and his acceptance was ratified on the sixteenth.[13]

Vitoria had never beheld a Pope before, not even one of the dubious Pontiffs of the Schism. It was not surprising that it was swept by enthusiasm.[14] The modern historian of the city writes: "Vitoria was crowded with bishops, grandees and throngs of people eager to pay homage to the new Pope, the only one who had been seen in Spain. The Council decreed a welcome befitting his high office, passed measures to ensure proper attendance on the great number of bishops, dignitaries and ambassadors who, accompanied by their followers and servants, converted our lowly city into a resplendant Court."[15]

The Admiral of Castile, Fadrique Henriquez, at the time a member of the Regency, was one of the truest representatives of the nobility and of the ancient tradition of their Catholic Majesties. He expressed the enthusiasm of the nobility in these words which he addressed to the Emperor: "It is as if God Himself had returned to the earth. He has called to his rest the Supreme Pontiff, and has chosen in his stead His Holiness Cardinal Adrian, once servant, now master, once son, now father. . . . I beg (your Majesty) that, mindful of your Crown, you enhance it by such good deeds that you may acquire a heavenly one. May your Majesty come to Spain soon. For God has revealed His Will that you become greater, since He has raised up in Spain the Supreme Pontiff. Such events, which were never seen or heard of before, are a sign that He wills your increase. That is why I desire that you set out for Castile."[16] In another letter the Emperor's journey was symbolically represented as having three stages or crosses, according to the medieval concept of the Empire: "The first, to win the Holy House (at Jerusalem); the second, the reform of the Faith; the third, the restoration and reformation of the Church."[17]

The new Pontiff kept aloof from these political interests which were so intermixed with religious ideals. He remained impartial in the rivalry between France and the Empire. For instance, he

[13]Ortiz, pp. 158, 161; Pastor, pp. 32 ff.
[14]Ortiz, p. 163: *"Oh felix Victoria tanto et tali Christi Vicario illustrata . . Tuae Provinciae primas gaudet."*
[15]Lizaralde, (II), p. 154: text by E. Serdan y Aguirregavidia.
[16]Danvila, V, p. 7: text of February 9, 1522 (erratum: January).
[17]Danvila, V, p. 10: letter of January 20.

not only avoided being in Spain while Charles was there, but
journeyed to Genoa through the territory of Francis I.[18] Yet, as
long as he was on the Catholic Peninsula, and while he was
receiving homage from all classes, he tried to bring concord and
to arouse an ever greater Catholic spirit among the people.

His reconciliation of the Constable of Castile with the Duke of
Najera, Iñigo's patron and relative, was the most important
instance of such intervention by the new Pope and former Regent.

We have noted instances of the antagonism between the
Constable, Iñigo Fernandez de Velasco, and the Duke of Najera.
This hostility became intense when the Viceroy entered Navarre
in triumph. For it put the entire Kingdom and the Agramontais,
the Constable's protegés, under his control. The Constable's
colleague, the Admiral of Castile, had written as early as June
twenty-first, 1521: "The Constable says that, now that Navarre
has been recovered, he will not consent to the Duke having it. I
say that the Duke should keep it until your Majesty orders otherwise. The Constable replies that the Duke of Najera is not going
to be a knife against his friends. I reply that he should not
regard as friends the traitors who did such disservice to your
Majesty. . . .[19]

The Admiral lost out. Velasco had the majority of votes on
the State Council.[20] He deprived the Viceroy of most of his
troops after the victory of Noain and the recovery of Pamplona.
When the new French invasion was threatened,[21] the Duke had
only five hundred lances and two thousand infantry.[22] He
regarded this as disapproval of his services, and an attempt to
ruin him. He was without funds, for he owed seventeen months'
pay to his troops and had not been paid his own salary for more
than twenty months. He had also "lost and spent all he possessed
in addition to the sacking of his palace."[23] He decided to write
the Emperor in protest and demanding justice. Meanwhile, he
withdrew to his estates in La Rioja[24] where he guarded his captive,
the Bishop Acuña.[25] The Regency then replaced him provisionally.

---

[18]Pastor, pp. 40 ff.
[19]Danvila, IV, p. 203.
[20]Danvila, IV, p. 190.
[21]As we have seen, this invasion began in September only to strike against
Fuenterrabia.
[22]Danvila, IV, p. 345.
[23]Danvila, IV, pp. 203-204.
[24]Danvila, IV, pp. 340-345; Salazar, II, p. 173.
[25]Lizarralde, (II), pp. 51-52.

First it appointed Beltran de la Cueva, and later on August twenty-seventh, the Count of Miranda, the Constable's nephew, whom it supplied abundantly with troops and money.[26] This is enough to show how difficult it must have been to reconcile these two haughty grandees of Spain. But the religious enthusiasm caused by the new Pope's election and the Pontiff's prudence and meekness, effected a reconciliation.

Adrian VI left Vitoria on March twelfth, 1522, for Catalonia, He went along the same route by way of La Rioja and Saragossa that Iñigo followed on his pilgrimage to Montserrat. He was accompanied by a brilliant cortege of nobles, headed by the Constable-Regent, Fernandez de Velasco. The cortege reached Santo Domingo de la Calzada on the fourteenth. There the Duke of Najera had arranged to present himself with his household to pay homage to His Holiness and offer him his estates. This meant he would meet the Constable. This encounter would be peculiarly delicate, for the chiefs of the Oñacinos and of the Gamboinos were present.[27] The Lord of Oñaz and of Loyola, Martin, the Duke's relative, must surely have been there.

The Constable saved the difficult situation. He went outside the city in person accompanied by a brilliant train of nobles to welcome the former Viceroy. They greeted each other amicably and then entered Santo Domingo in frank and easy conversation.[28]

Evidently the meeting had been pre-arranged. For the Pope's itinerary, as scheduled, had excluded Najera and Navarrete. The pretext was the rumor of pestilence in that neighborhood. Antonio managed to have the itinerary changed, and so had the honor of receiving the Vicar of Christ in his palace at Najera on August fifteenth. Later he accompanied him to Logroño and to Alfaro, but did not enter Tudela where the Count of Miranda, the new Viceroy, and his captains received the Pope.[29] The Pontiff's satisfaction with his host is proved by the favor he showed him. He wrote a letter to the Emperor that same month from Saragossa in which he commended his loyalty and merits and suggested he be made Viceroy of Naples.[30]

---

[26]Danvila, IV, pp. 372, 373: the Constable's letter.
[27]Ortiz, p. 163; Lizarralde, (II), 9 (1929), pp. 155-156.
[28]Ortiz, p. 163: *"Ambo alacres mutuo colloquentes . . . civitatem ipsam laeti intravere."*
[29]Ortiz, p. 166.
[30]Hofler, p. 157.

Charles V had already recognized the ex-Viceroy's services in the campaign of 1521. On February thirteenth he instructed Lachaulx, his representative in Spain, to inform the Duke "that I am fully satisfied with his attitude and deeds. . . . They have been such as he and his forebears have ever performed in the service of our Royal Crown. I have been greatly displeased that, due to no fault of mine and against my wish and his right to reward and favor, there has been an attempt made to injure him." He put off making any decision on the question of Navarre until his proximate arrival on the Peninsula. However, he asserted that "he would remember the many and distinguished services he has rendered and still renders me, that they may be rewarded as is right and as he deserves."[31] The Constable's conduct on March fourteenth shows that this letter had reached the Court, and that the Emperor's high regard for the Duke was known there.

3. We are now able to reconstruct the environment in which the Pilgrim of Loyola was about to carry out his high resolves. We can also appreciate the effectiveness of the pleas made by Martin and his other relatives.

The situation was known at Loyola by February. We learn that the Duke had sent several messages to the wounded hero.[32] It is likely, too, that he had told him that he intended to offer him "a good post", for instance, the permanent charge of his estate "on account of the credit he had won in the past." (13,380) Ignatius on his part had kept the Duke informed of his improvement. (12,378)

Adrian's election had a peculiar consequence for Iñigo. He would have to travel through Alava, La Rioja, Ribera, Saragossa and Catalonia to reach Montserrat. That was precisely the route chosen for the new Pontiff's triumphal procession. Iñigo wanted to avoid anything that would attract him to his former life, especially anything that might involve his enthusiasm and love for the Pope. Since he was obsessed by a fear of throngs, and was afraid lest any of his acquaintances recognize him, he began his journey eight or ten days before the cortege. He followed the

---

[31]Salazar, IV, p. 31: text.
[32]Ribadeneira, *Vida, lib. I, cap. III*: "The Duke had several times sent a representative to visit him in his illness."

same tactic he had used with his brother "to throw them off the track" and slipped away quietly.

He made no secret of his departure from Loyola. He had laid his plans carefully. First, he would pay a visit to the Duke, his patron. He would travel by mule, dressed in rich clothing worthy of being offered the Virgin of Montserrat.[33] Two Azcoitian squires: Andres de Narvais and Juan de Landeta would accompany him.[34] Then an unforeseen difficulty arose. His brother, the far-from-reformed Priest,[35] offered to go with him as far as Oñate,[36] where he wished to visit his sister, Magdalena, who had married in Anzuola Juan Lopez de Gallaiztegui.[37]

How, then, could Iñigo make the vigil at Aranzazu with which he intended to begin his pilgrimage? "On the way he persuaded" his brother and former companion in the sins of his youth, to make the vigil with him. It may well have been that some popular pilgrimage was scheduled to hold vigil that very night.[38] How could the priest brother refuse to accompany his soldier brother who had almost miraculously recovered from a serious illness in performing so Christian and Guipuzcoan an exercise of piety?

Father Lizarralde when he was archivist of the shrine wrote: "The nocturnal vigils at Aranzazu were characterized by certain symbolic portrayals of episodes in Our Lord's Passion. The pilgrims themselves were the actors. The scenes began in the shimmering candlelight as it were in the mystic shadows of Holy Week and lasted until dawn. Some of the most fervent pilgrims knelt on the floor with their arms outstretched; some dragged heavy iron chains or fastened their hands and feet in stocks; more commonly some carried crosses and walked about the church in imitation of Jesus, or extended their arms against the arms of the cross, or knelt beside it in prayer; some held in their hands the crown of thorns, the reed, the skull as subjects for meditation. Meanwhile the spectators recited the Rosary and other prayers, sang devout hymns or conversed about the appari-

---

[33]As we shall see that was what Iñigo had intended at first.
[34]Scripta, II, p. 821.
[35]Scripta, II, p. 189.
[36]Cros and Tacchi-Venturi, II, p. 23 maintain it was Pero Lopez. The Autobiography mentions no name.
[37]Fontes narrativi, I, p. 381, note 3.
[38]Father Lizarralde says it would have been strange if the shrine had been left open for a couple of pilgrims. Not in the case of the Loyolas and of a priest.

tion of the Virgin. All were contrite and confessed their sins, while the majority scourged their flesh to blood with disciplines."[39]

We do not know whether Iñigo disguised his first austerities beneath these devout practices of his own folk. It is certain that the future founder of the Society of Jesus began there, at least, the long course of his severe flagellations. Ribadeneira and a note found in the margin of the "Autobiography" tells *from the very day he left home* he was accustomed to discipline himself severely every night."[40] This was his first night away from home.

Ignatius offered the Virgin of the Basque shrine a gift more valuable than the first fruits of external mortification. Two years before his death he still remembered that night. In 1554 the Guipuzcoans begged him to obtain in Rome an indulgence to collect alms for rebuilding the church and hous at Aranzazu which had been destroyed by fire. He wrote Saint Francis Borgia: "For my part I have a special reason to desire this, for when God Our Lord gave me the grace to make some change in my life, I remember that I received *some advantage to my soul* as I stood watch by night in the body of that church."[41]

This tender recollection of the aged founder of the Society of Jesus is significant in the light of the fact that Iñigo made a vow of chastity at Aranzazu.[42] He not only abandoned the world in 1522, but from the very start armed himself against its attractions before he journeyed through the scenes of his worldly failings.

The Saint confided to Father Laínez a curious detail concerning that vow. Though it was fervent and acceptable to God, it was not "quite theologically correct" (*secundum scientiam*). . . . The Pilgrim had consulted no one before he came to Montserrat, so he made his vow not to God, but to Mary, the Lady of his new dreams. He undoubtedly misunderstood the passage from the Carthusian which we quoted previously.

Father Laínez says: "However God Our Lord, who had inspired him to make the vow, *used His Mother as His intermediary to help this creature.* He showed that He accepted the sacrifice and took him under His protection."[43] He left Aranzazu with new

[39]Lizarralde, (II), 8 (1928), pp. 15-16.
[40]Ribadeneira, *Vita, Lib. I, cap. III; Scripta* I, p. 44 b.
[41]*Epist. et Instruct.,* VII, p. 422.
[42]Iriarte, pp. 161-162: Ribadeneira seems to put the vow at the end of his journey to Montserrat. Cf. above p. 119 note 45.
[43]*Scripta,* I, p. 101; *Fontes narrativi,* I, p. 76, note 9.

strength for the journey. (13,380) Our Lady has confirmed there the work of purification begun in the alcove at the Castle.[44]

After the vigil was over, "he left his brother at Oñate at his sister's home and went on to Navarette." (13,380 As far as we know he never saw Pero Lopez again. For, when the Saint returned to Azcoitia in 1535, his priest-brother had died six years before in Barcelona on the way back from another visit to Rome.[45]

Iñigo does not mention the festivities in Vitoria in honor of the new Pope. He had other things on his mind. He by-passed the capital of Alava, for he was anxious to avoid meeting crowds and acquaintances. He probably stopped at Ozaeta to thank the family at whose home he rested when he was being carried on the litter to Loyola ten months before. Those ten months had been centuries for him and had opened up a new world.

He would soon, very soon, be free from all former ties. He reached La Rioja and stayed only long enough to pay his respects to the Duke. If we may judge from the "Autobiography" Providence facilitated this part of his plan. For when Iñigo came to Navarrete the ex-Viceroy was not in his palace.[46] He had left either for Najera or some other nearby place, perhaps, to arrange for the coming interview with the Pope and the meeting with the Constable. Had the Duke been in the city Iñigo would undoubtedly have paid him a personal visit, and have received the congratulations of his patron.

Since the Duke was absent, Ignatius presented a bill to the treasurer. This was for "some few ducats owed him by the Duke's household", (13,380) perhaps, what was still due him for the campaign in 1521. The Duke was both generous and grateful. When his treasurer told Iñigo there were no funds on hand, the Duke, when he learned of it, told him: "Though there may not be enough money for all, there is always enough for a Loyola."

After he had obtained the money he distributed it partly among those to whom he was indebted, for he had lived at the Manriques while he was in that city. The rest, in a typically Franciscan gesture, he spent on a statute of Our Lady. This statue "was in poor condition", and the money went for its

---

[44]Lainez here attributes the gift of chastity to this vow. As we saw the gift resulted from the earlier apparition at Loyola.
[45]Dudon, p. 613.
[46]Dudon, pp. 68-69.

repair. Probably it was in the church at Navarette which was dedicated then, as now, to Our Lady. Some thirty-one years later Ignatius recalled how, even before he offered his sword at Montserrat, he had spent his soldier's wages in his Queen's service, and that in the very theater of his sinful life.[47]

Now he had to rid himself of his Azcoitian servants. The Pilgrim gave them a few coins and sent them home bearing his farewell message to the family. The inhabitants of the valley must have repeated it a thousand times, for the curate, Miguel de Ipinza, and the Azcoitian notary, Juan de Ojanguren, recalled it in 1595. "Their master dismissed them because he was going to Montserrat on a pilgrimage of poverty and penance."[48]

This message must have been the only report heard of Iñigo in Loyola and Azpeitia for many years. The Azpeitian Martin Saez de Goyaz was astonished when he met Iñigo at Alcala in 1526.[43] He even persuaded him to write the lord of Loyola a short note. For the Saint had not written before, out of fear lest his name and even that of his country should reveal his noble origin and cause people to esteem him. "This fear so afflicted him that he did not dare to mention whence he came or where he had lived." (16,412)

4. Let us return to La Rioja and the first days of March, 1522. The Virgin's novice knight at last breathed freely, now that he was alone. Joyfully, and with heart filled with optimism, he turned his mule toward Tudela, Pedrola, and Saragossa. He had carried out his well laid plans to break with the past and had done so without revealing his secret. Now he could launch himself boldly on the broad expanse of his ambitions for holiness and austerity.

At this point we note a tone of chivalry in the "Autobiography" Up to now he had perforce to be realistic. The places through which he passed from Guipuzcoa and La Rioja had been familiar ground; the persons with whom he had to deal were relatives or acquaintances. He had to combine his pilgrimage with business and social obligations. But now all invited him to idealism;

---

[47]Martin paid the doctors' bills for his cure at Loyola. The sum was probably charged against his share in the inheritance.
[48]*Scripta*, II, pp. 800, 801, 821.
[49]*Scripta*, II, pp. 193-194.

the novelty of the surroundings, the security of not being recognized, the nearness of the goal. "His books of chivalry, in so far as they were not sinful, came into his inflamed imagination. He continued on his way to Montserrat, pondering as was his habit, the deeds he would perform out of love for God. Since his mind was filled with such things from *"Amadis"* and other novels, some things similar to them entered his mind." (17,386)

Two incidents which remind one of *"Amadis"* then occurred, which passed from the "Autobiography" into national literature and art, even into that Barroque art which universally characterized the Catholic Reformation: the encounter with the Moor, evidently a chance encounter, and the vigil of arms at Montserrat, deliberately decided upon beforehand.

Calderdon de la Barca has raised the encounter with the Moor to the sphere of religious drama in *"The Great Prince of Fez."* The theme is the conversion and entrance into the Society of Jesus of Muhummad At-tazi, Prince of Fez, who died at Madrid in 1667.[50] The dramatist has, of course, changed some details of the scene to satisfy the requirements of the theater and to fit his symbolic interpretation. In the vivid narrative of the "Autobiography" neither Iñigo nor the Moor are on foot. The Basque is riding a mule; the Moor a donkey. (15,382) There is another more important difference. Calderon's Loyola is already dressed as a penitent. Actually he was wearing the clothing of a rich noble and soldier. Witnesses testified later in the process that, when he reached the Catalan sanctuary, "his clothing was expensive and of fine quality" and that "he went about well dressed in the fashion of a soldier."[51]

The "Autobiography" does not tell us where the encounter took place. Ribadeneira tried to determine it because he was greatly angered at Father Maffei's remark that there were many Moors almost all over Spain: *"Hispania fere tota."* The Toledan wrote in the margin of Maffei's work: "false and insulting to Spain."[52] But he could not determine the place, and merely said that the Moor was one of those who still remained in the Kingdoms of Valencia and Aragon.[53] There is a passage in the "Itinerary of

[50]Calderon, Ed. Hartzenbusch, 'II, pp. 341-342.
[51]Albareda, pp. 62-63: texts.
[52]*Scripta*, I, p. 745.
[53]Ribadeneira, *Vita, lib. I, cap. III*, p. 17.

Adrian VI" by Blas Ortiz which may justify placing the encounter in the neighborhood of Pedrola.

This picturesque account of the new Pope's journey associates Pedrola with the Moors. There were the noisy celebrations at Logroño where he was saluted by salvos from cannon captured from the French. Then followed the official reception by the Viceroy of Navarre, Count of Miranda, at Tudela, a city almost ruined by the recent warfare. Then, ten or twelve days after Ignatius passed by, there was the reception given by Alonso de Gurrea y Aragon at his Moorish castle in Pedrola.[54] During the festivities, when Adrian baptized the Count's daughter, *"Moors entertained him with their dances."*[55] This note of Moors in close intimacy with Christians reappears in the encounter with the Moor, as told by the "Autobiography".

Besides the description of the place by Ignatius fits in rather well with the neighborhood of Pedrola. The road passes a short way from the town without entering it. Those who have made the trip by auto from Tudela to Saragossa will recall that this is not true of anywhere else along the route.[56]

Let us see the familiarity between Moor and Christian that is shown in Ignatius' narrative. Iñigo was riding along absorbed in his thoughts. It was the Moor who broke the ice. "As he was riding along the road a Moor overtook him." They must have entered into conversation, and what more natural than that the Moor should ask Iñigo where he was going. This gave the Pilgrim the chance to mention Montserrat and the Virgin. "And they chanced to speak of Our Lady."

Then the Pilgrim must have let slip some allusion to his Lady's purity. That was the secret object of his thoughts those days. The Moor had no fear of his companion's sword and dared to object: A virgin before giving birth, he admitted. But a virgin in giving birth, that "he could not believe, and he gave the natural arguments that came to his mind against it." The Virgin's champion became involved in a bitter dispute. He forgot the law of chivalry and the example of Saint Louis which forbade "a

---

[54]Thought to be the castle immortalized by Cervantes in the episode of the Duke's reception to don Quijote.
[55]Ortiz, p. 166: *"Mauri chorizantes exhilavere Pontificem."* Cf. his excellent account on Logroño and Tudela.
[56]The "Autobiography," however, speaks of a distance of but thirty or forty paces from road to town. The distance is greater at Pedrola, hence our opinion is but probable.

Knight" to dispute with an infidel but ordered him to slay him should he remain obstinate.[57] Iñigo not only permitted the thorny discussion, but even brought out "many reasons." One may well have been the comparison of the sun beam that passes through a stained glass window without breaking or discoloring it. Calderon uses it as a source whence flows a torrent of theological poetry.[58] (Appendix I)

The Moor remained unconvinced. "Which opinion, no matter how many reasons the Pilgrim gave, could not be changed. So the Moor, although he was not going far, rode ahead rapidly, and was soon lost to sight."[59] This brusque departure shows that the conversation had become heated and that the Moor wanted to avoid dangerous consequences. Iñigo "remained in suspense over what had happened with the Moor," while the latter was disappearing around the bend in the road.

What he did next is important, not so much because of its chivalrous tone, but because of his interior struggle. His election is determined by his experience in discerning the various spirits which moved him.

"At this time there came upon him certain *movements* that disturbed his soul, causing him to feel he had not done his duty, and also arousing *indignation* against the Moor, since he had acted wrongly in allowing a Moor to speak in such a way of Our Lady, and so was obliged to return and satisfy her honor. And there came to him the *desire* to go in search of the Moor and to slay him for what he had said. And when the conflict of these desires lasted a long time, he became perplexed as to what he should do. The Moor, who had gone on ahead, had told him he was going to a place somewhat further along the same road, very close to the royal highway, though the highway did not pass through it. . . ."

Ignatius, then, reached the fork which still exists where the main road continued and a secondary road to the town near the Moorish castle. There he stopped or even rode back a ways to give himself time to make a decision. He tells us later that, despite all his pondering, he came to no decision and "was worn out trying to find the right thing to do."

---

[57]*Acta SS. Augusti*, V, p. 577.
[58]*Jornada II, escena* 16.
[59]*Autobiografía*, 15, p. 46.

He saw that the road to the town "was wide and in good condition" and that there were only "thirty or forty paces" between the town and the highway. Both circumstances would naturally incline his mule to follow the road going to the town where it would find rest and fodder. . . . This common place observation, coupled, perhaps, with some recollection from his books of chivalry, gave the troubled knight of Mary a solution,[60] which in later years he looked upon as a special mark of divine Providence. That is why he related it so minutely, that it might be seen "how Our Lord dealt with this soul which was still blind, though greatly desirous of serving Him to the best of his knowledge." (14,382)

"And so, worn out trying to find out what would be the right thing to do, he came to this decision, *scilicet*, to give the mule its head at the fork in the road. Should the mule not go toward the town, but take the royal highway, he would let it go. And doing as he had resolved, *Our Lord willed* that, although the town was only thirty or forty paces from the road which was very wide and in good condition, the mule took the royal highway and not the one to town." (16,384) Afterward the knight remained tranquil. He had exhausted all means, even the natural instincts of his mount, and God had come to his aid. So he went back to his dreams as if nothing had happened.

5. He most likely did not stop at Saragossa with its famous *"Seo"* and *"Pilar."* Had he done so, he would have run into the crowds he was anxious to avoid. For the Regents had ordered special celebrations there to pay homage to the new Pontiff in the name of the entire nation. All the archbishops and bishops and the cream of Spanish nobility were assembled there. Four days after Iñigo's vigil at Montserrat the Holy Father entered the city.[61] Ortiz, who had been present at similar functions in Rome, tells us that the multitude at the solemn blessing on Palm Sunday surpassed any he had seen in the Eternal City. He says: "which well might happen, for what is rare is highly prized."[62]

Iñigo now had to outfit himself as a pilgrim. The thought of

---

[60]*Don Quijote, Libro I, Cap. IV*: Don Quijote mentions this custom peculiar to knights errant.
[61]Pastor, p. 40.
[62]Ortiz, p. 167: *"mea quidem opinione plures convenisse quam Romae crediderim. Quod contigere ideo potuit quia omne rarum pretiosum est."*

doing so had probably come to him as he rode along on his mule, reading through the notes he had jotted down at Loyola. For "he carried the note-book carefully protected" and "found great consolation' reading it. (18,388) He may have turned to some passage referring to Saint Francis' exchange of garments, or to Saint Onuphrius' unkempt hair and untrimmed nails. At any rate he decided to buy a "loosely woven, very coarse" sack-cloth tunic, a pilgrim's gourd and staff and also "a slipper" for his wounded foot "which was bandaged and in bad condition. . . . He thought this foot should be kept well-covered." (16,386)

At Igualada,[63] a large town near Montserrat, he bought the slippers and sack-cloth out of which he had a long tunic made. He did not put it on yet, for he had decided at Loyola not to remove his ordinary clothing until he reached his cell. So he put this last and most precious purchase on his saddle-bow and started up the holy Mount, dressed as a knight.

Even if he had worn his penitential garments and had gone on foot leading his mule laden with his fine clothes, no one would have paid him much attention. People were used to seeing the strangest kinds of penance performed, even by those who intended to stay in the world. Some pilgrims could be seen walking bare foot, others crawling along painfully on their knees, others carrying iron bars on their shoulders, others wearing ropes which they had tied about their necks or waists next to their skin, others disciplining themselves to blood.[64] The penitent of Loyola, who arrived a few days before the Annunciation, must have observed the pilgrims as they performed these various practices of mortification. We may imagine their effect on him, for in the next few months he would hardly be able to restrain his desires to imitate their austerities.

This is when the "Autobiography" tells us of the second chivalrous incident on his pilgrimage: his vigil of arms.

There are three laws relating to the rite of arming a knight in Alphonse the Wise's "*Siete Partidas.*" The XIIIth prescribes the cleanliness of body and soul required. The XIVth treats of the nocturnal watch of prayer to God before the act. The text reads: "and when this prayer is said, he is to remain kneeling or

---

[63]Creixell I, pp. 48-50; Albareda, p. 43 believes it was Lerida.
[64]Albareda, pp. 48-49: data from 1513-1552.

standing as long as he can. For the watch by the knights was established not in jest, nor for aught else save prayer to God which they and others present make that He protect them and direct and aid them, as men who enter upon a career of death."[65] Finally, the XVth law sets forth in detail the ceremony for arming the candidate.

Some authorities on Ignatius vigorously hold that this practical and religious law inspired Ignatius to stand watch before the altar of Our Lady. They reject the opinion that the inspiration came from his novels of chivalry. They argue that, as a man following the profession of arms, he would have been acquainted with this law which prescribed a rite much more like the one he followed in the Virgin's shrine, than the one contained in the two obscure passages in "Amadis:" the arming of don Galaor and of Celinda's son.[66] Besides, the vigil of arms was part of the coronation ceremonial of the kings of Aragon. King Pedro II, for instance, stood watch as a knight until dawn, assisted at Mass, and made his offering to the Virgin before going into battle.[67]

Two statements by Nadal seem to confirm this opinion. He wrote: "Recalling how novice knights were wont to be consecrated and dedicated for battle, he resolved to imitate them by devoting himself to God's service."[68] And again: "With this ceremony he began his new life, watching all night and praying before the holy Virgin's statue, in the manner that those who are about to be armed as knights stand watch over their arms, according to the solemn and ancient right of nobles."[69]

Undoubtedly this "solemn and ancient right" was the remote source of the Pilgrim's idea. From this remote source the rite and its details passed into chivalrous literature which became the immediate inspiration of Iñigo's vigil of arms. The "Autobiography" says so expressly, and surely we ought to accept the Saint's testimony in matters about which he alone can testify. The "Autobiography" says "And since his whole mind was full of these things, "Amadis" and other novels, some things similar to them entered his mind; and so he decided to stand watch over his arms," etc. (17,386) Besides, there are similar passages in

---

[65]Partida, II, tit. XXI, ley 14.
[66]Creixell I, pp. 79-80; Casanovas, pp. 88-89.
[67]Albareda, pp. 51-52; March, pp. 12-14.
[68]Scripta, I, p. 102; Fontes narrativi I, p. 76.
[69]Natalis Dialogi, fol. 296; unpublished text.

"Amadis" to which Ignatius referred, passages that present rather remarkable similarities of expression in addressing the Virgin as Protectress of Her Knights.

At the end of Book IV is found the scene in which the first-born and heir of Amadis and Oriana and his squires are consecrated knights. This passage crowns the entire work. The ceremony takes place in a chapel "adorned with gold and precious stones."

The unknown Princess Urganda assists the Prince don his armor. He is eager to go on a quest to liberate his grandfather, King Lisuarte. Other princesses attend the four squires. Then comes the nocturnal watch: "The four squires, with Esplandian in their midst, kneel *before the Virgin Mary's altar* and watch over their arms as was the custom of the time. Their hands and heads were uncovered and Esplandian stood among them, so handsome that his countenance shone as the rays of the sun, so that all marvelled beholding him *kneeling so devoutly and humbly imploring Her to be his advocate before Her glorious Son*, and to aid and direct him *so that being in Her service* he might be worthy of the great honor he was receiving, and to grant him grace through Her *boundless goodness*, that he and no other might restore King Lisuarte to his kingdom, should he still be alive. *Thus he stood the whole night* saying not a word, save for these prayers and many others, considering that no strength or valor no matter how great it might be, was of more worth and esteem than the dignity there bestowed upon him." Next morning, under quite fantastic circumstances, took place the solemn act of fixing spurs on the novice knight who leaves at once on his quest.[70]

There is little doubt that the Saint meant this passage when he spoke to Father Camara about *"Amadis."* Apart from the fantastic element, the central scene of the vigil is very poetic and devout. Such a scene would certainly inspire Iñigo to imitate it. We must keep in mind the Catholic and even pious nature of many passages in the Castilian version of the *"Amadis."* It was the current code of education among the nobility of the period. Menendez Pelayo says of the IVth Book to which this vigil scene belongs: "Perhaps one of the reasons the honorable Councilman of Medina, (the author of the Castilian version), had for adding

---

[70] *Amadis, lib. IV, cap. LII,* p. 400.

this episode was to marry Amadis and Oriana 'with benefit of clergy.' The author of the original who lived in the semi-pagan atmosphere of Celtic legend was little concerned with that."[71]

There were also chivalrous novels of a religious nature which adopted the literary form of *"Amadis."* Ignatius might mean them by the phrase "and similar books." There was, for instance, the Castilian version of *"El pelegrino de la vida humana,"* published in 1490, in which Lady Charity fastens and loosens the pilgrim's armor as he sets out for the heavenly city of Jerusalem.[72] In all this chivalrous literature there was an ingenuous Christian symbolism which Ignatius, the Saint of reason and purpose, immortalized by elevating it to spheres of a fecund and *modern* vitality.

6. The Pilgrim was absorbed by his purpose and transported with joy on seeing himself so near his Lady as he approached Montserrat on the morning of March twenty-first. He scarcely noticed the gigantic monoliths jutting from luxuriant vegetation which rose above the church and abbey, forming a background of cyclopean grandeur.

He threaded his way through the pilgrims who crowded the stables beneath the church, the Gothic cloisters, and the hostelry set aside for them.[73] He dismounted from his mule, stabled it and then, according to the "Autobiography" hastened to pray before the Virgin's altar and to arrange for an interview with a confessor. (17,386) He wanted to obtain permission to hold watch over his arms, and to reveal the secrets he had faithfullly guarded in his soul for eight months.

This long silence is rather surprising in the light of the stress which the "Exercises" put on the importance of guidance by a confessor or spiritual father. In the earliest rules for the discernment of spirits, Ignatius attributes to the devil the tactic of preventing such direction. He compares the devil to an illicit lover who dissuades the wife or young woman from revealing his evil designs to her husband or father.[74] He might well have found such counsels in the "Lives of the Saints," in particular of Saint

---

[71]Menendez Pelayo, p. 220.
[72]Vindel, XII, p. 124; Langlois, pp. 219-221.
[73]Albareda, pp. 47, ff. for this and other details.
[74]*Exercitia,* no. 326

Francis and of Saint Onuphrius, his favorite reading at Loyola.

He might have read in the "Life of Saint Francis": "One of his monks, who from all appearances was very mortified, kept apart from the others, and so strictly observed silence that he made his confession by signs. All esteemed him a saint, until one day Saint Francis came there and told them: 'My brothers, *do not praise the deceits of the devil,* rather urge him to confess once or twice each week, and if he does not do so *it is temptation and a snare of the devil.*' When the monks gave him this advice, he put his finger to his lips and shook his head as a sign he would not confess at all. A few days later he left the Order and returned to his sinful life."[75]

In the "Life of Saint Onuphrius," despite that Saint's extreme solitude and seclusion, there is the same emphasis on the need of guidance from a spiritual father as a safeguard against the snares and trials of so perilous a way. Not only did the monks of Hermopolis instruct him "carefully" before he went into the desert, but there, an ancient who dwelt in another cave taught him Our Lord's doctrine "for thirty days." The "Life" adds: "He showed me how to avoid the ambuscades of the devil with words of charity."[76]

None the less, despite these passages and the counsel which Ignatius himself gave in the "Exercises" in later years, the "Autobiography" tells us: "Up to that time he had revealed to no confessor"[77] the radical changes God was working in his soul. Of course, he went to confession at Loyola and Aranzazu. The text implies that when it says *"to no confessor"* it means that, although he confessed his faults and perhaps some sins of his past life, he neither made a general confession nor asked for any guidance in his spiritual experiences.

It is true that Ignatius was a Basque, by nature introspective, reserved, and self-reliant. However, this was not the real reason. Two elements enter into the explanation of his reticence. During all that period he felt no inner conflict nor anxiety such as later, at Manresa, required the direction of a confessor; and he was obsessed by the fear lest his acquaintances, becoming aware of his conversion, should look on him as a saint. The relevation had to

---

[75]*Flos Sanctorum,* fol. 142, col. 2a.
[76]Leturia, (IV), pp. 233-237. Texts and commentary.
[77]Codina, p. 49.

be made away from home where he would be unknown. Even in choosing his confessor, he picked one least acquainted with Guipuzcoa and Castile: a devout French priest, Jean Chanon, or in Castilian, Chanones. This confessor had formerly been pastor at Mirepoix, not far from Rosellon, and had retired to the abbey at Montserrat.[78]

Ignatius may also have heard of the reputation for doctrine and zeal that the confessors of Montserrat had earned. Dom Anselmo Albareda thinks this may have influenced his choice. Ignatius must have heard of these confessors while he was at Ferdinand's Court. As a matter of fact, King Ferdinand and Queen Isabella completed the reform of the monastery by sending there Fray Garcia de Cisneros, the famous Cardinal's cousin, with a group of monks from Valladolid. The holiness and observance of the community, and in particular of their abbot, were highly regarded at the Court during Ignatius' stay. If, then, he was aware of their reputation,[79] we can understand why he postponed manifesting his secret, until he could consult a learned and holy confessor at Montserrat.[80]

The "Autobiography" clearly shows that Ignatius himself proposed making the confession, and that the idea was not suggested to him by the Benedectine confessor.[81] "When he reached Montserrat, after he had prayed and had arranged for an interview with the confessor, he made a general confession in writing, and the confession lasted three days." (17,386) The arrangement mentioned here does not concern the vigil, for he speaks of that elsewhere, (17,386) but the confession, and how and when it was to be made. As we know, he made it in writing and during the few days still remaining before the Annunciation.

A passage at the very beginning of the prologue to the "*Vita Christi*" which Ignatius read and reread at Loyola, and from which he took many notes, seems to confirm this opinion. "The first thing (which the converted sinner is to endeavor) is to hearken to Our Lord Who invites sinners to pardon. . . . Let, then, the patient listen to the pious and solicitous Doctor, and let

---

[78]Albareda, pp. 56-57: for further information on Father Chanon.
[79]Further confirmation is the fact that many Guipuzcoans had recourse to the holy Mount "to unburden their consciences." We have mentioned the measures taken by the Provincial Council to ensure a supply of Basque confessors.
[80]Albareda, p. 38 .
[81]Ibid., pp. 110, 111. This is Dom Anselmo's opinion.

him come to Him *with deep contrition and diligent confession* and with a sincere resolve ever to shun evil and to do good. The second thing the sinner who is devout, ready and faithful to Christ and *reconciled with Him through penance* ought to do, is to strive diligently to unite himself to his Physician. . . ."[82] i.e. to Jesus Christ.

During his somewhat idealistic fancies on the way "he was resolved to perform great austerities, without as yet showing much concern for satisfying for his sins." (14,45) But, now, on reaching Montserrat, the memory of this counsel revived. Straightway he begged the Virgin's blessing and sought out a confessor with whom he might "make arrangements" for confession. Here, without his suspecting it, a new vista of spirit and life opened up before him.

---

[82]*Cartujano arromanzado,* fol. 4 v.

CHAPTER VII

VIGIL OF ARMS AT MONTSERRAT

1. Iñigo reached the abbey of Montserrat. At the beginning of the sixteenth century it was famous as a center of the Catholic reform which Isabella and Cisneros had started in Spain long before Protestantism was born.

Between 1500 and 1522 the community comprised some fifty monks, twelve hermits, forty lay brothers and lay assistants, and some fifteen children in the monastery school.[1] One of the lay assistants was procurator and administered justice within the exempt domain of the monastery. A constable kept order about the church and its adjuncts.[2] The soul of the community was the liturgy, as was traditional among the Benedictines. There was a printing press which was one of the oldest in Spain and had been set up expressly to provide missals and antiphonals for the "Congregation of Saint Benedict" in Valladolid.[3]

In addition to special concern for the liturgy, the reform cultivated meditation and methodical contemplation. This was a recent development of the *"devotio moderna"* which Abbot Peralta had initiated, and his successor, Fray Garcia de Cisneros, had fostered at the shrine.[4] By 1522 the monastery had produced contemplatives such as the Basque, Alonso de Vizcaya, who published in 1508 a treatise on "Spiritual Marriage,"[5] the Castilian, Pedro de Burgos, Cisneros' successor and abbot while Ignatius was there, and the Frenchman, Jean Chanon, his confessor and the future Master of Novices in Portugal.[6]

Father Chanon's piety and learning were of great help to the convert when he arrived at the shrine. He had entered Montserrat as a novice, knowing neither Castilian nor Catalan so was obliged to speak Latin.[7] By 1522, he was noted for his austerity and mortification, for his zeal in confessing pilgrims, for his devotion to liturgical and mental prayer, and for his special devotion to the

---

[1]Albareda, (I), pp. 54-55.
[2]Albareda, (I), p. 75: he was sometimes a lay assistant, sometimes a secular.
[3]Albareda, (II), pp. 39 ff.
[4]Leturia, (VI), pp. 379 ff.
[5]*Analecta Montserratensia* VII, pp. 145-146.
[6]Albareda, (I), p. 108 for many other names.
[7]*Scripta*, II, p. 441.

Rosary and to the Eucharist. These qualities stand out in his "Necrology," which was written after his death in 1568,[8] and are reflected in the life led by his disciple, Iñigo de Loyola, during the first months at Manresa.

However, we must attribute the efficacy of his providential encounter with Iñigo not only to his personal virtue but also to the school of prayer to which he belonged as a member of the community. The text-book of that school was the famous "Exercitatory of the Spiritual Life," written by Garcia de Cisneros, and printed in 1500 on the abbey press.

This work, the study of which belongs to the life of the Saint rather than to that of the Courtier Loyola, was intended to serve the novices as an introduction to the purgative way. It propounded to them a method of general confession[9] and seven meditations, chiefly based on the writings of the pious Hollander, Gerard of Zutphen, a predecessor of Thomas a Kempis.[10] Of more importance than the book itself, was its influence on the affective life of the novices and on the pilgrims who visited the Virgin's sanctuary from all parts of Spain and even from abroad.

The novices spent ten or twelve days in preparation for confession. They were assisted in the examining of their consciences by a manual of preparation for confession, or list of sins and virtues,[11] and by one of the seven meditations in the "Exercitatory." A compendium, which was composed at Montserrat, counsels non-religious to imitate the novices in this "as is customary in religious Orders at the beginning of their conversion by those who more perfectly serve God."[12]

Iñigo went to find Father Chanon, the confessor. The abbey was ideally suited to the execution of his high resolves: confession, penance, and then the vigil. He fitted easily into the new spiritual way divine Providence had opened up before him. On the morning of the twenty-first he "made arrangements for an interview" with the confessor. Father Ribadeneira, toward the

---

[8]*Scripta*, II, pp. 442-443.
[9]*Ejercitatorio*, p. 10. "It is proper, dear brethren, that he who wishes to exercise himself in the spiritual life, first purge his heart of all mortal sin by contrition and a general confession. because the impure of heart cannot receive the influence of the Holy Spirit."
[10]*Caps.* XII-XVIII; Leturia, (VI), pp. 380 ff.
[11]Albareda, (I), p. 112: unfortunately he seems not to know the text of the confessionary which would be of importance for the study of the "General Examen" in the "Exercises."
[12]Albareda, (I), p. 111: texts.

end of his life, wrote: "We of the Society ought to be grateful
to Our Lord that our blessed Father, after having been buffetted
by the waves and tempests of the world, should have reached
port so safely and have found so excellent a confessor and so
beneficial a book."[13]

Father Chanon introduced his generous penitent to the ascetical
and purgative method of the "Exercitatory," and gave him a copy
in Castilian. Fray Juan de Lerma, who had spent seven years at
the abbey with Father Chanon, wrote Ribadeneira[14] around
1583 that he had done so. Later, Fray Miguel de Santa Fe,
who was acquainted with him from 1553, as well as other monks
of the abbey, deposed substantially the same.[15]

The authors to whom Ignatius confided his life are less explicit.
There are some, however, who confirm the Montserrat tradition.
Thus, Father Nadal describes the Saint as preparing for general
confession by meditating, noting down whatever moved him, and
conferring with his confessor, a pious and learned man.[16]

2. When Iñigo came to the monastery which was situated outside the town, he sought lodging in the hostelry which was reserved for pilgrims. He had some difficulty, for he did not want
to tell his name as each pilgrim had to do. It is probable that
Father Chanon interceded for him, and obtained a dispensation
from that troublesome requirement.[17] He was given a cell, where
he would pray, write, and discipline himself. He would partake
of the soup which was furnished the pilgrims during these penitential days, and would sleep in some corner of the cloister when he
was not watching throughout the night in the sanctuary, as he
usually did. Juan Pascual related years later that Iñigo did not
remove his clothing those nights, not even his shoes, and fasted
on bread and water.[18]

What were Iñigo's emotions during those hours? He made
a thorough examination of his sinful past, diligently setting down
in writing a list of his iniquities. (22,392) In this, he may have
been helped by the Confession Manual. It is certain, however,

---

[13]Ribadeneira, II, p. 515.
[14]Ribadeneira in 1607: "Many years ago . . . he wrote me." Probably on the
occasion of the publication of the first edition of the "Life" in Castilian.
[15]Codina, pp. 168 ff.; Albareda, (I), pp. 133 ff.
[16]Natalis, IV, p. 826.
[17]Albareda, (I), pp. 51 ff.: details.
[18]Scripta, II, p. 83.

that here, as at Loyola, personal effort and self-analysis played the major role. This is shown in the definitive text of the "Exercises" particularly in the notes on the "Examen" and the "General Confession," which form the introduction to the "First Week."[19] Nevertheless, we can more fully appreciate his meditations during these days, thanks to the "Exercitatory" and Father Chanon's direction.

There is in the "Exercitatory" a consideration on sin which was already contained in the work by Gerard of Zutphen, classic also in his sources. It is found at the beginning of the purgative way, and is repeated with variations, at least thrice within a few pages.[20] Its moving, practical considerations are well adapted to strike the imagination of the reader.

The pious Benedictine counsels us to consider what we are to fear, and especially "the severity which is shown in the fall of Lucifer, who for *one single sin,* was hurled forever from Heaven. How, then, shall those who have committed many sins enter therein? This severity is manifested, too, in our father Adam's sin, *one single sin* for which he was banished from the terrestrial paradise, while the gate of Heaven was barred to him until Our Lord Jesus Christ opened it by His holy death. God's justice appears awesome and terrifying, even in this death and Passion, for He abandoned His most blessed Son into the hands of so cruel a people, as is shown by those fearful words He uttered on the Cross: "My God, My God, why hast Thou forsaken Me?" If this justice was exercised so sternly and so fearfully in the green wood, which is so filled with virtue, and upon One so loved by the Father, what will happen to us who are dry wood, bereft of virtue and burdened with sins?"[21]

The same thought, as terrible as it is just, recurs more insistently in the colloquies which Cisneros appends to the meditation on Hell: "Oh Lord, how many are in Hell, having committed one single sin? Then I, who have committed so many, what do I deserve, Lord? Rightly do I deserve condemnation, for I am worthy of all torment and unworthy of all beneficence."[22]

Nadal tells us that Iñigo chose from among the meditations for

---

[19]*Ejercicios,* nos. 24-44; Codina, pp. 48-49.
[20]*Ejercitatorio,* pp. 35, 41, 58.
[21]*Ejercitatorio,* p. XI, p. 35, and cap. XII, p. 41.
[22]*Ejercitatorio,* cap. XIV, p. 58.

his first general confession those considerations that moved him most, and noted them down in his note-book, the rudimentary sketch of the "Exercises." The fundamental outline described above appears in the first exercise of the "First Week." It is in the consideration on the "Triple Sin:" that of Satan, of Adam, and "of one, who because of one mortal sin, has gone to Hell, and of countless others, who have been condemned for fewer sins than I have committed."[23] This terrible thought, however, provokes in Iñigo's noble and generous soul, not so much fear, as shame and confusion "as if a knight should find himself before his King and all his Court, ashamed and confounded because he has offended so much him from whom he had received so many gifts and favors."[24]

The contemplation of the Crucified Christ, voluntary victim of our iniquities, at this point is interrupted by a colloquy: "as to how, being the Creator, He has deigned to become man, and being eternal, has come to a temporal death, and thus to die for my sins. Looking at myself, I, what have I done for Christ, what am I doing for Christ, what ought I do for Christ?"[25]

At this point, too, the "Exercitatory" and the notes taken at Loyola, with which he was so contented, must have helped Ignatius. Cisneros' outburst before the Crucified was admirably adapted to his exchanging his rich garments for the garb of a penitent: "Thou, Lord, naked on the Cross, and I dressed in vain and luxurious clothing. . . . What, then, will I do, Lord?"[26] And the "*Flos Sanctorum*": "Oh my Jesus, nailed to the Cross! Grant that I, whether I eat, or sleep or watch, may ever hear those cruel blows of the hammer when they nailed Thy sacred Hands and Feet. . . . May those nails, Lord, pierce the hardness of my heart. May those thorns pierce my soul in penance for my dissoluteness and sin. May I, Lord, contemplating Thy Passion, forego soft couches, comfortable clothing and exquisite foods. . . ."[27]

Ignatius was now within reach of the goal he had yearned after at Loyola. The joy he felt prevented the exercises of the

---

[23]*Ejercicios*, no. 52.
[24]*Ejercicios*, no. 74.
[25]*Ejercicios*, no. 53.
[26]*Ejercitatorio*, cap. XII, p. 45.
[27]Leturia (III), p. 344: complete text. Note that at the beginning at Manresa, Iñigo's devotion to the Passion is already prominent.

examen and of compunction for sin from resulting in a tempest of scruples and in agonies of interior desolation. The "Autobiography" and other early sources reveal that Iñigo experienced throughout the first months he spent at Manresa an inner joy (20,390) in the fulfillment of his hidden desires. (17,386) The result was that he "could hardly contain himself with pleasure," as Ribadeneira says in the fourth chapter of the "Life."

On the eve of the Anunciation he read the list of his sins to his confessor. He had drawn it up "diligently and in writing." (22,392) He had now taken definitive leave of his worldly habits of Azpeitia, Arevalo, Navarrete, and Pamplona. He had received absolution and, filled with consolation, he had but one concern: to exchange his garments and stand watch over his arms.

3. The "Autobiography" briefly remarks: "He arranged with the confessor to donate his mule to the monastery, and to have his sword and dagger put on the altar of Our Lady." (17,386) This might seem simple to do, but the process that refers to Montserrat and Manresa, reveals that a difficulty arose since the Pilgrim refused to tell his name. He still feared lest the world know he was a Loyola. The abbot hesitated to accept from an *anonymous* donor a fine mule, a Toledan sword and dagger, and the expensive clothing of a captain. Perhaps they would be demanded back some day or other, and the monks would be accused of having obtained them unjustly.[28] The abbot refused to accept the clothing, and was at first unwilling to take the mule. Through Father Chanon's intercession, Iñigo finally persuaded him to keep the mule, for he could conceive of no worthier destiny for his mount than that of serving the Virgin. The sword and dagger were accepted without difficulty and placed among the other ex-votos that covered the walls and the grill of the chapel.[29]

Iñigo was not present when the monks took over his mule which served many years at the monastery. It was still there when Father Araoz visited Montserrat in 1541.[30] The ex-soldier took off his sword and dagger, the weapons of Najera and Pamplona, and gave them to Father Chanon. The sacristan or one

---

[28]Albareda, pp. 63 ff.: further details. Such donations were often received but not anonymously.
[29]*Scripta*, II, p. 718. The sworn testimony of Francisco Capdepos of Manresa.
[30]*Scripta*, I, p. 725.

of the school children hung them on the grill which separated the Virgin's chapel from the main church. Fray Lorenzo Nieto recorded the fact in the process.[31] The sword and dagger remained for some time among the other ex-votos, until others took their place before Ignatius was known as a famous personage and the founder of the Society of Jesus.[32] The Virgin, who had smiled down upon Ignatius as he lay upon the couch at Loyola, now had before Her the trophies of Her victory.

Ignatius was now unarmed, but still wore his rich clothing. He had wanted to offer it to the Virgin,[33] but its very worth had caused them to reject it. He did not want to destroy it, or bury it on the mountain, as he might easily have done. He decided to wait until dark, and then find one of the beggars who swarmed in the cloisters and stables, and explain to him confidentially his reason for giving it as alms. Then he would be rid of the relics of his former vanity. The "Autobiography" relates: "He went at night, as secretly as possible, to a poor man, and despoiling himself of his clothing, including his shirt,[34] gave them to him and put on his longed-for sack-cloth." (18,386-388) In the simplicity of his fervor, he did not realize that this solution to his problem might not only compromise his incognito, but also the poor beggar who skulked off into the night laden with such suspicious alms. . . .!

While the beggar went blithely on his way with his prize, Christ's novice Knight was still more joyously crossing the cloister which was crowded with pilgrims, and entered the church. It was not a large edifice at the time, yet it blazed with its fifty silver lamps, one given by Charles V, and with its forty gigantic candle-sticks which bore the name of as many cities and towns of Catalonia, as well as with countless candles of varying sizes, which the pilgrims and anonymous donors had offered.[35] Ignatius ignores all these accessories in his "Autobiography." He gives us the essential fact in words that recall the devout passage in *"Amadis:"* "He put on his longed-for sack-cloth and went to kneel before Our Lady's altar. With staff in hand, he spent part of the night kneeling, part standing." (18, 47)

---

[31]*Scripta,* II, p. 385.
[32]*Scripta,* II, pp. 835-836. Editor's note: *Fontes narrativi,* I, p. 387, note 12.
[33]Albareda, p. 62: details.
[34]Ribadeneira, *Vida, lib. I, cap. IV.*
[35]Albareda, pp. 65-66: additional details.

Of course, he did not enter the Virgin's chapel, but stood before the grill. He was not alone. As he stood in the shadows touched by the sheen of the candles, he heard from time to time the murmured prayers of the pilgrims about him, and the harmony of psalmody and the strains of the organ. For at midnight, when the bell-ringer sounded the mystic summons on the "great bell," the monks intoned the Invitatorium of the Annunciation. Later, Matins and Lauds were crowned by the salutation to the Virgin, the "*Ave Stella Matutina.*"[36] Ignatius, who was extremely fond of the liturgical chant, must have joined ecstatically in the hymn to his Queen and Lady.

When the religious returned to their cells for mental prayer at two o'clock in the morning, Ignatius remained before the altar, now kneeling, now standing, as the code of chivalry prescribed. He meditated, too. In his note-book there is a passage which almost certainly was taken from the "*Vita Christi*" which treats of the feast of the Incarnation. Most critics admit that the passage in the Exercises in which the "Damascene field" is mentioned, was taken from his notes on the "*Vita Christi*" for the expression is found in the considerations on that great mystery.[37]

The devout Carthusian of Saxony paints a picture well adapted to Iñigo's state and to the feast day. One might say that it was intended to link the purgative meditations of the preceding triduum with the illuminative contemplations Iñigo is soon to consider. Following Saint Bernard, Ludolph depicts the sin of Lucifer and the fall of our First Parents. Then he continues: "and as a result, we were all doomed to the prison of Hell from which we could not escape nor could anyone help us. But the Father of mercies and the Lord of all consolation looked with clemency on our state of condemnation, and ordained that we be freed by Himself. And from the beginning of our creation, the sovereign mercy of God deigned to awaken contrition in men through *secret inspirations*, nor did it delay recalling to penitence man who had erred and gone astray, giving him hope of pardon."

This consideration makes the penitent realize that the merciful ways of Providence in the distant past still apply to him personally in the present. The conclusion the Carthusian draws is

---

[36]Albareda, pp. 67-68.
[37]*Vita Christi*, lib. I, cap. III, p. 1.

not that of Gerard and of Cisneros, one of shame and sorrow
for personal sins, but rather one of love and mercy, and places
the sinner before the Incarnate Word, and the lovable figure of
Mary in Her Immaculate Conception and fruitful virginity.

The chapter becomes a canticle of Mary's praises: "In watching,
She was ever the first, and, in the sublimest wisdom, the most
learned of all, and, in humility, the most profound, and in, singing the songs and psalms of David, the most charming and the
sweetest of voice, in charity, most loving and gracious, in purity,
most perfect, and most constant and unchanging in Her highest
resolves."

After this lyrical rhapsody come resolutions to imitate Her,
and then a colloquy, passionate, yet at the same time a pledge of
perfect chastity. This passage must have struck Iñigo when he
read it at Loyola. It may have induced him to vow chastity at
Aranzazu, and to renew that vow more solemnly in his penitential
sack-cloth before his Lady. "Thou, Lady, who art my sovereign
solace, direct all my life, and obtain for me from Thy Son the
grace to imitate all Thy virtues and examples in as far as in me
lies, and grand that Thy grace, Lady, be ever present to me.
Amen." The Virgin and Her Child smiled down upon him and
blessed him from Their throne of mercy. The "Autobiography"
does not say so, but the Saint's later life and even the history of
the Catholic Reformation prove it. . . .!

The devoted Knight was so affected by these and similar
thoughts that he determined then and there to postpone his journey to Barcelona and Jerusalem. He would stay in some nearby
obscure place where he could write at leisure all his new lights in
his note-book. (18,388) This was the simple and fertile election
he made at Montserrat!

He attended Mass before dawn at which the choir of school
children, dressed in black cassocks and white surplices, sang to
the organ the Mass of the Annunciation.[38] After Mass and Holy
Communion, he hastened to complete his vigil before dawn. As
he told Father Camara *when morning came he left at once,
lest he be recognized."* (18,388)

---

[38]Albareda (I), pp. 69-70: details.

4. This haste gives us an insight into certain of his thoughts during that night.

We have observed throughout the first phase of Saint Ignatius' spiritual life the fear he had of being recognized. It was almost an obsession. At Loyola he feared that his family might oppose his intention. Now he feared that he would be recognized at the shrine. He confided to Father Camara, even before he dictated his "Autobiography" to him, that this was a reaction to temptation to pride. When Father Camara had told him that he was assailed at times by temptation to pride, the Saint informed him "that he had been afflicted by like temptations, at the very beginning of his conversion, for two years. This temptation was so powerful that, when he embarked at Barcelona for Jerusalem, he dared not tell anyone where he was going, and so in other matters. He added that he had felt great peace of soul in this regard afterwards."[39] This purifying conquest over pride is significant in a century of humanist selfishness and Protestant individualism, especially in a personality so strong and self-reliant as that of Ignatius, who had followed his own way almost unaided, not only in his military career, but also in his conversion.

We can better understand his hurried flight from Montserrat in the light of this temptation. He had decided to postpone his journey to Palestine for a few days in order to quietly pray, do penance, and note in his book the new lights which had been given him while at the sanctuary. But he was not going to stay at the monastery, or in a hermitage, or in a nearby cave whence he would come down for Mass and to beg his meals.[40] He had noticed some of his former acquaintances at King Ferdinand's Court during his triduum[41] and feared lest they in turn might recognize him. He was afraid, too, that he would be pointed out as the courtier who had arrived in expensive clothing, and had secretly given it as alms to a poor man. If he should remain there, even for a few hours, clothed as he now was in the new uniform of a soldier of Christ, he would run the risk of exposure

---

[39]*Scripta*, I, p. 31; *Fontes narrativi* I, p. 356.
[40]Manresa, p. 12 (1936), pp. 158 ff. We refer to the days immediately after the vigil, for he might well have returned to Manresa later on.
[41]Saint Ignatius says later on, that, while on the road from Montserrat to Barcelona, he might meet many who would recognize him and esteem him. Perhaps he had seen among the pilgrims some acquaintances who would return to the city. He had known many Catalans at Court, and we know that the Duke of Najera's wife belonged to the noble Folch de Cardona, a family of Barcelona.

and be esteemed as a saint. Since the temptation assailed him to stay, he decided to remove himself from the scene. "When dawn came he left, lest he be recognized."[42]

But where should he go? The "Autobiography" gives the alternatives which presented themselves to him, and the choice he made: a hospital in one of the towns that dotted the road from Montserrat to Barcelona, or one in a town far from the road, and so, less frequented by caravans of travellers and pilgrims. His obsession led him to adopt the second course. "He went, not by the direct road to Barcelona, where there might be many who would know and esteem him, but turned off at a town called Manresa. . . ." (18,388), a name linked, and almost identified, with the fame of Loyola.

We do not know for certain who suggested this town to him. Juan Pascual, who was eleven years old at the time, testified seventy years later, that it was due to a chance encounter with his mother and some women from Manresa. The Saint had inquired of them whether they knew of a hospital in the neighborhood, where he might stay, so they brought him to Manresa.[43] But the many errors in this story[44] and Ignatius' clear idea of the route when he set out from Montserrat, lead us to think that he had made his decision before he left the monastery. It is likely Chanon advised him to go there. He must have been acquainted with many Manresans, and through them, have known of their piety, so well confirmed by later events.[45]

In the coolness of early morning, Ignatius "turned off" the road to Barcelona, rejoicing that he had broken the last bond that tied him to the world. Then an unexpected incident brought him down to earth.

We have mentioned that in the sixteenth century the abbey of Montserrat administered justice in its territory through a procurator, who had under him a constable who kept order in the church and its adjuncts.[46] This constable ran across the beggar to whom Iñigo had given his expensive clothing. The poor man's explanation of this "windfall" failed to convince either the constable or

[42]Albareda, pp. 95-96. This is an obvious reply to his observations.
[43]*Scripta*, II, pp. 83-84.
[44]Albareda, p. 98.
[45]Dudon, pp. 76-80: on the piety of the Manresans. Account taken from town archives.
[46]Albareda, p. 73 a: details.

the procurator. The "Autobiography" says they "ridiculed" his story and Polanco adds, they arrested him[47] which they would hardly have done had not the superior officer intervened. Then the beggar gave a detailed description of his benefactor which, incidentally, shows that Iñigos fear of being recognized was not an idle one. He told them of the nobleman, now dressed in sackcloth, who had given him the alms, and had left Montserrat a short while before,[48] and even told them in what direction he had gone. . . .

The constable decided to investigate so strange a case. He "hurried" down the road to overtake the Pilgrim. When he had caught up with him within a league of the sanctuary, he asked him whether he had given his clothing to a poor man. This unexpected question caused Iñigo to change color. He was even more confused when the constable, in reply to his prompt affirmation, asked him his name and nationality, and what he intended doing. Iñigo absolutely refused to answer these questions since the beggar was now cleared and they concerned him too intimately.[49]

The constable did not insist and the ex-courtier, though glad that the danger of exposure had passed, wept in his heart for the innocent man whom he had thoughtlessly jeopardized. The "Autobiography" says that he actually shed tears, (18,388) the first since he left Loyola, according to Lainez. Ribadeneira has preserved for us his inner reproach: "Alas, for you, sinner, that you do not know how, or cannot do good to your neighbor without bringing harm to him."[50] The sudden paleness in one who had faced the missiles at Pamplona, and those tender tears in one who had not shed a one throughout the butchery of his leg at Loyola, are the final acts by which Iñigo Lopez de Loyola took leave of his career as a courtier, to begin that of author of the "Spiritual Exercises" and of founder of the Society of Jesus. They indicate the effects of grace in his soul, but they also reveal the delicacy and tenderness of his heart.

And so he descended the holy Mount and calmly immersed him-

[47]*Chron.*, p. 18.
[48]*Chron.*, p. 18: *"Inde paulo ante recesserat."*
[49]*Chron.*, p. 20.
[50]*Scripta*, I, p. 101 (*Lainez*); *Fontes narrativi*, I, p. 76; Ribadeneira, *Vida, lib. I, cap. IV.*

self in those transcendental months at Manresa, which in later
years he called "his primitive church." For there he laid the new
foundation of his sanctity and gave us a new point of departure
for understanding his spirit. There, too, was the true origin of
the "Exercises" and of the Society of Jesus. Our book has given
but the façade of the temple. Ignatius himself, in the maturity of
his life, traced for us with sure hand, where the truly sacred
precincts began.

The grace that moved him was impulse rather than light, zeal
rather than discretion, until after he had passed four months at
Manresa. Despite his "retreat" at Loyola, on leaving the Castle,
he said his soul was "blind;" and despite Monteserrat, Chanon
and the "Exercitatory," he confesses that during the first months
at Manresa "he had no knowledge of spiritual things."

This evalution, made at the end of a long and enlightened
career, must be taken in a comparative sense, in contrast to the
splendors of divine light which shone upon him at Cardoner.
They do not entirely depreciate the real and beneficial influences
of other more external, though religious, factors which have been
described in the sources, and which burgeon even to this day in
certain passages of the "Exercises."

But, in the eyes of the author of the "Autobiography," all that
quite vanishes before the experiences of an extraordinary and
strictly personal spiritual life during his last months at Manresa.
But this is not the proper object of the present work, which aims
to portray the courtier, not the Saint.

CHAPTER VIII

WARTBURG AND LOYOLA

1. The dates of the wounding and conversion of Ignatius evoke once more the old topic of their coincidence with Luther's rebellion.

This chronological parallel attracted the attention of early biographers even before Ribadeneira's first "Life of Saint Ignatius" appeared. At first there was some confusion and disagreement. Ribadeneira placed the parallel in the year 1517, i.e. when Luther wrote his theses in Germany, and Iñigo was converted in Spain.[1] This was due to his erroneous belief that Iñigo, born in 1491, was converted when he was twenty-six. He did not know that the campaign in which Loyola was wounded took place in 1521, and so he simply added 1491 to 26 to get 1517, without further investigation.[2]

Some years later, around 1565, Nadal and Polanco learned that Ignatius was wounded in 1521. They then dated the providential parallel four years back. Polanco wrote: "It has been noted that this year 1521, the year in which Martin Luther, when he was cited by Charles V to appear at Worms, began to vomit his venom frankly and publicly against the Apostolic See and the Ecumenical Councils, (for hitherto he had declared he was willing to submit his doctrine to the Roman Pontiff), is the very year that Ignatius consecrated himself to the divine service." . . .[3]

The parallel is now more exact. Special interest is added by a circumstance, hitherto little noted: that the reaction to the Lutheran revolt began to be felt in Castile during the very years of Iñigo's formation and transformation.

The unity of the Church, the spouse of Christ, had inspired the songs and ballads which were composed at the Court, even in the days of the Catholic Kings. Fray Ambrosio de Montesino, Isabella's poet, hymned in winged verse the seamless robe of Our

[1]*Scripta*, I, p. 343, no. 18.
[2]Leturia, (I), pp. 46-47; *Fontes narrativi*, I, pp. 15-22. For further details. We have already shown in Chapter I that Ignatius contradicted himself when he stated he was converted at twenty-six, and that he was sixty-two in 1555.
[3]*Chronicon*, p. 18. It is not exact that Luther had not rejected the Councils up to Worms. He had already denied them in a controversy at Leipzig in 1519. However, Worms did mark a solemn and definitive break.

Saviour, in a poem dedicated to the Duchess of Najera, the viceroy of Navarre's mother. Doubtless the courtier Loyola heard of it.[4]

The sentiments of Catholic unity were deeply rooted among the nobility, clergy and people of Spain at the beginning of the sixteenth century. This is shown by the spontaneity with which they reacted in April 1521 to the first instances of Luther's propaganda which was then beginning to be translated and circulated on the Peninsula. The historian of the *Comunero* war observed that the report of the religious revolt in Germany and Charles' consequent embarrassment, produced a slackening in the support given to the *"Comuneros"* and a favorable change in the attitude of the nobility and of the people. It was not the right moment to deny the rights or demand the immediate presence of the Emperor on the Peninsula when in Germany "His Majesty" was defending "Our Holy Catholic Faith" and "the Roman Church, our Mother."[5]

These expressions occur in the Memorial of April twenty-first, 1521, a month before Iñigo was wounded at Pamplona. The Regents, the Grandees, and the Prelates of Aragon and Castile addressed the Emperor as follows:

"Most humbly we kiss Your Majesty's royal hands and feet, and inform you that in these your kingdoms and possessions, in various parts, we have learned of the tares and schism which the heresiarch, Martin Luther, has sown in Germany among your Majesty's subjects. We, as Catholic Christians, and zealous for the Faith, and for the service and honor of your Majesty, deeply regret that this is so. We are especially affected because we have learned that the seducer, not content with perverting and deceiving Germany, is striving by malicious and diabolical snares to corrupt and contaminate these your kingdoms and possessions in

---

[4]*Sancha, p.* 429: *De misterio no carece/ que esta santa vestidura/ tan entera permanece/ que pieza no le fallece,/ según dice la Escritura;/ Porque ella, según verdad,/ por ser toda sin costura,/ de toda la cristiandad/ y de su santa unidad/ fué figura./ Tanto quiso el Rey sagrado/ que entre nos cisma no haya,/ que nos lo dejó firmado/ con abrirnos su costado/ y con no romper su saya:/ Pues, según se me entiende,/ al que causa división/ eterna pena lo prende,/ porque más Cristo se ofende y su Pasión.*

(Of mystery there is not lack/ that this holy robe/ so whole remains/ that no piece is wanting/ as says the Scriptures;/ For it, in truth/ since it whole without hem,/ of all Christianity/ and of its holy unity was a figure. . . / So much the Sacred King willed/ that among us there be no schism/ that he left it to us established/ through the opening of His side/ and through the untorn robe:/ Hence, as it seems to me/ to the one who causes division/ eternal punishment overtakes him/ for rather offends he Christ and His Passion.)

[5]Danvila, III, pp. 579, 583.

Spain. For that purpose, with the assistance of some in these regions who desire to hinder the Holy Office of the Inquisition, he has had translated into Castilian his heresies and blasphemies, and has sent them to be circulated and published in this Catholic nation.

"And since, most Christian Lord, from a spark great conflagrations often spring, and, if such a disservice to God, Our Lord, and so great a danger to our Holy Catholic Faith be not remedied in time by your Majesty, there might result a great scandal and conflagration such as might not then be easily extinguished, the more so since some cities of your kingdoms are disturbed, therefore, in our own, and in the name of those absent, we humbly and earnestly beg your Majesty, as a most Christian Emperor and Catholic King, our Lord, the protector and defender of our Holy Catholic Faith and of the Roman Church, our Mother, imitating your glorious progenitors of immortal memory, to take this cause of the Faith for your own, as it truly is. . . .

"By so doing, besides accomplishing and performing what is right and obligatory upon you as the principal Christian Prince, you will grant us, the Grandees, Prelates and Knights of these your Kingdoms and possessions, both here present and absent, so great a favor and benefit that no one of us could imagine a greater, since it is for the cause of God, Our Lord."[6]

It would be absurd to think that the defender of Pamplona, wounded but a month after that letter was written, abandoned the earthly militia to become a soldier of the Faith and of the Church in a spiritual crusade against Luther. The future founder of the Society did not think of that even after several years had passed.[7] However, it is significant in the light of history that the future paladin of the Roman Catholic cause in its struggle with Protestantism, should have sprung from the environment that produced such a letter. Divine Providence ordained that Iñigo Lopez de Loyola be wounded and converted from May twentieth, 1521 to March of 1522, the period between the writing of that Memorial and the solemn homage paid a year later at Saragossa to the new Pope, Adrian VI, by the clergy, nobility and people of Spain.[8]

6Danvila, III, pp. 381, 382.
7Leturia, (II), pp. 81 ff.
8Cf. chapter on Adrian's reception throughout Spain.

2. Several years ago we noted an equally significant aspect in the coincidence of dates.[9]

A few days before Ignatius was wounded at Pamplona, on May fourth, 1521, a group of horsemen of the Elector of Saxony seized Luther in the neighborhood of Eisenach. They conducted him secretly to the famous castle at Wartburg, once made holy by Saint Elizabeth of Thuringia, but a half-abandoned and gloomy keep when Luther entered it. Frederick intended to keep Luther there under a feigned arrest in order to protect him from measures brought against him in unison by the Emperor and the Pope.

Luther, disguised as a farmer and using the alias of Junker George, spent in forced retirement at Wartburg Castle the very months Ignatius passed in "retreat" at the Loyola Castle. Iñigo left Loyola for Montserrat at the beginning of March, 1522. It was precisely on March first of the same year that Luther left Wartburg for Wittenberg.[10]

The activities of the two men in their respective castles are of more interest than the mere coincidence of dates.

Luther, during the first days of his stay at Wartburg, wrote the Augustinians of Wittenberg a vivid description of the crisis that had tormented his soul the preceding year. He wrote: "How often my heart trembled with fear when I posed this objection to myself, the only one, but very strong: Are you alone wise? Has everyone else been deceived and led astray for so long a time? What if you are the one who is deceived, and you drag down with you so many who will be lost forever?"[11]

He bares a different kind of struggle to Melancthon in a letter he sent him on July thirteenth, 1521: "I burn in the great fires of my untamed flesh. . . . For a week I have neither written, nor prayed, nor studied, partly because of the torment of carnal temptations, partly because of nervous strain. Pray for me, for I am buried in this solitude and drowned in sins."[12] It was in this solitude drowned in sins that he penned his tremendous libel on "Religious Vows," which brought ruin through desertion and scandal by monks and nuns to the monasteries of Germany.

He appreciated the force of the terrible argument his adver-

---

[9]Leturia, (II), pp. 47 ff. Based on a work written in 1921.
[10]Leturia, (II), p. 57.
[11]Grisar, I, p. 393.
[12]Grisar, I, p. 396.

saries brought to bear against him. He turns on them with rending and sharp sarcasm: "See how they open their jaws and say: 'Look how heavy this monk's habit hangs on him! How gladly he would take a wife!' Well, let them bite, the immaculate ones, the saints, those who think they are made of iron and stone. You, meantime, do not deny you are a man, a man of flesh and blood, and let God judge between the robust angelical heroes and the despised sinners. Then those who vaunt their great purity will stand revealed, and it will be found that their boasted chastity is not worth treading beneath a harlot's heel!"[13]

If Iñigo had heard him say this, his fiery Toledan blade would have leapt from its sheath, that blade so ready to dye itself in the blood of the Moorish blasphemer of the Virgin. The Moor had tarnished the honor of the Mother who was immaculate. Luther however, besmirched the honor of her children who were not so stainless. Ignatius had not been immaculate, nor did he trust in his own strength to fulfill his vow of chasitity which he conceived at Loyola and pronounced so sincerely at Aranzazu. His sorrow, his tears, his resolves and his vigil at Montserrat acquire new vigor and fresh splendor against this wider background of the providential history of the Church.

Papini has recently written: "Luther, too, immured himself in a castle, that of Wartburg, during these months, though unwounded in body . . . in order the better to strike at Rome. . . . This may seem a mere external coincidence, but chronology contains more mysteries than the confectioners of synopses and formulae can ever suspect. These two tormented spirits, (Ignatius at Loyola, and Luther at Wartburg) are the real antagonists of the first part of that century. In comparison, Charles V and Francis I seem but children quarreling over a broken toy. This is proved by reasons which are more profound than dates. This is true, not only because the Society of Jesus, founded by Ignatius erected a dike, strong even today, against the Lutheran flood from the north; but because of the absolute contrast presented by the spirits of the apostate friar and the transfigured Knight."[14]

3. Even this contrast does not exhaust the perspectives opened up by comparative chronology.

---

[13]Grisar, I, p. 400.
[14]Papini, pp. 124-125.

Luther, the self-styled renovator of the Gospel, formally held
that the Church had no vocation for the missions, but rather
they were the concern of the prince who conquered pagan lands.[15]
He adds in his own peculiar style, that as far as Jerusalem and
the Holy Sepulcher are concerned, God is just as interested in the
one and the other as He is in a Swiss cow. . . .[16]

Iñigo's ideal of Jerusalem assumes historical importance compared to such a concept. Though it is true that Iñigo, neither at
the Castle, nor during the vigil, was inspired by apostolic zeal,
none the less, the crusade of abnegation and penance, of which
the Pilgrim dreamed as he descended the slopes of Montserrat,
became a few months later at Manresa, another kind of crusade,
an apostolic crusade in which, following the footsteps of Christ
His King, he yearns "to conquer the entire infidel world . . . the
whole world and all His enemies."[17]

In this, too, Ignatius was a man of his country and of his
century. It was during these years, 1521 to 1522, that the conquest of Mexico by Cortes produced a wave of apostolic zeal
among the religious Orders of the Peninsula. Their pleas, particularly those of the Reformed Franciscans, had induced the
Emperor to request of the new Pope a solemn Bull which would
consecrate and regulate that generous missionary endeavor.

The Holy Father acceded in the following words: "You have
declared to Us your fervent desire to advance Religion and convert the infidels, chiefly those who through divine grace are subject to your jurisdiction and Empire in the regions of the Indies.
Hence you have insistently petitioned Us for the conversion and
right governance of souls whom Our Lord redeemed with His
precious Blood, and that We send to the said regions of the
Indies, Religious of the Mendicant Orders, and in particular, of
the Friars Minor of Regular Observance."[18]

The Pontiff's response to these pleas, known as *"Exponi Nobis"*
or *"Omnimoda,"* constituted for three centuries the charter of
missionary organization in Spanish America and in the Philip-
pines. The fact that the Bull was signed near Manresa a month
and a half after Iñigo's vigil of arms has escaped Saint Ignatius'

[15]Grisar, III, pp. 1022-1024.
[16]Grisar, II, p. 170.
[17]*Ejercicios,* pp. 93, 95; Leturia, (II), pp. 64-66.
[18]Hernaez, I, p. 384.

biographers. It was the most solemn and enduring of his acts and was granted when he was receiving the homage of the Church, the nobility, and people of Spain.[19]

The Mercedarians, Franciscans, Dominicans, and Augustinians set our for New Spain, New Granada and New Castile "to carry out the said undertaking, being certain that in as much as they imitate the disciples of Christ Our Redeemer in the task, they will share with them in the reward."[20] At that very time Loyola's new crusade gradually began to develop into a universal mission which, under the command of the Roman Pontiffs, was to give to the Orient a Francis Xavier, and to the West an Ignatius de Azevedo, a Roque Gonzalez and a Peter Claver. (Appendix I)

---

[19]Hernaez, I, p. 385; Torres, *Missionalia Hispanica*, 3 (1946), 7-52; "Given at Saragossa, under the Fisherman's seal, May 9, 1522."

[20]Hernaez, I, p. 385. "And that so holy a work be not lacking in the merit of obedience we order that all chosen or freely offering themselves, following the example of the disciples of Christ Our Redeemer, undertake the said work and carry out the directive, being certain that they, by imitating them in their work, will share with them in the reward."

APPENDIX I.

1. Stanzas to Our Lady from the *"Cancionero"* of Fray Ambrosio. Montesino.[1]

Aquella estrella del norte|tan sobida esperanza es y conforte|de mi vida.||Esta sola fué la estrella|tan bastante|que se hizo Dios por ella|pobre infante;||y del cielo triunfante|es servida,|la esperanza y el conforte de mi vida.||En tanto que, Reina noble,|no te veo,|es martirio y pena doble|mi deseo,||y tú eres la que creo|ser parida|del esfuerzo y de conforte|de mi vida.||Dios y tú solo mandáis|este siglo,|la vida dais y quitáis|de periglo;||y si yo, Reina, me libro|de caída,|es por tú ser el conforte de mi vida.

(That northern star so sublime is the hope and comfort of my life.|This star alone was so sufficing that God through it a poor Infant became and from Heaven triumphant deigns to be the hope and comfort of my life.|While I behold Thee not, noble Queen, martyrdom and double pain is my yearning,|and Thou art the One born to be the strength and comfort of my life.|God and Thou alone rule this world, give life and remove from peril;|and if I, Queen, am safe from fall, it is that Thou are the comfort of my life.)

2. Ballads in honor of Saint Francis by the same.[2]

Este perfecto caudillo|de póstolicos varones|guerra dió con homecillo|como roquero castillo|a tres bravas guarniciones.|| Al mundo, carne, Satán|quitó sus fuerzas e usos:|Oh bendito el capitán|por quien estos tres están|tan confusos.

(This perfect leader of apostolic men warred against hatred as a castle founded on rock triply garrisoned by the brave.|From the world, the flesh, and Satan he took away their force and power: Oh blessed the captain by whom these three are so confounded.)

La lanzada que ya muerto|no sintió crucificado,|tú, su alférez, la sentiste|de su mano traspasado;|deste misterio que-

---

[1]Ed. Sancha, pp. 461 ff.
[2]Ed. Sancha, pp. 420, 431-432.

daste|sucesor deificado|de su vida, y de su muerte|sobre
cuantos ha creado.||¿Quién dirá la fermosura|que ha tu
alma cobrado|si tu cuerpo, que es envés,|de tal gloria fué
dotado?

(The lance-thrust which already dead the Crucified did not
feel, you, His Captain, felt as His Hand pierced your side
and by this mystery you remained divinized successor of His
life and death above all He had created.|Who will tell the
beauty which your soul has gained if your body being less
with such glory was endowed?)

3. Ballad on the Way of the Cross by Montesino.[3]

    Pues, oh reina universal,|en quien Dios mejor se alberga,|
    paraíso oriental,|ante cuya faz real|los cielos parecen
    jerga.||Dulce mar de devoción,|muerte de todo letijo,|danos,
    danos relación|de las pensas y pasión, de tu Hijo. . . .||
    Nunca le vistes las manos|lindicas al lindo Infante,|ni los
    piececitos sanos|sin dolores inhumanos|pensando en lo de
    adelante. . . .|| Pues yo mísero mortal,|por estas llagas com-
    prado,|te pido, oh reina sin par,|que tu claro original|res-
    plandezca en mi traslado.

    (Then, oh Queen of the universe, in Whom God finds better
    shelter, oriental paradise before Whose queenly countenance
    the heavens seem gross.|Sweet ocean of devotion, death to
    all conflict, grant us, grant us the story of the Passion and
    Death of Thy Son. . . .|Never didst Thou clothe the pretty
    little hands of the pretty Babe, or cover the sturdy little feet
    without cruel sorrow thinking of the morrow. . . .|So I,
    wretched mortal, by these wounds purchased, beg of Thee,
    oh peerless Queen, that Thy original purity shine in me
    reflected.)

4. Stanzas addressed to Saints Peter and Paul from the *"Doce
    triunfos"* by Juan de Padilla.[4]

    Era muy rica la su vestidura|según requería su pontifical:|la
    broncha tenía de claro cristal|de perlas sembrada por la
    bordadura.||Dentro tenía sotil escritura|con cinco letricas en

---

[3]Ed. Sancha, p. 425.
[4]Ed. Sancha, p. 425.

forma de cruz,|la I con la E y la S con US:|y más que salía
de aquesta pintura,|por claro matiz, una cándida luz. . . .||Dos
llaves iguales y maravillosas|tenía por rica divisa poten-
te:|era la una del cielo fulgente,|otra de nuestras miserias
penosas|cuando nos cierra la puerta patente. . . .

(His garment was very rich as his pontifical dignity demanded: he held a sword of clear crystal, studded along its
length with pearls.|Behind him an ingenious I and E and S
with US, and further, from that picture there shone in clear
splendor a brilliant light. . . .|Two like and marvellous keys
he held as a rich and mighty device: one was of fulgent
heaven, the other penalty for our wretchedness when he
closes to us the open gate.)

Saint Paul then explains the vision to the poet[5]: Y ¿cómo
no gustas que vas navegando|en la gran nave de aqueste
varón? Conosce, conosce tan digno patrón|pues que su
barca te lleva remando.||Va con anzuelo de Cristo pes-
cando|los peces humanos, según te pescó;|éste la piedra pri-
mera fundó|del edificio, que va militando|con la bandera que
siempre venció.

(And why do you not want to go in the great boat of that
man? Know, know so worthy a patron for he bears you
rowing in his boat.|He fishes with the hook of Christ the
human fishes as he fished you. He it is who laid the first
stone of the building which is embattled under the standard
that ever triumphed.)

5. Ballad on Corruption at Court by Montesino.[6]

Este palacio que vedes|damas y prosperidades|sabed que es
lago de redes|que consume las mercedes|y se sorbe las
edades.||Pues dejad sus adherencias|envueltas en torpe
roña,|porque sus feas pendencias|mejor matan las con-
ciencias|que ponzoña. . . .||No llevéis como alquilados|la cruz
por solo interese,|en la ropa señalados|y en la renta sublima-
dos,|y vuestra alma que se mese!||Que al infierno va derecho|

5Ed Sancha, p. 330.
6Ed. Sancha, pp. 427-428.

el que se cruza de fuera,|si ojo tiene al provecho|y no, al
juicio estrecho|que se espera.||Y las damas cortesanas|en
peligros bien despiertas,|que con esperanzas vanas|no tienen
las honras sanas|y tienen las almas muertas.||Si mirasen bien
los fines|de las fiestas y galanes,|bien sé yo que sus chapines|
corrieran como (en) jardines|a la Cruz y a tus afanes. . . .||
Mas ¡ay! que nunca la hez|dejáis del mundo culpado,|hasta
dar en la vejez|en el desastre de preñez: ¡ mal pecado!

(This palace you see, ladies and men of wealth, know it is a
lair of snares that overcomes virtue and exhausts all ages.|So
leave its precincts scaly with sluggish rust, for its ugly en-
virons more surely kill consciences than does poison.|Do
not bear as hirelings the cross only out of interest, distin-
guished in garb, rich in income, and your soul in rags!|He
goes straight to Hell who crosses himself externally if he
looks to gain and not to the strait judgment that awaits.|And
the ladies of the court in perils skilled, who through vain
hopes have not their honor whole and have dead souls.|If
they would consider well the purpose of the banquets and
gallants, I know well that their feet would run as they do
in festive gardens to the Cross and to Your concerns. . . .|But
alas!, for never the dregs of the sinful world do you leave
until old age or in danger of pregnancy: deadly sin!.)

6. The *"Flos Sanctorum"*, Fray Gauberto M. Vagad's translation or revision of the *"Legenda aurea"* by the Dominican,
   Jacopo da Varazze.

At least seventy-four Latin editions, printed before 1500,
are known, and Potthast cites up to that date thirteen translations into Italian, eight into English, six into French, three
into Dutch, two into Bohemian, and one in German. His
failure to mention the Castilian versions shows his enumeration is incomplete. There were at least two up to 1500, five
up to 1525.

Before 1500 we find the edition by Meyer which was printed
at Toulouse around 1480, and another at Burgos around 1500.
This latter is the edition with prologue by Fray Gauberto
Maria Vagad, the exact date of which is undetermined.

There is the edition of Toledo in 1511, which is complete with prologue. A copy of this is in the archives at Loyola.

Finally there is the resumé of the "Life of Christ and of the Saints" in a single volume by Fray Pedro de la Vega, printed at Saragossa September 1521. The text of these translations of the "Lives of the Saints" is probably from the one made by the Jeronimin Friar, Gonzalo de Ocaña, Prior of the monastery of Santa Maria de Sisla in Toledo, who wrote around 1460. The difference in the various editions consists in additions and prologues.

We have already shown elsewhere that the edition used by Saint Ignatius was probably that of Vagad or a reprint of the Toledo version of 1511.[7]

The prologuist of the work, Fray Gauberto, of the Cistercian Order, was a well-known figure at Ferdinand's Court. He was born in Saragossa during the first quarter of the fifteenth century. He served in his youth as lieutenant to the brother of the King of Aragon, the Archbishop of that city, and Prince Juan (1458-1478). Disillusioned with the world, he professed at the monastery of Bernardos de Santa Fe in Saragossa, and devoted himself to works of piety and to literature. In his poem, *"El Razonamiento del monge con el caballero sobre la vida venidera"*, he contrasts his new life with his former vanities.

He detested some tendencies of the Italian Renaissance, and it is in this sense that his bitter criticism of Antonio Galateo must be understood, for he loved learning and the Renaissance itself. Of his works two of the lesser poems have come down to us: his satire, *"Contra los ginetes"*, notable for its rich vocabulary and mordant popular humor, and his famous *"Razonamiento"*, in which the ideal of holy knighthood serving an eternal King is developed.

The esteem which Fray Gauberto enjoyed at Ferdinand's Court was such that he was commissioned to write the "annals of the Kingdom of Aragon. After he had consulted the

---

[7]AHSI, V, (1936), pp. 10-11.

archives at San Juan de la Peña, Poblet, Montearagon, and
Barcelona, he published his "General Chronicle of Aragon"
in 1499, "to the honor and glory of God, Our Lord, and for
the exaltation of the Faith, and for the greater edification
and instruction of future Princes." This work, despite its
verbosity, its historical inaccuracies and omissions, would
have been better known in historiography, had it not been
displaced by the immortal "Annals" of Zurita.
In the *"Razonamiento"*[8] he contrasts the worldly knight with
the knight of God:

Tengo el sacro sacerdocio|la santa caballería|común
bien;|Vos el tiempo dado al ocio|la costumbre a tiranía|y a
desdén. . . .|Yo estoy a mesa de Rey|a manjares e convites|ce-
lestiales;|Vos en prado como buey, todo puesto en apetites
|de animales.| (I regard the sacred priesthood|holy knight-
hood|a common good;| But you spend your time in idle-
ness|given over to tyranny and disdain. . . . |While I at the
King's table|sit down to a banquet of|celestial food;:you
graze in the meadow as an ox,|immersed in|animal appetite.|)
He then describes the reward the knight awaits from his
King, though he is attracted rather by the goodness of the
King Himself:

¿E si los reyes mortales|e por mortales servicios|vemos
dar|mercedes tan inmortales,|tan crecidos beneficios,|tan sin
par,|que de viles facen nobles,|de aldeanos caballeros|pode-
rosos;| de sencillos facen dobles,|de mendigos herederos|cau-
dalosos;| Qué fará el que da el poder|de poder facer may-
ores|descendencias,|por le amar e obedecer,|por servicios e
loores,|abstenencias?|Ved que Dios para olvidalle,|para poder
defenderme|de seguille:|que amando, tan sin amalle,|me paga,
tan sin deberme,|su servile. . . .|

(And if mortal kings|and for mortal services|we see be-
stow|favors so immortal,|benefits so great,|so unequalled,|that
out of serfs they make nobles,|out of villagers|powerful
knights;|out of simple men men of doubled worth,|out of
beggars wealthy heirs;|What will He who gives power|to be

---

[8]Foulche-Delbose, II, pp. 705-709.

able to grant greater condescensions,|grant in return for
service and praise and mortification?|See what a God that I
should forget Him,|that I should fail|to follow Him;|who
loving without love in return,|rewards me, so undeserving,
his servant. . . .)

7. *The Life of Saint Onuphrius.*[9]

The Saint is described as he appeared when Paphnutius
encountered him in the desert. "A startling figure . . . for
his hair had grown so long that it covered his entire body,
and he wore ivy leaves girded about his loins." Yet, though
his appearance was frightening his speech was gentle. He
kindly called Paphnutius and told him the origin and conditions of "his penitence." He told him: "I am Onuphrius and
have been living in this desert some seventy years. . . .; instead of bread I have eaten herbs and have hidden my
miserable body in mountains, caves and valleys. And in so
many years you are the only man I have seen, and no one
ever gave me anything to eat."

A eulogy of the solitary life which he heard addressed to the
monks in the monastery of Hermopolis where he was reared
had led him to dwell in such extreme seclusion and rigor.
One of the hundred monks of the monastery had said:
"(Anchorets) live without human assistance while we
(monks) care for one another and recite the Office in common. Should one of us fall ill or suffer some other bodily
ailment then the religious must take care of us and help us.
We dwell in fine houses where we are sheltered from the heat
of the sun and from the rain and from the blasts of the
wind. But the monks of the desert receive no other consolation save that from God. Should they at times be troubled
or burdened or struggle with the devil, *the enemy of human
nature,* who will aid them? Certain it is that they who have
no human consolation will receive it from God."

Saint Onuphrius describes the effect this eulogy made upon
him in the following moving terms: "I thought within myself how wondrous a happiness they enjoyed in Heaven who
for love of God suffered on earth, and my heart was inflamed

and my thoughts seethed with the yearning and the resolve to leave wholly the pleasures of the world and unite myself with all my strength to God, as the Psalmist teaches us saying: 'It is fitting for me to draw near to God and place in Him all my hope.' "

So he left his monastery "secretly" by night, taking with him "a bit of bread and some vegetables which hardly lasted four days." An angel came to his assistance in the desert and an ancient hermit instructed him for *thirty days* in God's Commandments, this serving him as an introduction to his new life in which he dwelt alone *in another cave.*"

8. Montserrat.

The famous shine was well-known among the Guipuzcoans of the period. Gorosabel tells us that alms had been collected for Montserrat, and pilgrimages made to its sanctuary from time immemorial. The General Council of the Province had to intervene because of its increasing popularity. The representatives of the abbey were allowed to take up collections, but only on conditions that there be established at the shrine "two special choir seats in order that pilgrims from that province (of Guipúzcoa) might have fellow-countrymen to whom they could lay open their consciences in their own tongue." In the Synod of Pamplona in 1499, the decisions of which were published in 1501, appear the rights of the bishop over the churches to which he gives license to collect alms in the diocese: in the first place stands Montserrat and el Pilar with 14 pounds each.[10]

If we may judge from a declaration by the monks to the Councils of Guipuzcoa in 1688 the agreement mentioned above was made toward the end of the fourteenth century, and remained in effect throughout the fifteenth and sixteenth centuries.

This is confirmed in Guipuzcoa itself. We know, for instance, of the vow to make a pilgrimage to Montserrat taken by the lord of Arriaran. At Oñate, during the High Mass

---

[10]Data from Zunzunegui.

in the parish church the Montserrat basket was passed around
with that of the nearby Virgin of Aranzazu, and those of the
town confraternities.[11] Shortly after Ignatius' departure, we
find legacies left to Montserrat in wills made in Azpeitia. For
instance, Pedro Ibañez de Olaberria on March 6, 1524, willed
one Castilian real, and Maria Lopez de Eizaguirre another
of silver on August fifteenth, 1534.[12] There even exists on
the confines of the Province outside Fuenterrabia "near the
road and on the sierra of Aizquibel", a shrine to Our Lady
of Montserrat, which only later on changed its title to Our
Lady of Guadalupe.[13]

The Duke of Najera's family was devoted to Montserrat.
Iñigo must have noticed this during his service at Navarrete. The Duke's wife, Juana de Cardona, inherited this
devotion from his father, Juan, (+1513) a magnate of the
first Catalan nobility. He had been reared at the monastery
school, and was wont to invoke Our Lady throughout his
stormy career, as may be seen in his letters to Abbot Pedro
de Burgos.[14] The Duke's sister, Ana Manrique, figures also
in the annals of Montserrat because of the miracle the Virgin
worked in her behalf in 1535.[15] "The History and Miracles of
Our Lady of Montserrat" by Abbot Pedro de Burgos, printed
in 1514 at the abbey, and widely circulated throughout Spain
and Germany must surely have been seen in the Duke's palace by Iñigo.[16]

Their Catholic Majesties were especially devoted to the
shrine of Our Lady of Montserrat. . . . It is a place of great
devotion and pilgrimage, visited from all parts of the
world."[17] Queen Germaine, too, was devoted to the shrine
and we know that in 1508 she donated to the Virgin two
silver candle-sticks which held relics, and a lamp which
weighed six pounds.

---

[11]Data from Lizarralde.
[12]Arch. de Azpeitia, Protocols by Pedro Ibañez de Idarraga, 1521-1541 for respective dates.
[13]*Arch. Prov. de Guipuzcoa*: Mss History of "the town of Fuenterrabia", 1625.
[14]Albareda, p. 36; Creixell, I, pp. 22-24.
[15]Albareda, p. 36.
[16]*Span. Forschungen der Görresgesellschaft,* VIII (1838), p. 272 ff.
[17]Azpeitia, *Arch. de la Casa Emparan.*

9. Aranzazu.

The devotion of the Azpeitians toward the Virgin of Aranzazu is shown in documents which are contemporaneous with
Iñigo's conversion and departure from Loyola. Pero Martinez of Emparan wrote in his will of February fifteenth,
1518: "My said wife has promised to watch one night at
the monastery of Our Lady, Holy Mary of Aranzazu. . . .
I charge that some good person be sent to fulfill said promise."[17] While Iñigo was still at the Castle, Maria Echañiz,
the wife of Pedro de Castañalde, wrote on September twenty-seventh, 1521: "Inasmuch as I have promised to go on
pilgrimage to Holy Mary of Aranzazu, I donate three *"tar-
jas"*, (ancient Spanish coin worth about one quarter of a
real, as alms). I charge that, if I am unable to go in person,
two Castilian reales be sent to the said Monastery."[18] Other
documents specify that the pilgrimage is to be made carrying
two pounds of wax. (Teresa Ugarte, September twenty-seventh, 1525), or that an alms of "two reales of silver", be
set aside "for Masses to be offered by the friars of the said
monastery of Aranzazu." (Maria Martinez de Egurza, March
twenty-seventh, 1525.)

10. "The great Prince of Fez" by Calderon de la Barca.[19]
Jornada II, escena 16: . . . No hace, si miras|que el rayo
del sol penetra|la vidriera cristalina|y que, pasando sus
rayos,|luce, resplandesce y brilla,|quedándose la vidriera|
clara, pura, intacta, y limpia. . . . |Que si ese sol ilumina|por
un vidrio, sin que el vidrio|se empañe, turbe e resista,|¿por
qué no iluminará|Cristo, que es sol de justicia,|las entrañas
de una madre|sin daño e lesión, el día|que el Hijo de Dios,
de su seño|desciende a que la divina|naturaleza, la hu-
mana|en sí la abrace y admita?

(Tis not so, if you consider|how the sun beam passes
through|the pane of glass|and in passing its rays|lights, re-
flects and illumines|the glass remaining|clear, pure, whole
and clean.|So if that sun shines through a glass, without the
glass|being dimmed, obscured or resistant|why will not Christ

¹⁸Arch. de Azp., Protocols of the notary Pedro Ibañez de Idarraga, 1521-1541.
¹⁹Calderón, *Jornada* II, *Esc.* 16.

illumine|Christ, who is the sun of justice,|the womb of a
mother|without damage or injury, the day|that the Son of
God, from His bosom|descends in order that the divine|na-
ture|embrace and take unto itself the human?)

(Calderon then interprets the struggle that went on in Iñigo's
mind as to whether he should avenge Our Lady's honor by
slaying the Moor.)

Y pues tanto,|Ignacio, tu compañiá|ejercitándose maestra|de
la cristiana doctrina,|en no sé que oculto lejos|me asombra
y me atemoriza,|huiré de tí.|

(For so much|Ignatius, your company|exercising mastery of
Christian doctrine|in some far off future|afrights me and
terrifies me|that I shall flee from thee.|(Note the ingenious
play on the words: "compañiá" and "ejercitándose", la Compañia de Jesús and los Ejercicios espirituales.

(After the Moor flees, Iñigo cries):
Oye! ¡aguarda!|que no es bien de mí se diga|que oí de
María baldones|y no los vengue!

(Listen, wait,|for it is not well that it be said of me|that I
heard insults to Mary|and did not avenge them|)   Then
Calderon interprets the inner struggle as Iñigo ponders his
course of action.

Que siga|sus pasos, y a puñaladas|le mate, será accion dig-
na|Pero dónde voy? que ya|no es tiempo de bizarrias,|y la
milicia de Dios no es la pasada milicia.|El volverá por su
honra|sin que sea yo homicida,|haciendo que de su secta|
Reyes crean algún día que aquel común tributo,|María y
su Hijo se libran:|su Hijo por naturaleza,|y por la gracia
María.

To follow|after him, and with dagger thrusts|slay him, will
be a worthy deed.|But where am I going? For no longer|is
the time for adventures|nor is God's Knight the soldier of
the past? He will defend His honor|without my being a
murderer,|He will bring it to pass that|kings of his sect|will
one day believe|that from that common tribute (original
sin) Mary and Her Son are free:|Her Son by nature,|Mary
by grace.)

11. "La vela de armas" by Lope de Vega.[20]

The setting, action and the hero are depicted in a few strokes:

En aquel monte serrado|donde gusta de vivir|aquella serrana hermosa|más bella que Abigail,|a cuyo Niño le ponen|una sierra, por decir,|que instrumentos de Josef|no los aparta de sí;|un soldado viscaíno|y cansado de servir|guerras del mundo, en Navarra|contra las flores de lis)|la espada al altar ofrece,|porque se quiere ceñir|armas que conquistan almas:| que Dios se lo manda así.

(On that craggy mountain|whereon likes to dwell|that beauteous maid,|more beautiful than Abigail,|to whose Son they give|a saw, that is to say,|that Joseph's tools|He does not despise;| a Biscayan soldier| (and one wearied of serving in worldly warfare, in Navarre|against the Fleur de Lis)|offers his sword at the altar|because he wishes to gird on|weapons that conquer souls:|for so God wills.)

In the next verses attention is drawn not to Ignatius, or to the Virgin, but to the Child whose Name the Society will bear, and whose loveable infancy inspires the poetic imagination to play inoffensively on the concept of the cross of the sword and the wooden cross of the pilgrim staff.

Mirándole está Jesús,|y la boca de rubí|bañó de risa y de gloria|sobre su blanco marfil.|Porque ver que un viscaíno|la dorada trueque allí|por una cruz de madera,|los niños hará reír.|Mas dicen que fué alegriá|de ver que quiere esculpir|su santo nombre en los pechos|del más bárbaro gentil;|porque ha de hacer Compañiá|que por él vaya a morir, desde la dichosa España| hasta las islas de Ofir;|que adonde el fiero Luzbel|sembrada torpe maíz,|han de sembrar pan de cielo|con ricas aguas de abril.

(Looking at him is Jesus,|and His ruby mouth|bathed with laughter and glory|over the white ivory of his teeth. For to see that a Biscayan|trades a cross of gold|for one of wood, will make children laugh.|But tis said that it was for joy|on seeing that he wished to engrave|His Holy Name on

---

[20]Ed. Sancha, p. 124.

the breasts|of the most savage folk;| because he is to form a
Company|that for Him shall go to die,|far from blessed
Spain|even to the isles of Ophir;|that there where fierce
Lucifer sowed tares|they are to sow the Bread of Heaven|
watered by the fertile rains of April.)

Then the poet comments on Ignatius' lameness, as after the
vigil, he goes off to battle.

Mucho le pesa al soldado|de verse, cojo, al salir|a guerra tan
peligrosa,|que se han vuelto más de mil.|Pero díjole una
voz:|"Ignacio fuerte, partid,|que no ha menester los
pies,|quien ha de ser querubín.|Cubrid con alas la Iglesia,|que
el Jacob a quien servís,|de todas las Religiones|os quiere
hacer Benjamin."

(Much it pains the soldier|to see himself lame, on
leaving|for a war so perilous|that more than a thousand have
turned back.|But a voice said to him:|"Brave Ignatius, go
forth,|for there is no need of feet|for him who is to be a
Cherubim|Cover with your wings the Church,|for the Jacob
whom you serve|of all the Orders|wills you to be the Ben-
jamin."

Finally the poet addresses winged symbolic verses to Spain:

No se ha de preciar España|de Pelayo ni del Cid,|sino de
Loyola solo|porque a ser su sol venís.

(Spain has no need to boast|of Pelayo or of the Cid|
but only of Loyola|for to be her sun you come.)

APPENDIX II

BIBLIOGRAPHICAL INDEX

I. UNPUBLISHED SOURCES

Anonymous, *"Vita Patris nostri Ignatii"*, in Arch. Rom. Soc. Jesu, codex *"Memorie varie circa S. Ignazio"*, fol. 2-9. (Probably anterior to the first *"Vita"* by Ribadeneira, and in many details reveals Father Nadal's influence. Our opinion is that the author did not know of Saint Ignatius' "Autobiography".

Fondo Cros sobre San Ignacio, in the Archives of the Province of the Soc. of Jesus of Toulouse. (Comprises three main sections: first, four series of Opuscula on the life of the Saint; secondly, register of the researches made by the author from 1883 in the Archives at Loyola, Tolosa, Madrid, Alcala, etc.; thirdly, copies and photographs of some documents. We have made use of the second section in particular, on retouching our manuscript of 1936.)

Nat. Apol. Ad Doct. Paris, *"Apologia contra censuram quamdam editam . . . a Facultate Theologiae Parisiensi in Societatem Jesu."*. It is in the Arch. Rom. Soc. Jesu, codex *"Polanc. Hist. I, quad. 5."* (It is by Father Nadal and of 1557. Cf. Leturia (I), pp. 21-22.

Nat. Dial., *"Dialogi P. Ieronimi Natalis, S.I."* In Arch. Rom. Soc. Jesu in the codex" *Natalis Medit. et Dialogi de Instituto"*, fol 245-420. (They are of 1562-1565. Cf Leturia (I), pp. 27-28).

Nat. Exhortationes, *"Exhorationes quas habuit P. Natalis in Hispania anno 1554, excepit vero P. Emmanuel Sa ejus Socius . . . Del Principio de la Compañia."* In Arch. Rom. S.I., codex "Inst. 98," fol. 103-107.

Repartimientos, Original book of *Repartimientos*, 1516-1538, of the Council of Azpeitia, fol. 10-378. Found in the "Municipal Archives of Azpeitia".

Ribadeneira, *Historia de la Compañia de Jesus de las Provincias de España* . . . by Pedro de Ribadeneira, S.I. Mss in MHSI.

II. PUBLISHED SOURCES AND TREATISES.

Acta, "*Acta P. Ignatii, ut primum scripsit P. Ludovicus Gonzales excipiens ex ore ipsius Patris*". In MHSI "*Monumenta ignatiana*", Series IV, I, pp. 31-98. Madrid, 1904. At present a better edited work in *Fontes narrativi*, (Cf infra) pp. 355-507).

AHSI, "*Archivum historicum Societatis Jesu*". Rome 1932 ff.

Albareda (I) *Sant Ignasi a Montserrat*", by Dom Anselm Albareda, O.S.B., Montserrat, 1935.

Albareda (II) "*La imprenta de Montserrat*" (*segles xv-xvi*)", by Dom Anselm Albareda in "*Analecta Montserratensia*", 2 (1918), 11-166.

Aleson, "*Anales de Navarra*", by Father Moret, continued by Father Aleson, S.J. Volume 5°, Pamplona, 1776.

Amadis, cf. Gayangos.

Antonio (Nicolas), "*Bibliotheca hispana vetus*", by Nicolas Antonio. Madrid, 1788, 2 vol.

Ascunce, "*Iñigo de Loyola, capitan español*", by Father E. Ascunce, S.J. Pamplona (1940).

Astrain, "*Historia de la Compañia de Jesus*" *en la Asistencia de España*", by Father Antonio Astrain, S.J. Madrid, 1912.

BAE, "*Biblioteca de autores españoles de Ribadeneira.*" Madrid, 1870 ff.

BAH, "*Boletin de la Academia de la Historia.*" Madrid, 1880 ff.

Ballesteros, "*Historia de España*". . . . Barcelona, 1918 ff.

Barbieri, "*Cancionero musical de los siglos xv y xvi,*" transcribed and comments by Francisco Asenjo Narbieri. Madrid, 1890.

Bataillon, Prologue by Marcel Bataillon to '*Enquiridion o Manual del Caballero Cristiano*", by Erasmus, edition by Damaso Alonso, Madrid, 1932.

Beguierztain, "*Los origines de los Ejercicios de San Ignacio*", by Justo Beguiriztain, S.J. Buenos Aires, 1927.

Böhmer (I), "*Studien zur Geschichte der Gesellschaft Jesu. I. Loyola*". By Heinrich Böhmer. . . . Bonn, 1914.

Böhmer (II), "*Loyola und die deutsche Mystik*", by Heinrich Böhmer. Leipzig, 1921.

Boissonade, "*Histoire de la Reunion de la Navarre a la Castile*", by Father Boissonade, Paris, 1892.

Bonilla, *"Luis Vives y la Filosofia del Renacimiento"*, by Adolfo Bonilla y San Martin, Madrid, 1929, 3 tomes.

Bordenave, *"Histoire de Bearn et Navarre"*, by Nicolas de Bordenave. . . . Paris, 1873.

Calderon, *"Comedias de D. Pedro Calderon de la Barca"*. Ed. Hartzenbusch. Madrid, 1934. In BAE, vol. 9. Madrid, 1934.

Campion (I), *"Navarra en su vida historica"*. Second edition by Arturo Campion, Pamplona, 1925.

Campion (II), *"Gacetilla de la Historia de Navarra."* (Historical mosaic, by Arturo Campion in *"Euskariana"* (7th Serie). Pamplona, s.a.

Cartujano, *"Vita Christi Cartujano"*, translated into Romance by Fray Ambrosio (Montesino), O.F.M. Alcala, 1502 ff. 4 vol. in folio.

Casanovas, *"San Ignasi de Loyola"*, by Father Ignasi Casanovas, S.J. Barcelona, 1930.

Cedillo, *"El Cardenal Cisneros gobernador del Reino"*. . . . by His Excellency Count of Cedillo. Madrid 1921, 3 vol.

Cejador, *"Historia de la lengua y literatura castellana (desde los origenes hasta Carlos V)*. Tome 1°, 2 parte, by D. Julio Cejador y Fauca. Madrid, 1927.

Cisneros, Cf. *"Ejercitatorio"*.

Codina, *"Los origines de los Ejercicios de San Ignacio de Loyola"*. Historical study by Father Arturo Codina, S.J. Barcelona, 1926.

Constant, *"Saint Ignace de Loyola et les Dominicains"*, by Father M. D. Constant, O.P. Extract from *"Revue des Etudes Historiques"*, July-Sept., 1931.

Constitutiones, *Sancti Ignatii de Loyola Constitutiones Societatis Jesu.. Tomus primus. Monumenta Constitutionum praevia.* In MHSI, *"Monumenta ignatiana"*, Series III, Rome, 1934. Vol. I.

Coster, *"Juan de Anchieta et la famille de Loyola"*, by Adolphe Coster. Paris, 1930.

Creixell, *"San Ignacio de Loyola"*. . . . by Father Juan Creixell, S.J. Barcelona, 1922, 2 vol.

Cros, *"Saint François de Xavier. Sa vie et ces lettres"*, by Father J. M. Cros, S.J. 2 tomes. Toulouse, 1900.

Chron., *"Vita Ignatii Loiolae et Rerum Societatis Jesu"*. *Historia,* *auctore Joanne A. de Polanco, S.J.* In MHSI. Chronicon, I. Madrid, 1894.

Danvila, *"Historia critica y documentada de las Comunidades de Castilla"*, by Manuel Danvila, Madrid, 1897-1899, 6 vol. They are tomes 35-40 of the *"Memorial historico español"*.

Dudon, *"Saint Ignace de Loyola"*, by Father Paul Dudon, S.J. Paris, 1934.

Echegaray (I), *"Las Provincias vascongadas a fines de la Edad Media"*. Historical essay, by Don Carmelo de Echegaray. San Sebastian, 1895.

Echegaray (II), *"Provincia de Vizcaya"*, by Carmelo de Echegaray. In *"Geografia General del Pais Vasco-Navarro"*, directed by Francisco Carreras Candi. Barcelona (s.a.)

Echegaray (III), *"Monumentos civiles de Guipuzcoa"* . . . with prologue by Don Carmelo de Echegaray. Barcelona, 1921.

Eijan (I), *"Relaciones mutuas de España y Tierra Santa atraves de los siglos"*, by Fray Samuel Eijan, O.F.M. Santiago, 1912.

Eijan (II), *"España y el Santuario del Cenaculo"*, by Fray Samuel Eijan, OFM, in *"Archivo Ibero-Americano"*, 2 (1914) 5 ff.

Ejercitatorio, *"Ejercitatorio de la Vida espiritual"*, composed by V. P. Garcia de Cisneros, O.S.B. Edition Curiel. Barcelona, 1912.

Engelgrave, *"Coeleste Pantheon"* . . ., *auctore Henrico Engelgrave,* S.J. Coloniae, 1657.

Ep. et Instruct., *"San Ignatii de Loyola . . . Epistolae et Instructiones"*. In MHSI, *"Mon. Ignatiana"* Ser. I, vol. 12. Madrid, 1903 ff.

Ep. Mixt., *"Epistolae Mixtae ex variis Europae locis ab anno 1537 ad 1556 scriptae . . ."* In MHSI. Matriti, 1898 ff. 5 vol.

Exercitia, *"Exercitia spiritualia S. Patris Ignatii de Loyola"*. Spanish text et literal version. . . . Taurini, 1928.

Fabri Mon, *"Beati Petri Fabri . . . Epistolae"*. In MHSI. Matriti, 1914.

Feder (I), *"Aus dem geistlichen Tagebuch des hl. Ignatius von Loyola"*. Translated by Alfred Feder, S.J. Regensburg, 1922.

Feder, (II), *"Lebenserinnerungen des hl. Ignatius von Loyola.* Translated by Alfred Feder, S.J. Regensburg, 1922.

Finke, *"Papsttum und Untergang des Templerordens"*, by Heinrich Finke. Freiburg, 1907.

Fita (I), *"El mayorazgo de Loyola"*, by Fidel Fita, S.J. In BAH 22 (1893), 545-578.

Fita (II), *"San Ignacio de Loyola en la Corte de los Reyes de Castilla"*. Critical study by Father Fidel Fita, S.J., in BAH, 17, (1890), 492-520.

Fita, (III), *"Alonso Montalvo y San Ignacio de Loyola"*, by Father Fidel Fita, S.J. in BAH, 18, (1891), 75-78.

Flos Sanctorum, Legends of the saints vulgarly known as *"Flos Sanctorum"*. Prologues by Fray Gauberto, M. Vagad. Copy existing in Archives of Loyola, printed probably at Saragossa between 1490 and 1510.

Fontes narrativi, *"Fontes narrativi de S. Ignatio de Loyola et de Societatis Jesu initiis"*. *Vol. I. Narrationes "scriptae: Ediderunt D. Fernandez Zapico, S.J. et Candidus Dalmases, S.J., cooperante Petro Leturia*, S.I. In MHSI, vol. 66. *Romae* 1943.

Foronda, *"Estancia y viajes del Emperador Carlos V"*. by don Manuel de Foronda y Aguilera. Madrid, 1914.

Foulché-Delbosc, *"Cancionero castellano del signo xv"*, arranged by R. Foulché-Delbosc. Tomes 19 and 22 of the NBAE. Madrid, 1912 ff.

Fueter, *"Geschichte des europäischen Staatensystems von 1492-1559"*, by Eduard Fueter. München, 1919.

Gallardo, *"Ensayo de una biblioteca española de libros raros y curiosos formado con apuntamientos* (by B. J. Gallardo) Madrid, 1890, 4 vol.

Garibay, *"Los XL libros del Compendio historial de las Cronicas y Universal Historia de todos los Reinos de España"*, by Esteban de Garibay. Amberes, 1571.

Gayangos, *"Libros de Caballerias con un discurso preliminar y un catalogo razonado*, by don Pascual de Gayangos. Tome XL of BAE. Madrid 1875.

Genelli, *"Das Leben des heiligen Ignatius von Loyola"* by Father Christoph Genelli, S.J. Innsbruck, 1848.

Gomez Rodriguez (I), *"Levantamiento de Arevalo . . . y primera campaña militar de San Ignacio de Loyola"*, by Telesforo Gomez Rodriguez, in BAH, 19 (1892), 1-18.

Gomez Rodriguez (II) *"Levantamiento de la Villa de Arevalo . . . justificado ante la Historia. Diploma inedito del Emperador Carlos V"*, by Telesforo Gomez Rodriguez in BAH, 18 (1891), 385-401.

Gonzalez, *"Coleccion de cédulas, Cartas-patentes, provisiones, reales ordenes y otros documentos concernientes a las Provincias Vascongadas. . . . IV. Provincia de Guipuzcoa"*. (published by Tomas Gonzalez) Madrid 1829.

Gorosabel, *"Noticia de las cosas memorables de Guipuzcoa,* by don Pablo Gorosabel. Tolosa, 1899 ff. 6 vol.

Granero, *"La accion misionera y los metodos misionales de San Ignacio de Loyola"*, by Father Jesus Maria Granero, S.J. in *"Bibliotheca Hispana Missionum"*, III. Burgos, 1931.

Grausem, *"Le 'De Contemplatione' de Guigues de Pont"*, by Father J. P. Grausem, S.J., in *"Revue d'Ascetique et Mystique"*, 10 (1929), 259-289.

Grisar, "Luther", by Hartmann Grisar, S.J. Freiburg. 1911. 3 vol.

Guerra, *"Nobiliario y los palacios, casas solares y linajes nobles de la Muy Noble y Muy Leal Provincia de Guipuzcoa"*, by Domingo de Lizaso . . . with an introduction by don Juan Carlos Guerra. San Sebastian, 1901.

Hauser, *"Les débuts de l'âge moderne. La Renaissance et la Réforme"*, by Henri Hauser and Agustin Renaudet. Paris, 1929. Tome VIII *"Peuples et Civilisations"*.

Henao-Villalta, *"Averiguaciones de las antigüedades de Cantabria . . . a honor y gloria de San Ignacio de Loyola, cantabro de padre y madre"* . . ., by Father Gabriel Henao, S.J. . . . New edition, corrected by Father Miguel Villalta, of Las Escuelas Pias. Tolosa 1894, vol. I-VII.

Höfler, *"Papst Adrian VI"*, by C. von Höfler. Wien, 1880.

Huizinga, *"Herbst des Mittelalters"* . . ., by J. Huizinga. Translated into German by T. Jolles Monckeberg. München, 1924.

Huonder, *"Ignatius von Loyola, Beiträge zu seinem Charakterbild"*, by Father Anton Huonder, S.J. Edited by Balthasar Wilhelm, S.J. Köln, 1932.

Iriarte, *"Fijando el voto de castidad de San Ignacio de Loyola"*, by Joaquin Iriarte, S.J. in "Manresa", 3 (1927), 156-164.

Isasti, *"Compendio historial de la M.N. y M.L. Provincia de*

Guipuzcoa", by Dr. Lope de Isasti in 1626. San Sebastian, 1850.

Kolb, *"Das Leben des heiligen Ignatius von Loyola"*, by Viktor Kolb, S.J. S. J. Freiburg, 1931.

Kreiten, *"Zur Entstehung des Exercitienbüchleins"*, by W. Kreiten, S.J. in *"Stimmen aus Maria-Laak"*, 23 (1882), 42 ff.

Langlois, *"La vie spirituelle . . . d'après des écrits en français à l'usage des laïcs"*, by Ch. V. Langlois. Paris, 1928. . . . . . .

Latassa, *"Bibliotecas antigua y nueva de escritores aragoneses"* of Latassa, augmented and reedited by don Miguel Gomez Uriel. . . . Saragossa, 1886, 3 vol.

Leturia (I), *"Nuevos datos sobre San Ignacio. La labor de Polanco y Nadal en los origines de la biografia ignaciana a la luz de documentos inéditos'*, by Pedro Leturia, S.J. Bilbao, 1925.

Leturia (II), *"Apuntes ignacianos"* . . . by Father Pedro Leturia, S.J. Madrid, 1930.

Leturia (III), *"El Reino de Cristo y los prologos del Flos Sanctorum de Loyola"*, by Pedro Leturia, S.J., in *"Manresa"*, 4 (1928), 334-349.

Leturia (IV), *"El influjo de San Onofre en San Ignacio"* . . . by Pedro Leturia, S.J., in *"Manresa"*, 2 (1926), 224-238.

Leturia (V), *"Un texto desconocido del año 1556 sobre lu Santa Cueva"*, by Pedro Leturia, S.J., in *"Manresa"*, 1 (1925), 43-52.

Leturia (VI), *"La Devotio Moderna en el Montserrat de San Ignacio"* by Pedto Leturia, S.J., in *"Razon y Fe"*, 111 (1936), 379 ff.

Leturia (VII), *"La dama del Capitan Iñigo de Loyola"*, by Pedro Leturia, S.J., AHSI, 5 (1936), 88-91.

Lejarza, *"La Mision de Tierra Santa y el Patronato de los Reyes de España"*, by Fray Fidel de Lejarza, O.F.M., in *"Bibliotheca hispana Missionum"*, I. Barcelona, 67-94.

Lizarralde (*I*), *"Historia del Convento de la Purisima Concepcion de Azpeitia"*, by Fray José Adrian Lizarralde, O.F.M., Santiago, 1921.

Lizarralde (II), *"San Ignacio de Loyola penitente en Aranzazu"*, by Fray José Adrian Lizarralde, O.F.M., in review *"Aranzazu"*, 8 (1928), 13 ff.; 9 (1929), 51 ff.

Llanos y Torriglia, *"Contribucion al estudio de la Reina de Portugal, hermana de Carlos V, doña Catalina de Austria"*, by don Felix de Llanos y Torriglia. Madrid, 1923.

Lope de Vega, Cf. Sancha.

Lopez de Haro, *"Nobilario genealogico de los Reyes de Epaña"*, by Alonso Lopez de Haro. Madrid, 1622.

MHSI, *"Monumenta historica Societatis* Jesu," *Matriti*, 1894 ff.

Malexecheverria, *"La Compañia de Jesus por la Ilustracion del Pais Vasco en los siglos xvii y xviii"* . . . by Father José Malazecheverria, S.J. San Sebastian, 1926.

March (I), *"La vetlla de les armes de Sant Ignasi de Loyola a Montserrat en relacio amb la sagrada Liturgia i la Historia"*, by Father José M. March, Barcelona, 1922.

March (II), *"Niñez y juventud de Felipe II"*, by Father José M. March, S.J. Madrid, 1941. 2 vol.

Mariotti, *"Il Nome di Gesu et i Francescani"*, by Father Candido M. Mariotti, O.F.M. Fano, 1909.

Martyr, *"Opus epistolarum Petri Martyris"* . . . *Angheriae Compluti*, 1530.

Menéndez y Pelayo, *"Origenes de la novela. I. Introduccion. Tratado historico sobre la primitiva novela española"*, by don M. Menéndez y Pelayo . . Madrid, 1925. IN NBAE, vol. I. (In the citations we have changed for ease of reading the Roman numerals to Arabic of the pages.)

Mir, *"Escritores misticos españoles. Tomo I. Hernando de Talavera, Alejo Venegas, Francisco de Osuna, Alfonso de Madrid"*. With a preliminary discourse by don Miguel Mir . . . Madrid, 1911. In NBAE, vol. 16.

Montesino, Cf. Sancha y Cartujano.

Mujica (I), *"Provincia de Guipuzcoa"*, by don Serapio Mugica, in *"Geografia General del Pais Vasco-navarro,"* directed by Francisco Carreras y Candi. Barcelona (s.a.)

Mugica (II), *"El blason de Guipuzcoa"*. Monograph . . . by don Serapio de Mugica. San Sebastian, 1915.

Mugica (III), *"Las Comunidades de Castilla,"* by don Serapio Mugica, in *"Revista vascongada"*, 1897.

Mugica, S.J., *"Reminiscencias de la lengua vasca en el 'Diaro' de San Ignacio"*, by Father Placido Mujica, S.J., In RIEV, 27 (1936), 53 ff.

Muñoz y Romero, "*Diccionario bibliografico historico de España*". Madrid, 1858.

Nat, "*Epistolae P. Hieronymi Natalis, S.J.*". . . *Matriti*, 1898 ff. 4 vol. in MHSI.

Navarrete, "*Coleccion de viajes y descubrimientos que hicierion por mar los españoles desde fines del siglo xv*", by Father Fernandez Navarrete. Madrid, 1825 ff.

NBAE, "*Nueva Biblioteca de Autores españoles*," M. Menéndez y Pelayo. Madrid, 1911 ff.

Nueva recopilacion *de los Fueros, Privilegios, Buenos Usos y Costumbres, Leyes y Ordenes de la M.N. y M.L. Provincia de Guipuzcoa*". San Sebastian, 1919.

Olmedo, "*In Nomine Jesu*", by Father Felix Olmedo, S.J. In "*Razon y Fe*", 103 (1933), 148-156. Posteriorly to the edition of our work Father Olmedo has published in 1944 his "*Introduccion a la vida de S. Ignacio de Loyola*". Madrid.

Oñate "*Primer Congreso de estudios vascos. Recopilacion de los travajos de dicha Asamblea, celebrada en la Universidad de Oñate del l al 8 de septiembre de 1918*". *Bilbao*, 1919-1920.

Ortiz, "*Itinerarium Hadriani VI ab Hispania Roman usque . . per Blasium Ortizium . . . summa fide collectum*" (Toleti, 1548). Reproduced in Burmann. "*Hadrianus VI. Traiecti ad Rhenum*", 1727, pp. 153-243.

Ospina, "*Don Iñigo de Loyola. Retrato historico*", by Eduardo Ospina, S.J. Bilbao, 1921.

Papini, "*Gli Operari della vigna*", by Giovanni Papini. Firenze, 1929.

Pastor, "*Geschichte der Päpste . . . Adrian VI*", by Ludwig von Pastor, Freiburg. 1907.

Pedrell, "*Diccionario biografico y bibliografico de musicos españoles.*", by Felipe Pedrell (neither place nor date).

Pérez Arregui (I), "*San Ignacio en Azpeitia*". Historical Monograph by Juan Maria Pérez Arregui, S.J. Madrid, 1921.

Pérez Arregui (II), "*El Iñigo de Loyola visto por Adolfo Coster*", by Father Juan Maria Pérez Arregui, S.J. In "*Razon y Fe*", 95 (1931), 324-347; 96 (1931), 203-225; 97 (1931), 201-215; 98 (1932), 179-190.

Pfandl, "*Geschichte der spanischen Nationalliteratur in ihrer Blütezeit*", by Ludwig Pfandl. Freiburg. 1929.

Pol., Compl., *"Polanci Complementa. Epistolae et commentaria P. Joannis Alphonsi de Polanco e Societate Jesu"*. In MHSI Matriti, 1916-1917. II volumina.

Portillo, *"El original manuscrito de la primera edicion castellana de la Vida de N.P. San Ignacio por el P. Ribadeneira"*, by Father Enrique Pola Portillo, S.J., In *"Razon y Fe"*, 42 (1915), 289-298.

Potthast, *"Bibliotheca historica medii aevi"*. Berlin, 2, 1896.

Pulgar, *"Glosas a las coplas de J. Mingo Revulgo."*, by Fernando del Pulgar. Edition and notes by J. Dominguez Bordona. Madrid, 1929.

Rahner (I), *"Die Mystik des hl. Ignatius unde der Inhalt der Vision von La Storia"*. by Hugo Rahner, S.J. In *"Zeitschrift für Aszese und Mystik"*, 10 (1935), 202 ff.

Rahner, (II), *"Woher stammt der Name Ignatius?"* by Hugo Rahner, S.J. in *"Mitteilungen aus den deustchen Provinzen"*, 104 (1936), 13-18.

Renaudet, *"Les débuts de l'Age moderne. La Renaissance et la Réforme"*, by Henri Hauser and Augustin Renaudet. Paris, 1 1929.

Ribadeneira, *"Patris Petri de Ribadeneira. Confessiones, Epistolae aliaque scripta inedita"*. In MHSI. Matriti, 1920, 1923. 2 vol.

RIEV., *"Revista internacional de Estudios vascos"*. San Sebastian, 1935 ff.

Rodriguez, *"Historia da Companhia de Jesus na Assistência de Portugal"*. Father Francisco Rodriguez, S.J. Porto, 1931.

Rodriquez Villa, *"Doña Juana la loca"*. Historical study by Antonio Rodriguez Villa. Madrid, 1892.

Rohr, *"Franziskus und Ignatius. Eine vergleichende Studie"* by Erich Rohr, O.F.M. in the collection *"Zur religiosen Lage der Gegenwart"*, 14 (1926), 1-84.

Salazar, *"Historia genealogica de la Casa de Lara."*. by don Luis de Salazar y Castro. Madrid, 1697, 4 vol.

Salcedo, *"Literatura española"*, Madrid, 1916.

Sancha, *"Romancero y cancinero sagrados . . . sacados de los mejores ingenios españoles"*, by don Justo de Sancha. Madrid, 1925. In BAE tome 35.

Sandoval, *"Historia del Emperador Carlos V. Rey de España"*, by Master don Fray Prudencio de Sandoval, Bishop of Pamplona. Edition Madrid, 1846 ff.

Schnuerer, G. (I), *"Kirche und Kultur im Mittelalter"*, by Gustav Schürer. 3rd Vol. Paderborn, 1929.

Schnuerer, G. (II), *"Katolische Kirche und Kultur in Barockzeit"*. Paderborn, 1937.

Serrano, *"Cartulario de San Millan de la Cogolla"*, by don Luciano Serrano, O.S.B. Madrid, 1930.

Serrano y Sanz, *"El archivo Colombino de la Cartuja de las Cuevas"*. Historical and bibliographical study by don Manuel Serrano y Sanz. In BAH, 97 (1930), 144 ff.

Scripta, *"Scripta de San Ignacio de Loyola Societatis Jesu Fundatore"*. In MHSI, *"Monumenta Ignatiana"* Series IV, Madrid, 1904, 1918. 2 vol.

Sojo, *"El Capitan Luis Pizaño, por el coronel de ingenieros Sr. D. Fermin de Sojo y Lomba"*. In *"Memorial de ingenieros del Ejército"*, 44 (1927), 257 ff.

Susta, *"Ignatius von Loyola's Selbstbiographie"*, in *"Mittheilungen des Instituts für öster. Geschichtsforschung"*, 26 (1905), 80 ff.

Tacchi-Venturi, *"Storia della Compagnia di Gesu in Italia"*, by P. Pietro Tacchi-Venturi, S.J. Rome, 1922.

Talavera, Cf. Mir.

Tarin, *"La Real Cartuja de Miraflores (Burgos). Su historia y descripcion"*. by Francisco Tarin y Juaneda. Burgos, 1897.

Vagad, Cf. *"Flos Sanctorum"* and Foulché-Delbosc.

Van Ortroy, *"Manrèse et les origines de la Compagnie de Jesus"*, by Father Fr. van Ortroy, S. J., in *"Analecta Bollandiana"*. 27 (1908), 393-418.

Vita Christi, *"Vitae Jesu-Christi editio novissima ab L. M. Rigollot curata."* Parisiis, 1870, 4 vol. Cf. also Cartujano.

Vindel, *"Manual grafico-decriptivo del bibliofilo hispano-americano (1475-1850)"*, by Francisco Vindel, London, Madrid, Barcelona, Paris, 1930 ff. Up to the present 12 vol.

Watrigant (I), La *"Genèse des Exercises de S. Ignace de Loyola"*, by Henri Watrigant, S.J. Amiens, 1897.

Watrigant (II), *"Quelques promoteurs de la Méditation métho-dique au quinzième siècle"*, by Henri Watrigant, S.J. in *"Collection de la Bibliothèque des Exercises de Saint Ignace"*, n. 19 (1919), 1-83.

Xaveriana, *"Monumenta Xavierana ex autographis vel ex anti-guioribus exemplis collecta"*. Matriti, 1899-1912. In MHSI, 2 vol.

Yañez, *"Poema de Alonso onceno"*, by Rodrigo Yañez. In BAE, tome 57, p. 477 ff.

Yepes, *"Cronica general de la Orden de San Benito"*, by Antonio Yepes, O.S.B. Valladolid, 1613, 4 vol.

Yrizar (I), *"Las Casas Vascas. Torres, Palacio, Caserios, chalets, mobiliario"*, by don Joaquin de Yrizar, architect. San Sebastian 1929.

Yrizar (II), *"Arquitectura popular vasca."* Conference by don Joaquin de Yrizar at the Fifth Congress of Basque studies, Vergara, 1930. San Sebastian, 1934.

Yrizar (III), *"La Casa de Loyola"*, by don Joaquin de Yrizar. in *"Euskaleriaren Alde"*, 14 (1924), 41-48.

Ziesemer, *"Das Land der Basken. Skizzen aus der Heimat der Altesten Europäer"*, by Wilhelm Ziesemer. Berlin, 1934.

Zunzunegui, *"El Reino de Navarra . . . durante la primera época del Cisma del Occidente"*, by José Zunzunegui. San Sebastian, 1942.

Index of names and places

198 INIGO DE LOYOLA

This book* is a

Loyola
request
reprint

LOYOLA UNIVERSITY PRESS
Chicago, Illinois
is pleased to make
this out-of-print book
available once again
to its old friends

* **Reprinted by arrangement**
with the author
and/or the original publisher.
This book is now sold only by
Loyola University Press.